**Recent Developments in Phase Theory**

# Studies in Generative Grammar

**Editors**
Norbert Corver
Harry van der Hulst

**Founding editors**
Jan Koster
Henk van Riemsdijk

# Volume 139

# Recent Developments in Phase Theory

Edited by
Jeroen van Craenenbroeck
Cora Pots
Tanja Temmerman

ISBN 978-1-5015-2724-1
e-ISBN (PDF) 978-1-5015-1019-9
e-ISBN (EPUB) 978-1-5015-1013-7
ISSN 0167-4331

**Library of Congress Control Number: 2020937329**

**Bibliographic information published by the Deutsche Nationalbibliothek**
The Deutsche Nationalbibliothek lists this publication in the Deutsche Nationalbibliografie; detailed bibliographic data are available on the Internet at http://dnb.dnb.de.

© 2022 Walter de Gruyter, Inc., Berlin/Boston
This volume is text- and page-identical with the hardback published in 2020.
Typesetting: VTeX UAB, Lithuania
Printing and binding: CPI books GmbH, Leck

www.degruyter.com

# Contents

About the authors —— VII

Jeroen van Craenenbroeck, Cora Pots, and Tanja Temmerman
1    Recent developments in Phase Theory
     Introductory remarks —— 1

## Part I: Phases and ellipsis

Neda Todorović
2    Aspect interacts with phasehood: Evidence from Serbian
     VP-ellipsis —— 11

Barbara Citko
3    On top but not a phase: Phasehood inheritance and variation in
     sluicing —— 35

## Part II: Domain-internal phases

Andrew Simpson and Saurov Syed
4    Parallels in the structure of phases in clausal and nominal
     domains —— 61

Coppe van Urk
5    How to detect a phase —— 89

## Part III: Phases and labeling

Željko Bošković
6    On the Coordinate Structure Constraint, across-the-board-movement,
     phases, and labeling —— 133

Ivona Kučerová
7    Labeling as two-stage process: Evidence from semantic
     agreement —— 183

Index —— 213

## About the authors

**Željko Bošković** is Professor of Linguistics at the University of Connecticut. He is the author of *The Syntax of Nonfinite Complementation: An Economy Approach* (MIT Press), *On the Nature of the Syntax-Phonology Interface: Cliticization and Related Phenomena* (Elsevier), and *Minimalist Syntax: The Essential Readings* (with H. Lasnik, Blackwell). He has also published over one hundred journal articles and book chapters and has supervised over 40 Ph.D. dissertations.

**Barbara Citko** is a Professor of Linguistics in the Department of Linguistics at the University of Washington in Seattle. Her research focusses on minimalist syntax, syntax-semantics interface, and the syntax of Polish. Within these areas, she has worked on various types of relative clauses (free relatives, correlatives, appositives, and light headed relatives) and wh-questions (multiple wh-questions, across-the board wh-questions, wh-questions with coordinated wh-pronouns), coordination and ellipsis. On a more theoretical level, she is interested in the status of multidominance in the grammar. She is the author of two books: *Symmetry in Syntax: Merge, Move and Labels* and *Phase Theory: An Introduction*, and a number of journal articles. She is also an Associate Editor of the Journal of Slavic Linguistics.

**Ivona Kučerová** is associate professor of linguistics at McMaster University (McMaster University, Hamilton, ON, Canada). She specializes in the issues of syntax-semantics and syntax-morphology interfaces, and issues of computational complexity. She has published mainly on case, agreement, ergativity, and A-movement. She works on Romance, Germanic, Slavic, Semitic, Inuit and Mohawk.

**Cora Pots** is postdoctoral researcher at KU Leuven and member of the Center for Research in Syntax, Semantics, and Phonology (CRISSP). She obtained her Ph.D. from KU Leuven in 2020 with a dissertation entitled *Roots in Progress. Semilexicality in the Dutch and Afrikaans verbal domain*. Her main research interests are morphosyntactic variation, comparative syntax, Dutch and Afrikaans syntax, dialectal variation, syntactic optionality, and language change.

**Andrew Simpson** is Professor of Linguistics at the University of Southern California. His research focuses on the comparative syntax of East, Southeast and South Asian languages. He has produced seven books and over forty journal articles and book chapters, with papers in *Language, Natural Language and Linguistic Theory,*

*Linguistic Inquiry*, the *Journal of East Asian Linguistics*, *Linguistic Analysis*, and *Linguistics*. He is joint general editor of the *Journal of East Asian Linguistics*.

**Saurov Syed** is a Lecturer (US Assistant Professor) in the Linguistics department at the University of Auckland, New Zealand. He was previously appointed as a Lecturer at Harvard University, and he finished his Ph.D in 2017 from the Department of Linguistics at the University of Southern California. His research interests are focused on the syntax of Indo-Aryan languages, and he has published papers on negation, numerals, focus and DP-structure, yes/no questions in journals like *Natural Language and Linguistic Theory*, *Linguistic Inquiry*, and *Glossa*. His current research investigates cross-linguistic co-occurrence patterns of non-article determiners, as well as different syntactic phenomena in Madurese, an Austronesian language spoken in Indonesia. He is the Book Reviews Editor of the New Zealand based journal *Te Reo*.

**Tanja Temmerman** is Assistant Professor of Dutch Linguistics at Université Saint-Louis Bruxelles (Belgium). She also teaches English and is the head of the English Department at the same university. She obtained her Ph.D. from Leiden University in 2012 with a dissertation entitled *Multidominance, ellipsis, and quantifier scope*. Her principal research foci lie in (generative) syntax, issues at the syntax-phonology and syntax-semantics interfaces, Dutch dialectology and comparative Germanic syntax. Specific topics of interest include ellipsis, the internal and external syntax of idioms, phase theory, long distance dependencies, island effects, phrase structure, modals, and negation. She is co-editor of the *Oxford Handbook of Ellipsis*.

**Neda Todorović** is an Assistant Professor in Syntax at the University of British Columbia. Her primary research interest lie in the area of syntax, semantics and the syntax-semantics interface. Her work is primarily based on the interaction between syntax and semantics in the domain of Tense and Aspect in Slavic languages and languages of the Northern America. She is also actively involved in primary data collection in languages of British Columbia, Canada.

**Jeroen van Craenenbroeck** is Professor of Dutch Linguistics at KU Leuven, where he is also vice-president of the Center for Research in Syntax, Semantics, and Phonology (CRISSP). He is the author of *The syntax of ellipsis* (OUP) and co-editor of the *Oxford Handbook of Ellipsis*, and his research interests include ellipsis (sluicing, swiping, spading, VP-ellipsis), expletives, verb clusters, and the left periphery of the clause.

**Coppe van Urk** is a Senior Lecturer in Linguistics at Queen Mary University of London. He received his PhD from MIT in 2015. His research focuses on the syntax of understudied languages, with an emphasis on phrasal movement. He has published in particular on the syntax of long-distance dependencies in the Nilotic language Dinka, which offers especially clear evidence for successive cyclicity effects.

Jeroen van Craenenbroeck, Cora Pots, and Tanja Temmerman
# 1 Recent developments in Phase Theory Introductory remarks

## 1.1 Introduction

Throughout the history of generative grammar, there have been various ways of implementing locality effects, for example through Transformational Cycles (Chomsky 1965, Kayne 1975) or Barriers (Chomsky 1986). Phase Theory (Uriagereka 1999, Chomsky 2000, 2001) constitutes the most recent development in this line of thinking: it is argued that there exist discrete structural domains in natural language that exhibit a degree of syntactic, semantic, and phonological independence from the rest of the computation. Phase Theory offers a tool for investigating and understanding such domains. However, since the inception of phases, there have been many different proposals about the specific formalization of this concept, along with much debate about the ways in which (and the extent to which) phases can be evidenced empirically—and indeed whether they exist at all. The aim of this volume is to explore a number of recent developments (both empirical and theoretical) in Phase Theory, thus contributing to our overall understanding of the concept of phases.

The six chapters of this book have been organized around three current themes in Phase Theory: (i) the interaction of phases and ellipsis, (ii) the existence and properties of domain-internal phases, and (iii) phases and labeling. In order to reflect this thematic tripartition, the volume has been divided into three parts. In addition, there is a fourth theme, which surfaces in all of the chapters in one form or another; the question of whether the size of phases is fixed or flexible. In this introductory chapter, we introduce those four topics and indicate which position the individual chapters stake out with respect to them.

## 1.2 Phases and ellipsis

Given that phase heads signal Spell-Out points, i.e. points of Transfer to the PF-interface (Uriagereka 1999, Chomsky 2000, 2001), and given that one of the dominant approaches to ellipsis takes this process to involve deletion or non-pronunciation at PF (Merchant 2001), it seems only natural to try and link these two phenomena. Indeed, over the years, various authors have proposed that ellipsis sites can be reduced to phasal complements (Gengel 2007, Rouveret 2012) (though see Aelbrecht (2010) for an opposing view) and hence, that ellipsis can be used as a diagnostic for phasehood. In recent years, Bošković (2014) has brought this issue to the forefront of linguistic theorizing, by putting forward a very specific proposal in which *both* phasal complements and entire phases can undergo ellipsis, but no other constituents can. The impact of Bošković's (2014) proposal on the (ellipsis and phases) literature has been substantial, with researchers arguing both for and against it. Bošković (2014) has sparked an interesting debate regarding the extent to which ellipsis can be used to detect phasehood: exactly how tight is the relationship between phases and ellipsis? If the link between phases and ellipsis pans out, it has important repercussions for our understanding of phases. On the one hand, it confirms Chomsky's classical intuition that phases are 'PF-complete' in some sense, but on the other hand, the fact that both full phases and phasal complements are candidates for ellipsis does not mesh well with Chomsky's classical approach, which clearly distinguishes between the two. The first two chapters in this volume address Bošković's proposal, though from different perspectives and with a different conclusion.

Neda Todorović's contribution "Aspect interacts with phasehood: evidence from Serbian VP-ellipsis" shows that the hypothesis that both phases and phasal complements can be deleted yields the correct empirical results in describing VP-ellipsis in Serbian. There is a twist, however, and one that takes us beyond Bošković's proposal: Todorović argues that the phasal (complement) status of a constituent not only decides if that constituent can be elided, it is also the basis for an additional identity constraint on ellipsis. This phasal identity requirement states that phasal ellipsis sites need to have phasal antecedents, and phasal complement ellipsis sites need to have phasal complements as antecedents. To the extent that this identity condition in terms of phasal status is on the right track, it implies that phase theory is even more intimately connected to the mechanism of ellipsis than was previously assumed.

Barbara Citko takes a different stance in her chapter "On Top but not a Phase: phasehood inheritance and variation in sluicing". She focuses on Polish, as a representative of the so-called 'focus sluicing languages', whereby the remnant that survives after sluicing (typically a *wh*-phrase) resides not in the highest specifier of the left periphery (call it specCP), but rather in a lower one (typically identified as specFocP). The data patterns discussed by Citko suggest that phasal complements can be elided by sluicing, but entire phases cannot. Citko argues that FocP is a phase in Polish (on account of it triggering A'-movement) and then goes on to show that while the complement of Foc can be elided (leaving just the focused remnant and a complementizer to its left), ellipsis of the entire FocP (leaving just the complementizer) is illicit. As such, she argues against Bošković (2014) and presents an analysis that harkens back to earlier approaches to the interaction between phasehood and ellipsis (Gengel 2007, Rouveret 2012).

The fact that these two chapters disagree on the elidability of entire phases shows that the correctness of Bošković's (2014) conjecture is a still unresolved issue that needs further research. At the same time, it is worth speculating on why Todorović and Citko arrive at such different conclusions. One point to note is that they focus on different ellipsis mechanisms, and, as a result, on different phases: while Citko's discussion is concerned with the maximal clausal phase (CP), Todorović focuses on the lexical or 'mid-level' verbal phase ($v$P). It is not inconceivable that these represent two different types of phases, with different properties. That is precisely the issue that is taken up in part two of this volume.

## 1.3 Domain-internal phases

While many researchers agree that entire clauses and entire nominal constituents—'full' CPs and DPs, let's say—constitute phases, there is much less agreement about the question of whether there are also 'domain-internal phases' such as $v$P for the clausal domain, and NP, NumP, or QP for the nominal domain. If so, how can these be detected, and what is the evidence in favor of postulating such domain-internal phases? And even if one does assume both types of phases to exist, there is the additional question of whether they have exactly the same status and properties (see e. g. Rackowski and Richards (2005), den Dikken (2009), Keine (2016) for arguments that they do not). These questions are addressed in the next two chapters of this book.

Andrew Simpson and Saurov Syed focus on "Parallels in the structure of phases in clausal and nominal domains" in their chapter. Using data from word order patterns and other syntactic phenomena, they argue that the Bangla DP contains an internal phase boundary, which they identify as QP. They go to great lengths showing that this phasal domain is not identical to the highest nominal layer, i. e. DP, and that it behaves like a *bona fide* phase in hosting intermediate landing sites of (DP-internal) successive-cyclic movement and interacting with ellipsis (in a way predicted by Bošković (2014), see also section 1.2 above). As such, Simpson and Syed present arguments to the effect that both the clause and the noun phrase may be bi-phasal, a result that both solidifies the much-invoked but seldom demonstrated bi-phasality of the clause, and confirms the strong structural parallelism between clauses and nominal phrases. At the same time, Simpson and Syed's proposal leaves room for cross-linguistic variation, whereby some languages (such as Bangla or English) project a full, bi-phasal structure in their nominal domain, whereas others (such as Polish) project only up to the lowest phase.

Coppe van Urk takes a broader perspective in his chapter by examining "How to detect a phase". Based on a wide-ranging literature study, he shows that there is no difference in the range of successive cyclicity effects displayed at the CP- and at the *v*P-level: both argue for a view in which long-distance dependencies involve successive-cyclic steps of feature-driven movement that leaves copies. As far as the clausal level is concerned, then, the conclusions concerning domain-internal phases are clear: (i) they exist, and (ii) they have exactly the same status and properties as their domain-maximal counterparts. With respect to non-clausal domains—van Urk focuses in particular on DPs and PPs—the results are much less unequivocal. While there is some evidence that DP and PP function as locality domains, it is much scarcer than the successive cyclicity effects found at the clausal and verbal level. As such, an important contribution of this chapter is the realization that while diagnostics for successive cyclicity abound at the CP- and *v*P-level, they are harder to come by at the DP- and PP-level. More generally, the list of reflexes of successive cyclicity collected and categorized by Van Urk can serve as a yardstick against which to measure the potential phasehood of a particular projection.

## 1.4 Phases and labeling

The third and final part of this volume deals with labeling, in particular the extent to which and the ways in which Chomsky (2013)'s recent proposals on labeling interact with phasehood. While the two chapters in this part treat this issue from quite different perspectives, they converge on the importance of 'derivational timing', i. e. the order in which operations apply, or the order in which the adherence to certain constraints is evaluated.

Željko Bošković's contribution focuses "On the Coordinate Structure Constraint, Across-The-Board-movement, phases, and labeling". The gist of Bošković's analysis is as follows. Conjuncts are phases. Extraction from a phase triggers successive-cyclic movement via the phase edge. Under the assumption that such movement is not feature-driven—an assumption, we should point out, that runs counter to one of the conclusions of van Urk's chapter (cf. *supra*)—the resulting configuration leads to a labeling conflict: two XPs are merged but there is no joint feature that can serve as label for the overarching constituent. In Bošković's terms, this movement operation 'delabels' the constituent. Add to this the Law of the Coordination of Likes (LCL), and it becomes clear why extraction from a conjunct is disallowed, i. e. why the Coordinate Structure Constraint exists: movement to the edge of the conjunct delabels that conjunct and, as a result, it is no longer of the same category as the other conjunct, and the LCL is violated. By that same token, the analysis correctly predicts that extraction from both conjuncts—of which ATB-movement is the most well-known instantiation—is well-formed: now both conjuncts are delabeled, and as a result the LCL is no longer violated.

Whereas Bošković focuses on labeling conflicts that arise in the absence of Agree-driving features, Ivona Kučerová examines the labeling process in the presence of such features in her chapter "Labeling as two-stage process: evidence from semantic agreement". Just as in Bošković's chapter, however, derivational timing once again plays an important role. In particular, Kučerová argues that the labeling process should be split up into two stages. The first one is purely syntactic, driven by features projected from narrow syntax, whereas the second one involves labeling by the syntax-semantics interface. The role of phase heads is then to map narrow syntax features (first labeling stage) onto features within the phase label making them legible to the semantics module (second labeling stage). Empirical support for the proposal comes from nominal, anaphoric, and conjunct agreement in Italian, Czech, and English.

## 1.5 The rigid vs. flexible nature of phases

As should have become clear at various points in the above discussion, the organization of the six chapters into three themes should not be taken to mean that there are no common points between chapters that belong to different themes. That holds in particular for the question of whether phases are rigid/absolute or flexible/context-sensitive, a topic that shows up in one form or another in most, if not all chapters in this book. In its essence, this issue boils down to the question of what the inventory of phases looks like. For example, does it always include CP, DP, and $v$P, or can these projections in some languages, in some constructions, in some contexts, also *not* be phasal? Influential proposals in this respect are Bošković (2014) and Wurmbrand (2017), who argue that the highest head in the extended projection of a lexical head is a phase head, regardless of the precise identity or featural content of that head. As such, a nominal domain that only projects up to, say, $n$P has this projection as its phase level, while in one that goes all the way up to DP, this same $n$P is non-phasal (but DP is). A different take on phasal variability can be found in den Dikken (2007)'s work on Phase Extension and Gallego (2010)'s discussion of Phase Sliding. What these accounts have in common is that a projection can gain or lose phasehood as a result of a derivational operation (typically movement).

The chapters in this volume also grapple with this issue, and present various ways of dealing with it. Bošković (not surprisingly) adopts his own contextual approach to phases in accounting for why conjuncts are phases even when the constituents making up those conjuncts are not necessarily phasal in isolation. For example, in a coordination of IPs selected by a single C-head, the ConjP-projection intervenes between (the two) IP(s) and CP, breaks up the extended projection of the verbal head inside the conjuncts and hence, causes the coordinated IPs to be phasal. A similar line of reasoning can be found in Todorović's chapter. She examines various types of aspect in Serbian, and depending on their precise properties, takes them to be part of the verbal extended projection or not. If they are, the heads hosting this aspectual information are phasal (because they close off the extended verbal projection). If they are not, it is the immediately lower head that is phasal.

Citko addresses crosslinguistic variation with respect to phasehood (Wurmbrand 2017), with the C-head being a phase head in some languages, and the Foc-head being a phase head in others. Moreover, in her chapter, she presents an interesting twist on the derivational approaches to phasal flexibility such as those found in den Dikken (2007) and Gallego (2010). While in those works, the phasehood of a particular projection is raised up to a higher projection (as a result of head movement to the head of that projection), Citko proposes a scenario whereby the phasehood of CP is *lowered* onto FocP. She sees this mechanism as an extension of Chomsky (2007, 2008)'s notion of Feature Inheritance, an operation she terms Phase Inheritance.

Simpson and Syed argue that their biphasal approach to the nominal domain is compatible with Bošković (2014)'s contextual approach to phases, i. e. his position that it is the highest nominal projection that constitutes the phase in the nominal domain. Echoing a sentiment also found in van Urk's chapter, they point out that evidence in favor of the domain-internal phase might simply be harder to come by in the nominal domain, though for largely orthogonal reasons.

The two chapters that address the rigid vs. flexible nature of phases least explicitly are also the ones that most closely adhere to the traditional, absolute view on phases. In van Urk's literature review, the domain-internal phase is very specifically identified as *v*P, i. e. the projection hosting the external argument in its specifier, independently of what the entire extended projection of the verb looks like. Similarly, Kučerová seems to adopt the view—altough admittedly, the issue remains largely implicit—that phase heads are those heads that carry uninterpretable features, as in Chomsky (2008).

## 1.6 Conclusion

As evidenced by the chapters in this volume, Phase Theory is not only a lively and interesting research topic in and of itself, it also interfaces with many other linguistic topics that are currently under debate. We have little doubt, then, that these issues will remain at the forefront of linguistic theorizing for the foreseeable future and believe that the present volume can make a meaningful contribution to that debate.

## Bibliography

Aelbrecht, Lobke. 2010. *The syntactic licensing of ellipsis*. John Benjamins Publishing Company.
Bošković, Željko. 2014. Now I'm a phase, now I'm not a phase: On the variability of phases with extraction and ellipsis. *Linguistic Inquiry* 45:27–89.
Chomsky, Noam. 1965. *Aspects of the theory of syntax*. Cambridge, Massachusetts: M.I.T. Press.
Chomsky, Noam. 1986. *Barriers*. Cambridge, Massachusetts: MIT Press.
Chomsky, Noam. 2000. Minimalist inquiries: The framework. In *Step by step: Essays on minimalist syntax in honor of Howard Lasnik*, ed. Roger Martin, David Michaels, and Juan Uriagereka, 89–156. Cambridge, MA: MIT Press.
Chomsky, Noam. 2001. Derivation by phase. In *Ken Hale: A life in linguistics*, ed. Michael Kenstowicz, 1–52. Cambridge, Massachusetts: MIT Press.
Chomsky, Noam. 2007. Approaching UG from below. In *Interfaces + Recursion = Language? Chomsky's minimalism and the view from syntax-semantics*, ed. Uli Sauerland and Hans-Martin Gärtner, 1–30. Berlin and New York: Mouton de Gruyter.
Chomsky, Noam. 2008. On phases. In *Foundational issues in linguistic theory*, ed. Robert Freidin, Carlos Otero, and Maria Luisa Zubizarreta, 133–166. Cambridge, MA: MIT Press.
Chomsky, Noam. 2013. Problems of projection. *Lingua* 130:33–49.
den Dikken, Marcel. 2007. Phase extension. Contours of a theory of the role of head movement in phrasal extraction. *Theoretical Linguistics* 33:1–41.
den Dikken, Marcel. 2009. Arguments for successive-cyclic movement through specCP: a critical review. *Linguistic Variation Yearbook* 6:89–126.
Gallego, Angel. 2010. *Phase theory*. Amsterdam: Benjamins.
Gengel, Kirsten. 2007. Phases and ellipsis. *Linguistic Analysis* 35:21–42.
Kayne, Richard S. 1975. *French syntax: the transformational cycle*. Cambridge, Massachusetts: MIT Press.
Keine, Stefan. 2016. Probes and their horizons. Doctoral Dissertation, University of Massachusetts at Amherst.
Merchant, Jason. 2001. *The syntax of silence: sluicing, islands, and the theory of ellipsis*. Oxford: Oxford University Press.
Rackowski, Andrea, and Norvin Richards. 2005. Phase edge and extraction: A Tagalog case study. *Linguistic Inquiry* 36:565–599.

Rouveret, Alain. 2012. Vp ellipsis, phases and the syntax of morphology. *Natural Language and Linguistic Theory* 30:897–963.
Uriagereka, Juan. 1999. Multiple spell-out. In *Working minimalism*, ed. Samuel Epstein and Norbert Hornstein, 251–282. Cambridge, Massachusetts: MIT Press.
Wurmbrand, Susi. 2017. Stripping and topless complements. *Linguistic Inquiry* 48:341–366.

Part I: **Phases and ellipsis**

Neda Todorović
# 2 Aspect interacts with phasehood: Evidence from Serbian VP-ellipsis

**Abstract:** This paper shows that VP-ellipsis is available in Serbian, but with certain restrictions – it is aspect-sensitive, i. e. the availability of VP-ellipsis depends on the aspectual specifications of the antecedent and the target. The paper addresses VP-ellipsis in several cases of aspectual mismatches of the antecedent and the target and it shows that VP-ellipsis is allowed only with some such mismatches. It is shown that the division between the mismatches that allow for it and those that do not can be captured in a systematic fashion: the distribution of VP-ellipsis is captured under a phase-based approach to ellipsis, whereby only phases and complement of phases can be elided, as argued in Bošković (2014). However, I argue that, when it comes to Serbian, the requirement is stricter than that – the target and its antecedent need to be identical in terms of their phasal status, i. e. either both are phases or both are phasal complements. I argue that an approach which takes into consideration the phasal status of both target and the antecedent can successfully capture the VP-ellipsis patterns in Serbian discussed in the paper.

## 2.1 VP-ellipsis in Serbian

When it comes to VP-ellipsis, Serbian allows Aux-stranding VP-ellipsis, i. e. non-finite VP can be deleted, with the Auxiliary being stranded. This is shown in (1), in which the elided parts are the participle (part of a periphrastic past form), and infinitive (part of a periphrastic future form), respectively. Note that the antecedent can be either non-finite form (participle in (1a), infinitive in (1b)).

(1) a. Aca je redovno pobeđi-va-o Anu, a Iva je samo
Aca is regularly win-**IMPF**-PART.MASC.SG. Ana and Iva is only
jednom ~~pobedi-o~~ ~~Anu~~/ će ovaj put ~~pobedi-ti~~ ~~Anu.~~
once win.**pf**-PART.MASC.SG Ana will this time win. **IMPF**-INF Ana
'Aca has always been defeating Ana, while Iva has (defeated Ana) once/ will (defeat Ana) this time.'

b. Ako nastave ovako, Aca će više puta pobedi-ti ~~Anu~~ a
if continue this.way Aca will more times win.**IMPF**-INF Ana and
Iva je samo jednom ~~pobedi-o~~ ~~Anu~~/ će samo ovaj put
Iva is only once win.**pf**-PART.MASC.SG Ana will only this time
~~pobedi-ti~~ ~~Anu.~~
win. **IMPF**-INF Ana
'Aca has always been defeating Ana, while Iva has (defeated Ana) once/ will (defeat Ana) this time.'

The availability of VP-ellipsis in Serbian has previously been discussed by Stjepanović (1997). She argues that VP-ellipsis is finiteness-sensitive in Serbian, i. e. antecedents and targets need to match in finiteness. This is shown in (2), where, in constrast to (1), the ellipsis of non-finite VPs is unavailable. Unlike in (1), the antecedent in (2) is finite. Thus, VP-ellipsis seems not to tolerate this mismatch.

(2)  *Aca čita knjigu, ali Iva nikad nije
Aca read.**IMPF**.3SG.PRES book but Iva never not.is
~~čita-o~~ ~~knjigu~~/ nikad neće ~~čita-ti~~ ~~knjigu.~~
read.**IMPF**-PART.MASC.SG book/ never not.will read.**IMPF**-INF book
'Aca is reading the book, but Iva never has (read the book)/ but Iva never will (read the book).'

Stjepanović's analysis successfully captures the discrepancy between (1) and (2). However, if we consider more data, in particular, if we focus on the aspectual values of the antecedent and the target (aspect is always overtly marked in Serbian), we observe that: 1) VP-ellipsis is not as restricted with finite antecedents as it appears to be, given the data she discussed, 2) when the antecedent and the target differ in their aspectual specifications, finiteness mismatches become irrelevant – under each aspectual mismatch, VP-ellipsis is equally permitted or not permitted with both finite and non-finite antecedents. The discussion in the paper will focus on certain aspectual mismatches (see Todorović 2016 for a complete paradigm).

I start by showing that finiteness differences seem not to matter even under the aspectual matching. Consider, e. g., (3), with the VP specified for the perfective. In (3a), a finite Aorist form is the antecedent to an infinitival and participial target, respectively. Importantly, VP-ellipsis is allowed. The ellipsis is also allowed with a non-finite antecedent, as in (3b). Thus, non-finite targets can be elided with both finite and non-finite antecedents in (3).

(3) a. Oni ne pobedi-še    Mariju a  ni Petar neće  ~~pobedi-ti~~
they not win.**PF**-3PL.**AOR**. Marija and nor Petar not.will win.**PF-INF**
~~Mariju/~~ a  ni Petar još nije  ~~pobedi-o~~    ~~Mariju~~.
Marija. and nor Petar still not.is win.PF-**PART**.MASC.SG Marija
'They haven't defeated Marija, and Petar won't either/and Petar still hasn't either.'
b. Ivan je jedanput pobedi-o    Mariju a   Petar je dvaput
Ivan is once    win.**PF-PART**.MASC.SG Marija and Petar is twice
~~pobedi-o~~     ~~Mariju/~~ će dvaput ~~pobedi-ti~~   ~~Mariju~~
win.**PF-PART**.MASC.SG Marija  will twice  win.**IMPF-INF** Marija
'Ivan has defeated Marija once, while Petar has (defeated Marija) twice/ will (defeat Marija) twice.'

Todorović (2016) provides numerous examples where it is shown that, under the same aspectual specification of the antecedent and the target, VP-ellipsis is equally permissible with either finite or non-finite antecedents. I. e., finiteness does not affect the availability of VP-ellipsis is Serbian. It is only root imperfectives that show the difference between the finite and non-finite antecedents, and when controlling for factors such as polarity, only participial targets turn out to be sensitive to finiteness. Todorović (2016) argues that the peculiarity of participial targets can independently be explained and that VP-ellipsis in Serbian still remains finiteness-insensitivity. Curiously, root imperfective is exactly the aspectual specification of the example in (2), which Stjepanović uses to argue for the finiteness-sensitivity of VP-ellipsis in Serbian.[1]

Note further that, in addition to aspectually identical antecedent and the target, we can test for VP-ellipsis in which the two VPs do not completely match in as-

---

[1] Assuming a featural matching requirement for ellipsis, Todorović suggests that there is a feature present only with non-finite forms and not with finite root imperfectives; in the case of participial targets, this feature is present at the level of evaluation of feature identity, making the participle VP and finite VP featurally distinct, whereas with infinitives, the feature is introduced after the point when featural identity between the antecedent and the target is evaluated. Note also that finiteness mismatches do not pose an obstacle in (3a), and for some speakers, Aorist is more easily acceptable than present tense with participial perfective targets. Todorović proposes that Aorist forms, despite being synthetic on the surface, actually contain a silent Aux, which is the locus of their back-shifted interpretation. Aorist is in that sense similar to periphrastic past forms, with the difference being in the overt/covert presence of Aux. This might suggest that Aorist is more similar to non-finite forms than to finite forms, with the lexical verb entering into a feature-checking relation with the Aux, in the similar vein that participles do (see Bošković 1997). This feature is then present in both the Aorist antecedent and the participle target, in turn allowing for feature matching, making them more tolerant antecedents than the present tense form.

pect. In those cases, the lack of finiteness-sensitivity becomes even more evident. Under aspectual mismatches, VP-ellipsis is equally permissible or not permissible with both finite and non-finite antecedents. Consider one example of a mismatch: the target is a root perfective, i. e. a perfective form whose aspectual specification is contained in the verbal root, as in (4a), and the antecedent is also a perfective, but a derived perfective, a prefixed verbal form where a prefix is added to the perfective base, as in (4b). As shown in (5), ellipsis is disallowed, equally with finite and non-finite antecedent.[2]

(4)    a.    ba**ci**-ti                   b.    **iz**-baci-ti
         throw.**PF**-INF                       *out*-throw.**PF**-INF
         'to throw' (pf.)                      'to throw out' (pf.)

(5)    a.    *Aca je u petak iz-baci-o                    flaše, a    Ana je u
             Aca is in Friday *out*-throw.**PF**-PART.MASC.SG bottles and Ana is in
             sredu        ~~baci-la~~           ~~flaše~~/ će u sredu
             Wednesday throw.**PF**-PART.FEM.SG bottles will in Wednesday
             ~~baci-ti~~        ~~flaše.~~
             throw.**PF**-INF bottles
             'Aca threw the bottles out on Friday, while Ana threw the bottles away on Wednesday/will throw the bottles away on Wednesday.'
   b.    *Aca svakog petka iz-baci               flaše, a    Ana je u
             Aca every Friday *out*-throw.**PF**.3SG.PRES bottles and Ana is in
             sredu        ~~baci-la~~           ~~flaše~~/ će u sredu
             Wednesday throw.**PF**-PART.FEM.SG bottles will in Wednesday
             ~~baci-ti~~        ~~flaše.~~
             throw.**PF**-INF bottles
             'Aca throws the bottles out every Friday, while Ana threw the bottles away on Wednesday/will throw the bottles away on Wednesday.'

In (5), both the antecedent and the target are perfective, i. e. they have the same aspectual value, yet VP-ellipsis is not permitted. On the other hand, there are cases in which the antecedent and the target do not match in aspect, yet VP-ellipsis is allowed. For example, when the target is perfective, and the antecedent is a derived (henceforth secondary) imperfective, imperfective derived by adding a suffix *–va* to the perfective stem, as in (6), the ellipsis is allowed, as in (7). Again, finiteness of the antecedent does not affect the availability of VP-ellipsis.

---

[2] The example in (5) is felicitous when the target is derived perfective and it completely matches the antedent.

(6)  iz-baci-ti           ->   iz-baci-va_**IMPF**-ti
     out-throw.**PF**-INF       out-throw.pf-**IMPF**-INF
     'to throw out' (**pf.**)   'to throw out' (**impf.**)

(7) a.  Aca je redovno iz-baci-va-o                  flaše  a   Ana je
        Aca is regularly *out*-throw-**IMPF**-PART.MASC.SG bottles and Ana is
        jedanput ~~iz-baci-la~~            ~~flaše~~/ će  ovaj put
        once     *out*-throw.**PF**-PART.FEM.SG bottles will this time
        ~~iz-baci-ti~~         ~~flaše.~~
        *out*-throw.**PF**-INF bottles
        'Aca was throwing the bottles out regularly, while Ana has (thrown the
        bottles out) once/will (throw the bottles out) this time.'
    b.  Aca redovno iz-bacu-je                 flaše  a   Ana je jedanput
        Aca regularly *out*-throw-**IMPF**.3SG.PRES bottles and Ana is once
        ~~iz-baci-la~~           ~~flaše~~/ će  ovaj put ~~iz-baci-ti~~
        *out*-throw.**PF**-PART.FEM.SG bottles will this time *out*-throw.**PF**-INF
        ~~flaše.~~
        bottles
        'Aca is throwing the bottles out regularly, while Ana (thrown the bottles
        out) once/will (throw the bottles out) this time

The examples in (5) and (7) show that finiteness is not at issue here. Instead, the aspectual specification of the antecedent and the target is a relevant factor and what remains as a question is whether the patterns in (5) and (7) can systematically be captured in some way. I will argue that they can. In section 2.2, I present the assumptions about the nature of aspect in Serbian. In section 2.3, I propose a phase-based account of the availability of VP-ellipsis, in which only phases and phasal complements can be elided, as proposed in Bošković (2014). However, I argue that this requirement is even stricter in Serbian in that the target and the antecedent need to match in their phasal status – either both are phases or both are phasal complements. This analysis can then further capture additional patterns of VP-ellipsis under aspectual mismatches, as shown in section 2.4, and it can also capture an apparently problematic VP-ellipsis of another type of perfective, i. e. superlexical perfective, as shown in section 2.5. While exploring the interaction of aspect and phasehood with a number of aspectual mismatches, the paper aims to provide new insights regarding phasal partitioning of the clause, and establish a more fine-grained structure for the middle field.

## 2.2 The nature of aspect in Serbian

This section discusses the nature of aspect in Serbian. In terms of semantic contribution, there are two types of aspect: a) lexical aspect, which, *i. a.*, specifies the type of the situation denoted by the predicate, such as activities, states, achievements, accomplishments, and semalfactives, affects durativity and dynamicity of the predicate, interacts with the thematic structure of the predicate, and contributes idiosyncratic meanings; b) viewpoint aspect, which, *i. a.*, refers to viewing the situation from the outside as either bounded, i. e. seeing its beginning and end, or as unbounded with respect to a time interval, and which interacts with the temporal component. Structurally, it is argued that lexical aspect is within the VP (Travis 2010, cf. Marantz 2001, 2007, *i. a.*), whereas viewpoint aspect is in AspP (see von Stechow 2002, Pancheva 2003, Travis 2010, *i. a.*). I propose that Serbian manifests both lexical and viewpoint aspect, but that those are different both in terms of syntax (VP-internal vs. external aspect, cf. Travis 2010) and semantics (telicity vs. boundedness, cf. Borik 2002, Borik and Reinhart 2004, Travis 2010, *i. a.*).

Let us consider Serbian in more detail. Aspect is always specified on the root, as in (8). In addition, there are derived forms, i. e. derived perfectives and secondary imperfectives. Derived perfectives are further subdivided, as discussed below.

(8) bac**i**-ti    -> bac**a**-ti
    throw.**PF**-INF    out-throw.pf-**IMPF**-INF
    'to throw' (**pf.**)    'to throw' (**impf.**)

Milićević (2004) notes that there are two types of prefixes in Serbian: lexical and superlexical.[3] Lexical prefixes are prefixes that change lexical properties of verbs, contributing idiosyncractic meanings, and sometimes affecting their thematic structure. Unlike (9a), when the prefix *pre-* is added to the stem *skočiti* 'to jump-pf.' as in (9b), it requires an NP argument. Assuming that lexical aspect is VP-internal, I propose that lexically derived perfectives (henceforth lexical perfectives) introduce an additional VP projection on the top of a VP containing root perfective, as in (10).[4]

---

[3] For the same division in other Slavic languages, see Babko-Malaya (1999), Di Sciullo and Slabakova (2005), Romanova (2004, 2006), Svenonius (2004, 2008), *i. a.*

[4] These prefixes can also be added to root imperfectives, as in (ii). Similarly to (8) and (9) above, the contrast between (i) and (ii) shows that lexical prefixes affects the thematic structure of the verb.

(9) a. Skoči-o        je.
       jump.**PF**-PART.MASC.SG is
       'He has jumped.'
   b. Pre-skoči-o       je potok.
       *over*-jump.**PF**-PART.MASC.SG is stream
       'He jumped over the stream.'

(10)  [$_{VP2}$ lexical pf. [$_{VP1}$ root pf. ]]

In terms of the difference between prefixes, Milićević notes that in, e. g., (11), a prefix *iz-* that is closer to the stem makes the same contribution as the prefix in (9b), whereas the word initial *iz-* marks the completion of the event, but it does not contribute any lexical change. Prefix *po-* in (11) contributes distributive reading (cf. Filip 2000). What both word initial *iz-* and *po-* do is introduce predictable changes in meaning (distributivity, cumulativity). Note also that they can be added only to the secondary imperfective base, as in (12), in which case they change the boundedness of the event, and interact with the temporal domain of the clause; the contrast between (13) and (14) shows that, while secondary imperfectives (13) are felicitous with a present tense form under the Utterance Time interpretation, just adding superlexical perfective (14) makes this interpretation unavailable.

(11) Iz-po-iz-baci-va-o              je sve flaše  iz   kuhinje.
     cmpl-dstr-out-throw.**PF**-**IMPF**-PART.MASC.SG is all  bottles from kitchen
     'He threw out all of the bottles from the kitchen.'
     (Milićević 2004:293)

(12) a. iz-baci-ti       – iz-baci-**va**-ti
        *out*-throw.PF-INF  *out*-throw.PF-**IMPF**-INF
   b. iz-baci-ti          – **iz-po**-iz-baci-**va**-ti
                             CMPL-DSTR-*out*-throw.PF-**IMPF**-INF
   c. iz-baci-ti          – *****po**-iz-baci-ti
                             DSTR-*out*-throw.**PF**-INF
   d. iz-baci-ti          – *****iz-po**-iz-baci-ti
                             CMPL-DSTR-*out*-throw.**PF**-INF

---

(i) Skaka-o          je.
    jump.**IMPF**-PART.MASC.SG is
    'He was jumping.'

(ii) Pre-skaka-o          je potok.
     *over*-jump.**IMPF**-PART.MASC.SG is stream
     'He was jumping over the stream.'

(13)  Trenutno iz-bacuje                      sve flaše  iz   kuhinje
     currently *out*-throw.PF.**IMPF**.3SG.PRES all  bottles from kitchen
     'He/she is throwing out all of the bottles from the kitchen right now.'

(14)  *Trenutno iz-po-iz-bacuje                sve flaše  iz
     currently CMPL-DSTR-*out*-THROW.PF.**IMPF**.3SG.PRES all bottles from
     kuhinje.
     kitchen
     'He/she is throwing out all of the bottles from the kitchen right now.'

Following Milićević (2004), I take the difference between the prefix *iz-* that is closer to the stem, on the one hand, and the word initial *iz-* and *po-* on the other, to be the difference between lexical and superlexical prefixes, where superlexical prefixes are structurally higher than the lexical ones (see also Svenonius 2004)). Given that superlexical prefixes are built on the secondary imperfective base, I propose that they are located in a projection above secondary imperfective. I return to the exact nature of this projection in section 2.5, and I define secondary imperfectives immediately.[5]

Secondary imperfectives, common across Slavic languages (see Isačenko 1960, Forsyth 1970, Zucchi 1999, Filip 2000, Ramchand 2004, *i.a*) are formed by suffixation of either root or lexical perfectives. Secondary imperfective has been classified in the higher domain, the domain of viewpoint aspect (Borer 2005; cf. Zucchi 1999, Filip 2000, Svenonius 2004 *i. a.*). In Serbian, secondary imperfective also shows the viewpoint aspect properties: it does not affect the telicity of the event, and it does not change the lexical properties of the verb. Rather, it only changes the boundedness of the event (15) (cf. (16)). It also interacts with Tense, affecting the availability of a present tense form with the Utterance Time interpretation (17) (cf. (18)) (Todorović 2015).

(15)  Jovan je u  kontinuitetu pobedji-va-o            protivnika.
     Jovan is in continuity    win-**IMPF**-PART.MASC.SG rival
     'Jovan was continuously defeating his rival.'

---

[5] Note that distinguishing between lexical and superlexical prefixes is far from trivial. However, when talking about superlexical prefixes, I restrict myself to prefixes which contribute a predictable meaning change (e. g. distributivity) and which are added to the secondary imperfective base only, changing the boundedness of the event in that case. Thus, I posit them higher in the structure than what I label as lexical perfectives, which do not necessarily introduce predictable changes in meaning and affect the structure in the manner described above. Regardless of the exact position of these prefixes, it is relevant that they are in a structurally different position, with superlexical prefixes being higher.

(16) Jovan je tom prilikom pobedi-o protivnika
 Jovan is that occasion win.**PF**-PART.MASC.SG rival
 'Jovan defeated his rival then.'

(17) *Jovan repriča knjigu Marku.
 Jovan retell.**PF**.3SG.PRES book Marko
 'Jovan has retold the book to Marko (just now).'

(18) Jovan prepričava knjigu Marku.
 Jovan retell.**IMPF**.3SG.PRES book Marko
 'Jovan is retelling the book to Marko (right now).'

Given the patterns in (15) to (18), I propose that secondary imperfective is exclusively a marker of viewpoint aspect in Serbian (see also Milićević 2004), and as such it is located in the AspP (cf. Svenonius 2004, Borer 2005, Travis 2010, *i. a.*), as in (19). Superlexical perfective is located in the projection above AspP, as in (20).

(19) [$_{AspP}$ secondary impf. [$_{VP2}$ lexical pf. [$_{VP1}$ root pf.]]]
 *iz-baci-va-ti* 'to throw out' – **impf**.

(20) [ superlexical pf. [$_{AspP}$ secondary impf. [$_{VP2}$ lexical pf. [$_{VP1}$ root pf.]]]]
 *po-iz-baci-va-ti* 'to throw out one by one'– **pf**.

Armed with the above distinction between the types of perfective and imperfective, and with their location in the structure, we can proceed to the analysis of the VP-ellipsis data under aspectual mismatches.

## 2.3 The role of phases in VP-ellipsis

In a phase-based approach to ellipsis developed in Bošković (2014), only phase and/or the complement of a phase head (referred to as phasal complement below) are eligible for ellipsis, e. g. the complement of a phasal complement is not. Most phase-based approaches share the intuition that a phasal complement can be elided (Boeckx 2009, Bošković 2014, Gengel 2009, van Craenenbroeck 2010, Rouveret 2012, M. Takahashi 2011, *i. a.*); this is illustrated in (21) in which CP is a phase and a phasal complement TP is elided. Where Bošković's approach differs is that for him, in addition to the phasal complement, the phase is also an eligible domain for ellipsis (see also Holmberg 2001, who argues that only phases can undergo ellipsis).

(21) John bought something, but I don't know [_CP_ what [_TP_ ~~John bought~~]].
(Merchant 2001)

Bošković (2014) argues that the ellipsis of full phases happens, for instance, with argument ellipsis, allowed in Japanese, Korean, Turkish, Chinese, and American Sign Language, i. a. (see Şener and Takahashi 2010, D. Takahashi 2008a, 2008b, Takahashi 2014, Koulidobrova 2012, i. a.), and argued to target full phases. Consider Japanese. In (22), the availability of a sloppy reading of the phonetically null embedded CP is taken as an indicator of ellipsis ('____' indicates the ellipsis site). In other words, (22) is taken to involve the ellipsis of the argument CP, a phase.

(22) Hanako-wa [_CP_ zibun-no teian-ga    saiyoosareru to] omotteiru
Hanako-TOP    self-GEN proposal-NOM accepted-be that think
ga    Taroo-wa    omotte inai.
though Taroo- TOP think   not
Hanako$_i$ thinks that her$_i$ proposal will be accepted, but Taroo$_j$ does not think that her$_i$/his$_j$ proposal will be accepted.'
(Shinohara 2006)

In terms of the availability of eliding either of the two phasally relevant domain, Bošković argues that such an option accounts for the discrepancies in the availability of A'-extraction out of an ellipsis site: extraction seems to be acceptable out of elided phasal complements, e. g. sluicing, but not out of elided phases, e. g. argument ellipsis. In addition, he argues that the proposed model provides the right cut in terms of VP-ellipsis possibilities in English multiple auxiliaries constructions, as in (23). Assuming crucially contextual approach to phasehood (e. g. Bobaljik and Wurmbrand (2005, 2013), Bošković (2005, 2013, 2014), den Dikken (2007), Gallego and Uriagereka (2007), Wurmbrand (2013), i. a.), in particular a version where the highest projection in the extended domain of a lexical projection is a phase, Bošković (2014) argues that in (23a) and (23b), AspP$_1$ is a phase, and only AspP$_1$ and VPf$_2$, a phasal complement, can be elided, as in (24); crucially, VP, a phasally non-relevant domain, cannot, hence the ungrammaticality of (23c).

(23)    Betsy has been being hassled by the police, and Peter
   a. has too.
   b. has been too.
   c. *has been being too.
       (Sag 1976)

(24) [TP Peter_k has_i [VPf1 t_i [**AspectP1** be_j+en [VPf2 t_j [AspectP2 ing [VPf3 be [VP hassled t_k by the police]]]]]]]
(Bošković 2014)

## 2.3.1 Applying phase-constrained approach to Serbian

Regarding the VP-ellipsis with aspectual mismatches in Serbian, I argue that those can be accounted for if both phases and phasal complements are eligible for deletion. However, I argue that VP-ellipsis in Serbian needs to meet an additional requirement: the general parallelism requirement on ellipsis extends to the parallelism in terms of phasal status between the antecedent and the target, as in (25) i. e., the part of the antecedent which I call the strict aspectual antecedent and define it in (26), needs to have the same phasal status as the target.

(25) **Identity in terms of phasal status**: If the target is a phase, its strict aspectual antecedent also needs to be a phase; if the target is a phasal complement, its strict aspectual antecedent also needs to be a phasal complement.

(26) **A strict aspectual antecedent**: Part of the VP antecedent that completely matches the VP target in terms of aspectual properties, both lexical and functional.

Regarding what counts as the strict aspectual antecedent, consider (27), which corresponds to (5) and which will be discussed in more detail in section 2.4. In (27), we are deleting a VP, and its strict aspectual antecedent is a VP$_1$ in the antecedent. Since the target VP is a phase and VP1 is a phasal complement, there is no match in terms of their phasal status and the ellipsis in (27) is predicted to ungrammatical.

(27)

| Antecedent | Target |
|---|---|
| [VP2=phase lex. pf. [VP1 root pf.]] | [VP=phase root pf.] |

Regarding phasehood, I follow Bošković (2014) and Wurmbrand (2013), who assume that the highest projection in the extended domain of all major categories constitutes a phase.[6] This is contextual approach in that the amount of projected structure cross-linguistically, but also within a language, affects which particular

---

6 Note that this differs from Grimshaw's (1991) proposal, where the verbal domain would extend all the way up to the CP. Bošković (2014) and Wurmbrand (2013), place pure temporal projections (and CP) outside of the extended domain of VP. Under the current approach, purely functional

phrase within a major category will count as a phase.[7] For example, assuming that articles languages do not project a DP (Corver (1992), Zlatić (1997), Bošković (2005, 2008, 2012)), in a contextual approach to phases, NP will count as a phase in such a language, since it is the highest projection in the nominal domain.[8] In article languages, however, where a DP is projected on the top of the NP, DP counts as a phase. Interestingly, Despić (2011, 2013), and Bošković (2013, 2014) show that numerals and certain quantifiers project a phrase above an NP in Serbian. Bošković shows that when QP is projected on the top of an NP in an NP-language, NP is all of a sudden not a phase, and QP becomes a phase; the relevant evidence is based on the extractability of phasal complements – assuming that phasal complements cannot move (Abels 2003), Bošković shows that the complement of a noun cannot move in the configuration in (28a), but it can in (28b) and (28c). Importantly, variability of a phasal status of a phrase is argued to also occur within a single language, depending on what the highest projection is within a particular domain.

(28)    a.    [$_{NP=phase}$      (Serbian)
       b.    [$_{DP=phase}$ [$_{NP}$      (English)
       c.    [$_{QP=phase}$ [$_{NP}$      (Serbian)

When it comes to Serbian VP, the contextual approach to phases makes the highest VP in a series of VPs a phase. I illustrate the specifics for each particular case.

With root perfectives, a VP containing a root perfective is a phase, since there is no additional VP phrase on top of it.

(29)    [$_{VP=phase}$ root pf. ]      *baciti* 'to throw' **pf.**

With lexical perfectives, the situation is different. I proposed in (10) that they project an additional phrase within the VP-domain and close the VP domain. This higher VP then counts as a phase (VP$_2$), while the VP containing root perfective (VP$_1$) suddenly ceases to be a phase, and becomes a phasal complement.

(30)    [$_{VP2=phase}$ lex. pf. [$_{VP1}$ root pf.]]      *iz-baciti* 'to throw out' **pf.**

---

(semantically impoverished) temporal, but also viewpoint aspectual projections are outside of the extended VP-domain.

**7** Cf. Wurmbrand (2013) who, on the basis of QR, provides evidence that highest projection of a cyclic domain, i. e. AspP, count as a phase.

**8** For Serbo-Croatian as an NP language, see also Corver (1992), Zlatić (1997), Bošković (2005, 2008, 2012), Marelj (2008), Despić (2011, 2013), Runić (2013); Cf. Progovac (1998), Leko (1999), Aljović (2002), Rutkowsky and Progovac (2005), Caruso (2012), Stanković (2014a, 2014b) for Serbo-Croatian as a DP language.

Finally, there are secondary imperfectives, instances of viewpoint aspect. As discussed above, unlike lexical aspect, viewpoint aspect does not affect the telicity of the event, it does not change the lexical properties of the verb, but it does change the boundedness of the event and it interacts with Tense. I propose that, due to different contribution of lexical and viewpoint aspect in Serbian, lexical aspect, located within the VP domain, and viewpoint aspect, located in AspP, are parts of different phasal domains, i. e. viewpoint aspect in AspP is outside of the VP phasal domain. This further means that secondary imperfective does not affect the phasal status of phrases within the VP domain, since it belongs to a phasal domain outside of VP.

(31)    $[_{\text{AspP}}$ sec. impf. $[_{\text{VP=phase}}$ lex. pf. $[_{\text{VP}}$ root pf. ]]]
       *iz-baci-va-ti* 'to throw out' **impf**.

## 2.4 Deriving VP-ellipsis under aspectual mismatches

We finally have all the ingredients to deal with VP-ellipsis patterns discussed in section 2.1. Consider again the case of ellipsis of root perfectives with lexical perfective as in (5), repeated in (33); the ellipsis is disallowed. As shown in (32), the target and the antecedent project different level of structure within the VP. What makes VP-ellipsis unavailable is failure to satisfy the phasal identity requirement. In particular, the target is a phase, since the VP containing root perfective closes the phasal domain. Its strict aspectual antecedent is $VP_1$. $VP_1$, however, is not a phase, since there is an additional phrase on top of it which acts as a phase, $VP_2$. Given that there is no match in terms of phasal status between the target and its strict aspectual antecedent, ellipsis is correctly predicted to be unavailable.[9]

---

[9] An anonymous review wonders whether the acceptability of (5)/(33) can be due to recoverability of deletion: the antecedent contains aspectual information which is not contained in the target. It is true that this information is semantically non-vacuous (brining in additional meaning, affecting the thematic structure, etc.) and that when added to the root perfective, lexical perfective changes the meaning of the antecedent – it is this part outside of the strict aspectual antecedent that creates the problem in this case, not the target (the same goes for (35) below). While such a semantic solution is possible, note that the same problem would arise with otherwise felicitous (7) – the antecedent contains additional aspectual information not otherwise present in the target. Even more, secondary imperfectives can serve as targets of root perfectives and lexical perfectives, respectively, from which they are created, which would be difficult to explain under

(32)

| Antecedent | Target |
|---|---|
| [$_{VP2=phase}$ lex. pf. [$_{VP1}$ root pf.]] | [~~$_{VP=phase}$ root pf.~~] |

(33) a. *Aca je u petak iz-baci-o                    flaše, a    Ana je u
       Aca is in Friday *out*-throw.**PF**-PART.MASC.SG bottles and Ana is in
       sredu       ~~baci-la~~           ~~flaše/~~ će u sredu
       Wednesday throw.**PF**-PART.FEM.SG bottles will in Wednesday
       ~~baci-ti~~      ~~flaše.~~
       throw.**PF**-INF bottles
       'Aca threw the bottles out on Friday, while Ana threw the bottles away on Wednesday/will throw the bottles away on Wednesday.'
   b. *Aca svakog petka iz-baci           flaše, a    Ana je u
       Aca every   Friday *out*-throw.**PF**.3SG.PRES bottles and Ana is in
       sredu       ~~baci-la~~           ~~flaše/~~ će u sredu
       Wednesday throw.**PF**-PART.FEM.SG bottles will in Wednesday
       ~~baci-ti~~      ~~flaše.~~
       throw.**PF**-INF bottles
       'Aca throws the bottles out every Friday, while Ana threw the bottles away on Wednesday/will throw the bottles away on Wednesday.'

Let us look at the pattern in (7) now. What we have seen in (32) is that VP-ellipsis is precluded when there is a difference in the level of structure projected within the VP in the target and its strict aspectual antecedent. If this is so, then VP-ellipsis should not in principle be blocked when there is no structural difference between the target and its strict aspectual antecedent, because this would also mean no difference in the phasal status of the target and its strict aspectual antecedent. We can actually test this. In (7), repeated in (35), lexical perfectives are targets and secondary imperfectives are antecedents. (34) shows that the target VP and its strict aspectual antecedent, $VP_2$, are both phases – viewpoint aspect in AspP is a part of a phase outside of VP, so AspP in the antecedent does not affect the phasal status of the strict aspectual antecedent, $VP_2$. Given that the target VP and its strict aspectual antecedent match in their phasal status, VP-ellipis is correctly predicted to be acceptable.

(34)

| Antecedent | Target |
|---|---|
| [$_{AspP}$ sec.impf [$_{VP2=phase}$ lex. pf. [$_{VP1}$ root ~~pf.~~]]] | [~~$_{VP2=phase}$ lex. pf. [$_{VP1}$ root pf.~~]] |

---

the semantic account; see Todorović (2016) for how these mismatches can straight-forwardly be captured in a phase-based approach.

(35) a. Aca je redovno iz-baci-va-o flaše a Ana je
Aca is regularly *out*-throw-**IMPF**-PART.MASC.SG bottles and Ana is
jedanput ~~iz-baci-la~~ ~~flaše/~~ će ovaj put
once *out*-throw.**PF**-PART.FEM.SG bottles will this time
~~iz-baci-ti~~ ~~flaše.~~
*out*-throw.**PF**-INF bottles
'Aca was throwing the bottles out regularly, while Ana has (thrown the bottles out) once/will (throw the bottles out) this time.'

b. Aca redovno iz-bacu-je flaše a Ana je jedanput
Aca regularly *out*-throw-**IMPF**.3SG.PRES bottles and Ana is once
~~iz-baci-la~~ ~~flaše/~~ će ovaj put ~~iz-baci-ti~~
*out*-throw.**PF**-PART.FEM.SG bottles will this time *out*-throw.**PF**-INF
~~flaše.~~
bottles
'Aca is throwing the bottles out regularly, while Ana (thrown the bottles out) once/will (throw the bottles out) this time.'

We can now extend the analysis to the additional set of data. Note first that in (34), secondary imperfective is formed by suffixation of lexical perfective. We can retain that same antecedent as in (34), but change the target to root perfective, as in (36). In this case, ellipsis should be precluded – the target is a phase, since VP containing root perfective closes the VP domain, but its strict aspectual antecedent is a phasal complement. Unlike in (34), the additional structure in the antecedent is now within the VP domain (as well as in AspP), i. e. in VP$_2$; VP$_1$ in the antecedent ceases to be a phase and becomes a phasal complement. We are facing the same problem as in (32) above – adding structure within the VP in the antecedent affects the phasehood of strict aspectual antecedent and makes it phasally unequal to the target. Ellipsis is correctly predicted to be unavailable (37).

(36)

| Antecedent | Target |
|---|---|
| [$_{\text{AspP}}$ sec.impf [$_{\text{VP2=phase}}$ lex. pf. [$_{\text{VP1}}$ V root pf.]]] | ~~[$_{\text{VP=phase}}$ root pf.]~~ |

(37) a. Aca je satima iz-baci-va-o ~~smeće~~ a Ana za
Aca is hours *out*-throw-**IMPF**-PART.MASC.SG trash and Ana for
pola sata ~~baci-la~~ ~~smeće/~~ će za pola sata
half hour throw.**PF**-PART.FEM.SG trash will for half hour
~~baci-ti~~ ~~smeće~~
throw.**PF**-INF trash
'Aca was throwing the bottles out regularly, while Ana has (thrown the bottles out) once/will (throw the bottles out) this time.'

b. Aca redovno iz-bacu-je smeće a Ana je jedanput
Aca regularly *out*-throw-**IMPF**.3SG.PRES trash and Ana is once
~~baci-la~~ ~~smeće~~/ će ovaj put ~~baci-ti~~ ~~smeće.~~
throw.**PF**-PART.FEM.SG trash will this time throw.**PF**-INF trash
'Aca is regularly taking the trash out, while Ana has (throw the trash) once/while Ana will (throw the trash) once.'

Note, however, that secondary imperfectives can also be formed by suffixation of root perfective, as in (38). What happens if we use them as antecedents to root perfective targets? We predict ellipsis to be available. This is because, even though there is an additional structure within the antecedent, i.e. AspP, this phrase is outside of the VP-domain, as in (39). As in the cases above, AspP does not affect the phasal status of the phrases within the VP. So, when the target VP needs to match with its strict aspectual antecedent VP, this antecedent is still a phase, just like the target – no problems arise. VP-ellipsis is correctly predicted to be possible, as in (40).[10]

(38) [AspP secondary impf. [VP root pf.]]
*pobeđi-va-ti* 'to win' **impf.**

(39)

| Antecedent | Target |
|---|---|
| [AspP sec. impf [VP=phase root pf. ]] | ~~[VP=phase root pf.]~~ |

(40) a. Aca je redovno pobeđi-va-o Anu a Iva je jedanput
Aca is regularly win.**IMPF**-PART.MASC.SG Ana and Iva is once
~~pobedi-o~~ ~~Anu~~/ će ovaj put ~~pobedi-ti~~ ~~Anu~~
win.**PF**-PART.SG.MASC Ana will this time win.**IMPF**-INF Ana
'Aca has always been defeating Ana, while Iva has (defeated Ana) once/ will (defeat Ana) this time.'

---

**10** This paper does not discuss VP-ellipsis of root imperfectives, but those cases can be captured under the same approach. Note first that root imperfectives are non-permissible targets under any aspectual mismatch. However, the ellipsis of these targets under aspectual mismatches runs in the same problems as the ellipsis of root perfectives does and can be captured under the same analysis that has been proposed in this section. The only case where root perfectives can be elided and root imperfectives cannot is with secondary imperfective antecedents. These cases are independently excluded because secondary imperfectives can never be added directly to the root imperfective base. They, however, can be added to lexical perfectives derived from root imperfectives, and as such act as antecedents to root imperfectives, but then the VP-ellipsis is excluded for the same reason that (36) is ungrammatical.

b. Aca redovno pobeđuje Anu a Iva je jedanput
Aca regularly win.**IMPF**.3SG.PRES Ana and Iva is once
~~pobedi-o~~ Anu/ će ovaj put ~~pobedi-ti~~ ~~Anu~~
win.**PF**-PART.SG.MASC Ana will this time win.**IMPF**-INF Ana
'Aca is always defeating Ana, while Iva has (defeated Ana) once/ will (defeat Ana) this time.'

## 2.5 Superlexical perfective

In section 2.2, I briefly discussed superlexical perfectives. I have shown that they make a predictable change in meaning (e. g. distributivity), affect boundedness and interact with the temporal clausal domain. Given that they can be added only to secondary imperfective base, I proposed that they introduce an additional projection on top of secondary imperfective AspP (repeated in (41)). However, I left the nature of the projection open. All we know so far is that, since this projection is outside of VP, we expect it not to affect the availability of the ellipsis of the VP target.

(41) [ superlex. pf. [$_{AspP}$ sec. impf. [$_{VP2=phase}$ lex. pf. [$_{VP1}$ root pf.]]]]

Surprisingly enough, VP-ellipsis with superlexical perfectives is highly restricted. In particular, superlexical perfective antecedents allow for the ellipsis only under the complete identity with the target, i. e. when the target is also superlexical perfective:

(42) a. Aca je u sredu po-iz-baci-va-o flaše, a
Aca is in Wed. DSTR-*out*-throw.**PF-IMPF**-PART.MASC.SG bottles and
Ana je u p. ~~po-iz-baci-va-la~~ ~~flaše/~~ će u
Ana is in Fri. DSTR-*out*-throw.**PF-IMPF**-PART.FEM.SG bottles will in
petak ~~po-iz-baci-va-ti~~ ~~flaše.~~
Friday DSTR-*out*-throw.**PF-IMPF**-INF bottles
'Aca threw all the bottles away on Wednesday, and Aca threw all the bottles away /will throw all the bottles away on Friday.'
b. *Aca ponekad poizbacuje flaše, a Ana
Aca sometimes DSTR-*out*-throw.**PF-IMPF**-3SG.PRES bottles and Ana
je samo jedanput ~~po-iz-baci-va-la~~ ~~flaše/~~ će
is only once DSTR-*out*-throw.**PF-IMPF**-PART.FEM.SG bottles will
samo jednom ~~po-iz-baci-va-ti~~ ~~flaše.~~
only once DSTR-*out*-throw.**PF-IMPF**-INF bottles
'Aca sometimes throws away all the bottles, and Ana has (thrown all the bottles away) /will (throw all the bottles away) only once.'

Consider, for example, secondary imperfective targets. Although minimally different from its antecedent, ellipsis of this target is not available:

(43) a. *A. je ovog puta po-iz-baci-va-o flaše, a
A. is this time DSTR-*out*-throw.**PF-IMPF** PART.MASC.SG bottles and
Ana je redovno ~~iz-baci-va-la~~ ~~flaše/~~ će
Ana is regularly *out*-throw.**PF-IMPF**-PART.FEM.SG bottles will
redovno ~~iz-baci-va-ti~~ ~~flaše.~~
regularly throw.**PF-IMPF**-INF bottles
'Aca threw out all the bottles this time, while Ana was (throwing the bottles out) regularly/ will be (throwing the bottles out) regularly.'

b. *A. ponekad po-iz-bacuje flaše, a Ana je
A. sometimes DSTR-*out*-throw.**PF-IMPF**.3SG.PRES bottles and Ana is
redovno ~~iz-baci-va-la~~ ~~flaše/~~ će redovno
regularly *out*-throw.**PF-IMPF**-PART.FEM.SG bottles will regularly
~~iz-baci-va-ti~~ ~~flaše.~~
throw.**PF-IMPF**-INF bottles
'Aca sometimes throws all the bottles out, Ana was (throwing the bottles out) regularly/ will be (throwing the bottles out) regularly.

Note also that secondary imperfectives can otherwise be elided when their antecedent is secondary imperfective:

(44) a. Aca je redovno pobeđi-va-o Anu a Iva je povremeno
Aca is regularly win.**IMPF**-PART.MASC.SG Ana and Iva is sometimes
~~pobeđi-va-o~~ Anu/ će povremeno ~~pobeđiva-ti~~ ~~Anu~~
win.**IMPF**-PART.MASC.SG Ana will sometimes win-**IMPF**-INF Ana
'Aca was defeating Ana regularly, while Iva was occasionally/will occasionally be (defeating Ana).'

b. Aca redovno pobeđuje Anu a Iva je povremeno
Aca regularly win.**IMPF**.3SG.PRES Ana and Iva is sometimes
~~pobeđi-va-o~~ Anu/ će povremeno ~~pobeđiva-ti~~ ~~Anu~~
win.**IMPF**-PART.MASC.SG Ana will sometimes win-**IMPF**-INF Ana
'Aca keeps defeating Ana regularly, while Iva was occasionally/will occasionally be (defeating Ana).'

Furthermore, superlexical perfectives are also infelicitous antecedents to lexical perfectives:

(45) a. *Aca je ovog puta po-iz-baci-va-o                          flaše, a
        Aca is this time DSTR-*out*-throw.**PF-IMPF**-PART.MASC.SG bottles and
        Ana je prošlog puta ~~iz-baci-la~~                         flaše/ će narednog
        Ana is last      time *out*-throw.**PF**-PART.FEM.SG bottles will next
        puta ~~iz-baci-ti~~       ~~flaše.~~
        time *out*-throw.**PF**-INF bottles
        'Aca has thrown away all the bottles this time, and Ana threw the bottles out last time/ will throw the bottles out next time.'
    b. *Aca redovno poizbacuje                    flaše, a    Ana je
        Aca regularly DSTR-*out*-throw.**PF-IMPF**-3SG.PRES bottles and Ana is
        samo jedanput ~~iz-baci-la~~              flaše/ će samo sada
        only once      *out*-throw.**PF**-PART.FEM.SG bottles will only now
        ~~iz-baci-ti~~      ~~flaše.~~
        *out*-throw-**PF**.INF bottles
        "Aca regularly throws away all the bottles, and Ana has (thrown the bottles out) only once/ will (throw the bottles out) only this time.'

The unavailability of ellipsis in (45) poses an apparent problem for the current analysis. Namely, as shown in (46), the target is a phase, since VP$_2$ is the highest projection in the VP domain. Within the antecedent, if secondary imperfective and superlexical perfective are parts of a phasal domain outside of the VP phasal domain, then they should not affect the phasal status of VP projections. I. e., the strict aspectual antecedent, i. e. VP$_2$, is also a phase. Given that the target and its strict aspectual antecedent have identical phasal status, is not clear why ellipsis is disallowed.

(46)

| Antecedent | Target |
|---|---|
| [superlex. pf.[$_{AspP}$ sec.impf.[$_{VP2=phase}$ lex. pf. [$_{VP1}$ root pf.]]]] *poizbacivati* 'to throw out one by one'-pf. | [~~$_{VP2=phase}$~~ ~~lex. pf.~~ [$_{VP1}$ ~~root~~ ~~pf.]~~] *iz-baciti* 'to throw out'-pf. |

I propose that specifying the exact nature of the projection hosting superlexical perfective reveals why (45) is precluded. In particular, superlexical perfectives make predictable contribution in meaning (distributive, cumulative), so they are to some extent lexical in nature, which, I suggest, places them within the VP-domain. But, they also change boundedness of the predicate and interact with the temporal domain, which also makes them functional in nature. I propose that they are some sort of a VP-projection, potentially semi-lexical/functional projection (cf. Koizumi's (1995) implementation of Larsonian (1988) shells in terms of split VP; see also Travis 2010). The proposal is then that when superlexical perfectives are present in the structure, due to the verbal-like nature of the projection which hosts them, they close the verbal domain, making the entire domain one phase, as shown in (47).

(47)  [$_{=phase}$ superlex pf. [$_{AspP}$ sec. impf. [$_{VP2}$ lex. pf. [$_{VP1}$ root pf.]]]][11]

With the new structure in mind, we can reconsider the availability of ellipsis with superlexical perfective antecedents. What we see is that the patterns fall out straightforwardly.

Consider first the ellipsis of secondary imperfectives with these antecedents. Since the ellipsis of secondary imperfectives is in principle available (44), secondary imperfectives are either a phase or a phasal complement in the domain crucially outside of the VP phasal domain. However, assuming (47), its strict aspectual antecedent AspP is a phasal complement, but still a part of the verbal phasal domain.[12]

(48)

| Antecedent | Target |
|---|---|
| [[$_{=phase}$ superlex. pf. [$_{AspP}$ sec. impf. [$_{VP2}$ lex. pf. [$_{VP1}$ root pf.]]]] *poizbacivati-* 'to throw out one by one'-pf. | [$_{AspP=phase/phasal compl.}$ sec. impf. [$_{VP2=phase}$ lex. pf. [$_{VP1}$ root pf. *izbacivati-* 'to throw out'-impf.]]] |

The newly proposed structure lets us also account for the problematic lack of ellipsis of lexical perfectives (cf. (45)). The target is a phase (and in principle elidable), as in (49) – VP$_2$ closes the VP domain. However, the problem is superlexical perfective in the antecedent – by extending the phasal domain of the VP all the way up, it renders the strict aspectual antecedent, i. e. VP$_2$, a complement of a complement of a phasal head. The lack of identity in terms of phasal status precludes ellipsis. Thus, an apparent problem is actually accounted for, at the same time revealing the nature of projections in the VP-domain and the middle field.

---

**11** Note that according to the analysis proposed above, there's no option whereby VP$_2$ in (47) counts as a phase (as it did in the examples above), because in (47), a projection hosting superlexical perfective closes off the verbal domain and hence counts as a phase; this rendeds VP$_2$ complement of a complement of a phase.

**12** Another option is that secondary imperfective target projects only a VP domain (only in those limited case when secondary imperfective is not overt; see Todorović (2016) for a cross-linguistic support), and acts as a phase, while its strict aspectual antecedent, VP$_2$, is the complement of the complement of a phase, given (47).

(49)

| Antecedent | Target |
|---|---|
| [₌phase superlex. pf. [AspP sec. impf. [VP2₌phase lex. pf. [VP1 root pf. ]]]] *poizbacivati* 'to throw out one by one'-pf. | [VP2₌phase lex pf. [VP1 root pf.]] *iz-baciti* 'to throw out'-pf. |

The Table 2.1 summarizes the patterns of (un)available aspectual mismatches between the antecedent and the target:

**Table 2.1:** Availability of VP-ellipsis under certain aspectual mismatches.

| Antecedent | Target | Ellipsis |
|---|---|---|
| secondary imperfective derived from lexical perfective | lexical perfective | √ |
| secondary imperfective derived from root perfective | root perfective | √ |
| secondary imperfective derived from lexical perfective | root perfective | * |
| lexical perfective | root perfective | * |
| superlexical perfective | derived imperfective | * |
| superlexical perfective | lexical perfective | * |

## 2.6 Conclusion

This paper explored how the aspectual specification of VP affects the availability of VP-ellipsis in Serbian. It was shown that VP-ellipsis in Serbian, rather than being finiteness-sensitive, is aspect-sensitive – it is not permitted with certain aspectual mismatches between the antecedent and the target. It was proposed that the discrepancies in the availability of VP-ellipsis under these aspectual mismatches can be accounted for under a phase-constrained approach to ellipsis. Following Bošković (2014), I argued that, in order to be elidable, the target needs to be a "phase-privileged" domain, i. e. either a phase or a phasal complement. However, I proposed that in VP-ellipsis in Serbian, the antecedent also has a significant role. Namely, in addition to the target being "phasally relevant", its strict aspectual antecedent, i. e. the part of the antecedent that matches with the target in lexical and viewpoint aspectual specifications, also needs to be either a phase or a phasal complement. This is due to the idea that the general parallelism requirement on ellipsis extends to a parallelism in terms of the phasal status between the antecedent and the target, i. e. either both are phases or both are phasal complements. I showed that, with respect to VP ellipsis in Serbian, the requirements of

1) phasal relevance and 2) phasal parallelism successfully account for a number of seemingly unsystematic patterns involving ellipsis with aspectual mismatches. While exploring VP-ellipsis in Serbian, we hopefully also gained insights into the nature of projections within the VP and the middle field.

## References

Abels, Klauss. 2003. *Successive cyclicity, antilocality, and adposition stranding*. Doctoral dissertation, University of Connecticut, Storrs.

Aljović, Nadira. 2002. Long Adjectival Inflection and Specificity in Serbo-Croatian. *Recherches linguistiques de Vincennes* 31:27–42.

Babko-Malaya, Olga. 1999. Zero Morphology: A Study of Aspect, Argument Structure, and Case. Doctoral dissertation, Rutgers University.

Bobaljik, Jonathan, and Susanne Wurmbrand. 2005. The domain of agreement. *Natural Language and Linguistic Theory* 23:809–865.

Bobaljik, Jonathan, and Susanne Wurmbrand. 2013. Suspension across domains. In *Distributed Morphology Today: Morphemes for Morris Halle*, ed. by A. Marantz and O. Matushansky, 185–198.

Boeckx, Cedric. 2009. On the locus of asymmetry in UG. *Catalan Journal of Linguistics* 8:41–53.

Borer, Hagit. 2005. *Structuring Sense: The Normal Course of Events*. Oxford: Oxford University Press.

Borik, Olga. 2002. *Aspect and reference Time*. Doctoral dissertation, Utrecht University.

Borik, Olga & Tanya Reinhart. 2004. Telicity and Perfectivity: Two Independent Systems, In *Proceedings of the Eighth Symposium on Logic and Language, University of Debrecen*, ed. by L. Hunyadi, G. Rakosi, E. Toth, 12–33.

Bošković, Željko. 1997. *The Syntax of Nonfinite Complementation: An Economy Approach*. MIT Press, Cambridge, Mass.

Bošković, Željko. 2005. On the locality of left branch extraction and the structure of NP. *Studia Linguistica* 59:1–45.

Bošković, Željko. 2008. On the operator freezing effect. *NLLT* 26:249–287.

Bošković, Željko. 2012. On NPs and clauses. *Discourse and grammar*. ed. by G. Grewendorf and T. Zimmermann, 179–242. Mouton de Gruyter.

Bošković, Željko. 2013. Phases beyond clauses. In *Nominal Constructions in Slavic and Beyond*, ed. by L. Schürcks, A. Giannakidou, U. Etxeberria, and P. Kosta, 75–128.

Bošković, Željko. 2014. Now I'm a phase, now I'm not a phase: On the variability of phases with extraction and ellipsis. *Linguistic Inquiry*: 27–89.

Caruso, Đurđica, Željka. 2012. The Syntax of Nominal Expressions in Articleless Languages: A Split-DP Analysis of Croatian Nouns. Doctoral dissertation, University of Stuttgart.

Corver, Norbert. 1992. On deriving left branch extraction asymmetries. *Proceedings of NELS* 22:67–84.

Despić, Miloje. 2011. *Syntax in the Absence of Determiner Phrase*. Doctoral dissertation, University of Connecticut, Storrs.

Despić, Miloje. 2013. Binding and the Structure of NP in Serbo-Croatian. *Linguistic Inquiry* 44:239–270.

den Dikken, Marcel. 2007. Phase extension: Contours of a theory of the role of head movement in phrasal extraction. *Theoretical Linguistics* 33:1–41.

Di Sciullo, Anna Maria and Roumyana Slabakova. 2005. Quantification and Aspect. In *Perspectives on Aspect*, ed. by H. J. Verkuyl, H. de Swart and A. van Hout, 61–80. Dordrecht: Springer.

Filip, Hana. 2000. The quantization puzzle. In *Events as Grammatical Objects*, ed. by C. Tenny and J. Pustejovsky, 39–96. Stanford, CA: CSLI.

Forsyth, John. 1970. *A grammar of aspect: usage and meaning in the Russian verb*. Cambridge, UK: Cambridge University Press.

Gallego, Ángel J., and Juan Uriagereka. 2007. Conditions on sub-extraction. In *Coreference, Modality, and Focus*, ed. by Luis Eguren and Olga Fernández-Soriano, 45–70. Amsterdam: John Benjamins.

Gengel, Kirsten. 2009. Phases and ellipsis. *Linguistic Analysis* 35:21–42.

Holmberg, Anders. 2001. The syntax of yes and no in Finnish. *Studia Linguistica* 55:141–175.

Isačenko, Aleksandr. 1960. *Grammatičeskij stroj russkogo jazyka. Morfologija. Častj vtoraja. Vydavatelstvo Slovenskej Akadémie vied*, Bratislava.

Grimshaw, Jane. 1991. Extended Projection. Ms, Brandeis University, Waltham, MA.

Koizumi, Masatoshi. 1995. Phrase structure in minimalist syntax. Doctoral dissertation, Massachusetts Institute of Technology.

Koulidobrova, Elena V. 2012. *Why choose a language and what happens if you don't: Evidence from bimodal bilinguals*. Doctoral dissertation, University of Connecticut, Storrs.

Larson, Richard. 1988. On the Double Object Construction. *Linguistic Inquiry* 19:335–391.

Leko, Nedžad. 1999. Functional Categories and the Structure of the DP in Bosnian. In *Topics in South Slavic Syntax and Semantics*, ed. by M. Dimitrova-Vulchanova and L. Hellan, 229–252. Amsterdam: John Benjamins.

Marantz, Alec. 2001. Words. *West Coast Conference on Formal Linguistics, University of South California*. Los Angeles. [http://web.mit.edu/marantz/Public/EALING/WordsWCCFL.pdf].

Marantz, Alec. 2007. Phases and words. In *Phases in the theory of grammar*, ed. by S.-H.Choe, 191–222. Seoul: Dong In.

Marelj, Marijana. 2008. Probing the relation between binding and movement. *Proceedings of NELS* 37:73–86.

Merchant, Jason. 2001. *The syntax of silence: Sluicing, islands, and the theory of ellipsis*. Oxford University Press: Oxford.

Milićević, Nataša. 2004. The lexical and superlexical verbal prefix *iz*- and its role in the stacking of prefixes. In *Nordlyd 32*, ed. by P. Svenonius, 279–300.

Pancheva, Roumyana. 2003. The Aspectual Makeup of Perfect Participles and the Interpretations of the Perfect. In *Perfect Explorations*, ed. by A. Alexiadou, M. Rathert, and A. von Stechow, 277–306. Mouton de Gruyter.

Progovac, Ljiljana. 1998. Determiner Phrase in a language without determiners. *Journal of Linguistics* 34:165–179.

Ramchand, Gillian. 2004. Time and the event: the semantics of Russian prefixes. In *Nordlyd 32*, ed. by P. Svenonius, 323–361.

Romanova, Eugenia. 2004. Superlexical. vs. Lexical Prefixes. *Nordlyd* 32:2. 255–278.

Romanova, Eugenia. 2006. Constructing Perfectivity in Russian. Doctoral dissertation. University of Tromsø.

Rouveret, A. 2012. VP ellipsis, phases and the syntax of morphology. *Natural Language and Linguistic Theory* 30:897–963.

Runić, Jelena. 2013. A new look at clitics. In *The Proceedings of FASL 21*, ed. by S. Franks, M. Dickinson, G. Fowler, M. Witcombe, and K. Zanon, 275–288. Michigan Slavic Publications.

Rutkowsky, Pawel, and Ljiljana Progovac. 2005. Classification Projection in Polish and Serbian: The Position and Shape of Classifying Adjectives. In *Annual Workshop on Formal Approaches to Slavic Linguistics 13: The South Carolina Meeting, 2004*, ed. by Steven Franks, Frank Y. Gladney, and Mila Tasseva-Kurktchieva, 289–299. Ann Arbor: Michigan Slavic Publications.

Sag, I. 1976. *Deletion and logical form*. Doctoral dissertation, MIT, Cambridge, Mass.

Stanković, Branimir. 2014a. Arguments for DP-Analyses of Serbo-Croatian Nominal Expressions. In Nominal Structures: All in Complex DPs, edited by L. Veáselovská and M. Janebová, 29–48. Olomouc: Palacký University.

Stanković, Branimir. 2014b. Sintaksa i semantika odredjenog i neodredjenog pridevskog vida u srpskom jeziku. Doctoral dissertation. University of Kragujevac.

von Stechow, Arnim. 2002. German *Seit* 'Since' and the Ambiguity of the German Perfect. In *More than Words: A Festschrift for Dieter Wunderlich*, ed. by B. Stiebels and I. Kaufmann, 393–432. Berlin: Akademie Verlag.

Stjepanović, Sandra. 1997. VP Ellipsis in a Verb Raising Language and Implications for the Condition on Formal Identity of Verbs. In *'Is the Logic Clear?': Papers in Honor of Howard Lasnik, University of Connecticut Working Papers in Linguistics 8* ed. by J-S. Kim, S. Oku, and S. Stjepanović, 287–306.

Svenonius, Peter. 2004. Slavic prefixes inside and outside VP. In *Nordlyd 32*, ed. by P.Svenonius, 205–253.

Şener, Serkan and Daiko Takahashi. 2010. Ellipsis of argument in Japanese and Turkish. *Nanzan Linguistics* 6:79–99.

Shinohara, Matsunaka. 2006. On some differences between the major deletion phenomena and Japanese argument ellipsis. Ms., Nanzan University

Takahashi, Daiko. 2008a. Noun phrase ellipsis. In *The Oxford Handbook of Japanese Linguistics*, ed. by S. Miyagawa and M. Saito, 394–422. New York: Oxford University Press.

Takahashi, Daiko. 2008b. Quantificational null objects and argument ellipsis. *Linguistic Inquiry* 39:307–326.

Takahashi, Daiko. 2014. Argument Ellipsis, Anti-Agreement, and Scrambling. In *Japanese Syntax in Comparative Perspective*. ed. by Mamoru Saito, 88–116.

Takahashi, Masahiko. 2011. *Some consequences of Case-marking in Japanese*. Doctoral dissertation, University of Connecticut, Storrs.

Todorović, Neda. 2015. Tense and Aspect (in)compatibility in Serbian matrix and embedded clauses. *Lingua* 167:82–111.

Todorović, Neda. 2016. On the presence/absence of TP: Syntactic properties and temporal interpretation. Doctoral dissertation, University of Connecticut.

Travis, Lisa. 2010. *Inner aspect: The articulation of VP*. Dordrecht: Springer.

van Craenenbroeck, Jeroen. 2010. *The syntax of ellipsis: Evidence from Dutch dialects*. New York: Oxford University Press.

Wurmbrand, S. 2013. QR and selection: Covert evidence for phasehood. In *Proceedings of the NELS 42*, ed. by S. Keine and S. Sloggett, 277–290. Amherst: University of Massachusetts, GLSA.

Zlatić, Larisa. 1997. The structure of Serbian noun phrase. Doctoral dissertation, University of Texas.

Zucchi, Alessandro. 1999. Incomplete events, intensionality and imperfective aspect. *Natural Language Semantics* 7:179–215.

Barbara Citko
# 3 On top but not a phase: Phasehood inheritance and variation in sluicing

**Abstract:** This paper examines the consequences of Deal's (2016) proposal that TP selected by a relative C becomes a phase for the so-called Focus sluicing languages like Polish, in which the Focus head, rather than the C head, licenses sluicing and triggers wh-movement. It shows that there is no reason to treat a relative TP as a phase in Polish. It attributes the crosslinguistic variation with respect to sluicing to the mechanism of *phasehood inheritance* (Chomsky 2015): a process by which a lower head can inherit phasehood (not just uninterpretable features) from a higher phase head.

## 3.1 Introduction

There are three phase-theoretical issues that I address in this paper.[1] The first one concerns the relationship between ellipsis and phasehood. On some views, only complements of phase heads can be deleted (see Gallego 2010; Gengel 2007; Rouveret 2012; Wurmbrand 2017, among others). On others, both complements of phase heads and entire phases can be deleted (Bošković 2014). And yet on others, there is no direct relationship between phasehood and ellipsis (Aelbrecht 2009). The second issue concerns the range of variation with respect to phasehood. For Bošković (2014) and Wurmbrand (2017), the highest head in an extended projection of a lexical head is a phase head.[2] For others, the same head can be a phase head in one context but not in others, regardless of whether it is the highest head in the extended projection or not. This is the view taken by Den Dikken (2007) or

---
[1] I would like to thank the audience at the 9th Brussels Conference on Generative Linguistics, two anonymous reviewers and the volume editors for insightful questions, comments and suggestions. Since the conference took place in December of 2016, and the paper was written in 2018, the paper may not do justice to the more recent research on phases. I alone remain responsible for any errors and omissions.
[2] This leads to a fair amount of crosslinguistic variation. If a language lacks a DP layer, the highest nominal projection will be a phase. So in some languages, it will be a DP, and in others an NP, as proposed by Bošković 2014 (see, however, Pereltsvaig 2007, 2013 and the references therein, for arguments against treating noun phrases in article-less languages as NPs).

Gallego (2010), for example, who argue in favor of the so-called Phase Extension (in Den Dikken's terms) or Phase Sliding (in Gallego's terms). For Deal (2016), TP is a phase or not depending on whether it is in a relative clause environment or not. And the third issue concerns the mechanisms that can affect phasehood. The view I defend in this paper is that only complements of phase heads can be deleted. Furthermore, it is not always the case that the highest head in an extended projection is a phase head. More specifically, I suggest that in so-called Focus sluicing languages (in Van Craenenbroeck and Lipták's terms), the Focus head inherits phasehood from C. This explains why that the Focus head, rather than the C head, licenses sluicing and triggers wh-movement.

I start with Deal's (2016) proposal that TP becomes a phase when it is selected by a relative C. This can provide a simple account for the contrast in grammaticality between sluicing in questions and relative clauses in English. However, Van Craenenbroeck and Lipták (2006, 2013) show that the ungrammaticality of sluicing in relative clauses is subject to crosslinguistic variation, and that in languages in which the Focus head licenses wh-movement, it also licenses sluicing. This raises two questions *for these languages*: (i) if the Focus head licenses sluicing and wh-movement, is there any reason left to treat CP as a phase?, and (ii) is there any evidence that the relative TP is a phase? To address these questions, I focus on Polish, a language in which (like in Hungarian), Focus movement has been shown to license sluicing, and I provide evidence that the conditions on ellipsis in questions and relative clauses are the same, and that the differences between relative sluicing and non-relative sluicing are due to independent factors.

I proceed as follows. In Section 3.2, I elaborate on the contrast between sluicing in questions and relative clauses and present a phase-theoretical account of this contrast. In Section 3.3, I turn to Polish, a Focus sluicing language in Van Craenenbroeck and Lipták's terminology, and show that Polish violates the No Embedded Stripping Generalization of Wurmbrand (2017). As noted by Wurmbrand herself, this suggests crosslinguistic variation with respect to phasehood, with the C head being a phase head in some languages and the Focus head being a phase head in others. In Section 3.4, I attribute this variation to Phasehood Inheritance. In Sections 3.5, I turn to sluicing in relative clauses, and the question of whether there are any differences between sluicing in relative clauses and sluicing in questions that might suggest different licensing heads. And in Section 3.6, I summarize the main findings of this paper.

## 3.2 Sluicing in interrogative versus relative clauses

Deal (2016) proposes that TP becomes a phase when it is selected by a relative C:

(1)  *Lower Phase Conjecture*
 The TP sister of relative C/Fin is a phase.
 (Deal 2016: 465)

This is how she accounts for the contrast between questions and relative clauses with respect to the so-called *that-trace* effect, illustrated in (2a–b) (Bresnan 1972; Perlmutter 1971):

(2) a. Who do you think **(\*that)** studies syntax?
 b. The students **\*(that)** study syntax are smart.

She relies on Pesetsky and Torrego's (2001) account of the *that*-trace effect in questions, the basic tenets of which are summarized in (3a–d).

(3) a. Nominative Case is uT (uninterpretable Tense feature) on the subject.
 b. The uT feature is checked in the specifier of TP but it is not deleted till CP/phase level so it can also check the uT feature of C.
 c. *that* is the realization of T to C raising.
 d. Economy rules out *that* with fronted subjects (*that*-trace effect)

In the grammatical case of subject extraction given in (4a–b), the subject wh-phrase can check both the wh-feature and the uT feature of C when it moves to [Spec, CP]. By contrast, the derivation of the ungrammatical example (5a), given in (5b), involves both T to C movement, realized as *that*, and movement of the subject to the embedded [Spec, CP]. Since the subject can check the uT feature of C, T to C movement is redundant and violates economy.

(4) a. Who do you think studies syntax?
 b. [$_{CP}$ who$_{[uT, wh]}$ do you think [$_{CP}$ ~~who~~$_{[uT, wh]}$ C$_{[uT, uwh]}$ [$_{TP}$ ~~who~~ T [$_{VP}$ studies syntax]]]]

(5) a. \*Who do you think **that** studies syntax?
 b. \*[$_{CP}$ who$_{[uT, wh]}$ do you think [$_{CP}$ ~~who~~$_{[uT, wh]}$ [$_T$ **that**]$_i$-C$_{[uT, uwh]}$ [$_{TP}$ ~~who~~ T$_i$ [$_{VP}$ studies syntax ]]]]

Relative clauses are well-known to differ from wh-questions with respect to the *that*-trace effect (Bresnan 1972). Deal accounts for this difference by proposing that the TP inside the relative clause is a phase (per her conjecture in (1)). This means that the checked uninterpretable features contained inside the TP are deleted; the [uT] feature on the subject in [Spec, TP] is not accessible to C, and the only way for the uT feature on C to be checked is via T to C movement. This is schematized in (6a–d).[3]

(6) a. *students that study syntax*
 b. [TP [DP **OP**]₍ᵤT, wh₎ T [VP study syntax ]]
 c. [CP C₍ᵤT, wh₎ [TP [DP **OP**]₍ᵤ̶T̶, wh₎ T [VP study syntax ]]]
 d. [CP [DP **OP**]₍wh₎ [T **that**]ᵢ-C₍ᵤ̶T̶, ᵤ̶w̶h̶₎ [TP O̶P̶ T̶ᵢ [VP study syntax ]]]

---

**3** This is not by no means the only way to account for the contrast between movement from complement clauses and relative clauses with respect to the *that*-trace effect, and there are many alternatives that do not rely on phasehood (see Pesetsky 2017 for an overview). Rizzi (1990), for example, hypothesizes that the lack of the *that* trace effect in relative clauses has to do with the fact that a null operator cannot agree a null complementizer. More recently, Gallego (2007) derives the obligatorily presence of the complementizer in relative clauses from the assumption that null operators cannot pied-pipe. Douglas (2017) attributes it to a difference in size. CPs in clauses containing a complementizer are split into at least ForceP and FinP, whereas CPs without a complementizer remain CPs. In relative clauses without a complementizer, the promoted head moves from [Spec, TP] to [Spec, CP], as shown in (ia-b).

(i) a. *students study syntax
 b. [CP studentsᵢ C [TP tᵢ T [VP tᵢ study syntax ]]]

This movement, however, is too short; it violates the anti-locality of Erlewine (2016), given in (ii). (see, however, Abels 2003 and Grohmann 2000 for other versions of anti-locality, which would not rule out the movement in (ib).

(ii) A'-movement of a phrase from the Specifier of XP must cross a maximal projection other than XP.
 (Erlewine 2016: 445)

In relative clauses with *that*, on the other hand, movement is longer; it crosses FinP:

(iii) a. students that study syntax
 b. [ForP studentsᵢ [For' that [FinP [TP tᵢ T [VP tᵢ study syntax ]]]]]

However, anti-locality also rules out the standardly assumed derivation for successive cyclic movement from complement clauses, given in (ivb), leading Douglas to pursue an alternative account of successive cyclic movement.

(iv) a. Who do you think studies syntax?
 b. [CP C [do you think [CP **who**ᵢ [C' C [TP tᵢ T [VP tᵢ studies syntax ]]]]]]

What is interesting about Deal's proposal that TP is a phase in relative contexts is that it can provide a simple account for the difference between sluicing in questions and relative clauses. As shown by the contrast between (7a) and (7b) and the ungrammaticality of the examples in (8a-b), sluicing is banned in relative clauses (Lobeck 1995; Merchant 2001).

(7) a. Someone stole the car but they couldn't find out **who**.
    b. *Someone stole the car, but they couldn't find the person **who**.
       (Merchant 2001: 59)

(8) a. *Someone wants to talk to Mary, but the person **who** __ is too shy to approach her.
    b. *Although the place **where** __ is unclear, the time when the meeting is to be held is posted on the door.
       (Lobeck 1995: 57)

On the assumption that ellipsis is the pronunciation of the *spell-out domain* as zero, which means that *only* complements of phase heads can be deleted (as in Gengel 2007; Rouveret 2012; Wurmbrand 2017, but contra Bošković 2014, who allows both phases and complements of phase heads to be deleted), this contrast can be attributed to the fact that in wh-questions, the complement of a phase head is deleted (as shown in (9a)), but in relative clauses, the entire phase is, as shown in (9b). Crucially, this account only works if TP is a phase in relative clauses (but not in wh-questions) and only complements of phase heads can be deleted (as opposed to both complements of phase heads and entire phases). If CP remains a phase in (9b), then both (9a) and (9b) are predicted to be possible, contrary to fact. And if both phases and complements of phase heads can undergo ellipsis, both are incorrectly predicted to be possible as well.[4]

(9) a. wh-questions

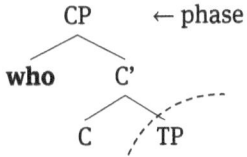

---

4 Thank you to one of the reviewers for asking me to be explicit about this point.

b. relative clauses

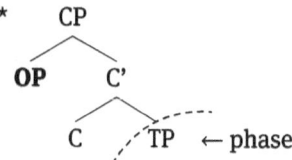

Such a phase-theoretical account departs from accounts that rely purely on the featural make-up of the C head licensing sluicing. Lobeck (1995), following Rizzi (1990), takes the complementizer in relative clauses to be marked [−WH]. If sluicing is only licensed by a [+WH] complementizer with an agreeing wh-phrase in its specifier, the ungrammaticality of sluicing in relative clauses can be accounted for. Merchant (2001) builds on this account, and attributes the ungrammaticality of sluiced relatives to a condition on the E feature (the Ellipsis feature); this feature is only 'compatible' with interrogative environments.

(10)   English sluicing: $E_{[uwh*, uQ*]}$

However, it is also well-known that sluicing is subject to a fair amount of crosslinguistic variation (Van Craenenbroeck and Lipták 2006; Lipták and Aboh 2013; Lipták 2015, the contributions in Merchant and Simpson 2012, among many others). In the next section, I turn to Polish, one of the languages identified by Van Craenenbroeck and Lipták as Focus sluicing languages, and to the question of what heads count as phase heads in Focus sluicing languages.

## 3.3 Focus sluicing in Polish

Van Craenenbroeck and Lipták (2006) propose the following parameter to account for variation in sluicing, tying it to variation with respect to wh-movement. The gist of their proposal, given in (11), is that the head that triggers wh-movement is the head that licenses sluicing.

(11)   *The Wh/Sluicing Correlation*
       The syntactic features that the [E]-feature has to check in a certain language are identical to the strong features a wh-phrase has to check in a regular constituent question in that language.
       (Van Craenenbroeck and Lipták 2006: 257)

Even though their data come mostly from Hungarian, they include Spanish, Basque, Polish, Russian and Hebrew in the same group of languages, i.e. languages in which the E feature is dissociated from the wh-feature and is linked to the Operator feature instead, hosted by the Focus head. More concretely, they posit the following difference between the properties of the E feature in English and Hungarian:

(12) a. Hungarian: E $_{[uOp*]}$
 b. English: E$_{[uwh*, uQ*]}$
  (Van Craenenbroeck and Lipták 2006: 258)

Polish is like Hungarian is that the Focus head can license sluicing (see Grebenyova 2006, 2007, for relevant discussion and examples from Russian and Polish). We see this not only in embedded wh-questions (13a), but also in embedded yes-no questions (13b) and in embedded declarative clauses (13c).

(13) a. *Wiem, kto studiował składnię, ale nie wiem,* **kto fonologię**.
  know who studied syntax but not know who phonology
  'I know who studied syntax but I don't know who (studied) phonology.'
 b. *Wiem, że Maria studiowała składnię, ale nie jestem pewna,* ***czy***
  know that Maria studied syntax but not am sure if
  ***fonologię***.
  phonology
  'I know that Maria studied syntax but I am not sure if (she studied) phonology.'
 c. *Wiem, że Maria studiowała składnię, ale nie wiedziałam,* ***że***
  know that Maria studied syntax but not knew that
  ***fonologię***.
  phonology
  'I know that Maria studied syntax but I didn't know that (she studied) phonology.'

Even though it is tangential to the issue of the Focus head being a phase head or not, it is also worth noting is that the remnant in Focus sluicing can be a negative polarity item (NPI), as shown in (14).[5]

---

5 Polish is a strict negative concord language, in which clausemate negation is required to license NPIs (see Błaszczak 2001; Giannakidou 2000; Przepiórkowski and Kupść 1999; Zeijlstra 2004, among many others).

(14)  *Wiem, kto kogoś  zaprosił, ale nie wiem,* **kto  nikogo.**
  know who someone invited   but not know who anyone
  'I know who invited someone but I don't know who (didn't invite) anyone.'

This example also shows that Focus sluicing allows polarity mismatches; the antecedent clause is positive but the elided clause is negative, as evidenced by the presence of the NPI, which requires clausemate negation. This goes against Merchant's (2013) generalization, which states that larger ellipsis types (i. e. sluicing and sentence fragments) disallow polarity mismatches.[6]

While sluicing in embedded wh-questions remains grammatical when the focused remnant is absent, it becomes ungrammatical in embedded *yes/no* questions and in embedded declaratives. Example (15a) parallels in grammaticality example (13a) above, but the examples in (15b–c) contrast in grammaticality with the examples in (13b–c).[7,8] I take this to mean that it is the Focus head with a focused remnant in its specifier that licenses ellipsis, not the C head.

---

**6** Polarity mismatches are allowed only if some element that indicates the difference in polarity (e. g., NPI or a polarity particle) survives ellipsis. Not surprisingly, sluicing with wh-remnants does not allow polarity mismatches: (ia) allows the interpretation in in (ib), where the antecedent clause and the elided clause match in polarity, but it disallows the interpretation in (ic), where the two do not match.

(i)  a.  *Ktoś  wyszedł, ale nie wiem,* **kto.**
      someone left    but not know who
      'Someone left but I don't know who.'
   b.  = *Ktoś  wyszedł, ale nie wiem,* **kto wyszedł.**
      someone left    but not know who left
      'Someone left but I don't know who left.'
   c.  ≠ *Ktoś  wyszedł, ale nie wiem,* **kto  nie wyszedł.**
      someone left    but not know who not left
      'Someone left but I don't know who left.'

**7** The examples in (15a–c) are not direct counterparts of (13a–c), with just the focus remnant missing. They have been modified slightly to control for control for independent factors. For example, (i), which would be a more direct counterpart of (13a), is infelicitous for the same reasons its non-elided variant is.

(i)  #*Wiem, kto  studiował składnię, ale nie wiem,* **kto.**
    know who studied   syntax    but not know who
    'I know who studied syntax but I don't know who (studied syntax).'

**8** The inability of *yes/no* and declarative complementizers to license sluicing extends to C sluicing languages like English and is well documented in the relevant literature. For example, Lobeck (1995) attributes it to the strong agreement requirement, where only heads agreeing with phrases in their specifiers can license sluicing. Merchant (2001) attributes it to the E feature specification.

(15) a. Wiem, że ktoś studiował składnię, ale nie wiem, **kto.**
know that someone studied syntax but not know who
'I know that someone studied syntax but I don't know who (studied syntax).'

b. *Jan wie, że Maria studiowała składnię, ale ja nie jestem pewna,
Jan knows that Maria studied syntax but I not am sure
**czy.**
if
'Jan knows that Maria studied syntax but I am not sure if (she studied syntax).'

c. *Jan słyszał, że Maria studiowała składnię, ale ja nie wiedziałam,
Jan heard that Maria studied syntax but I not knew
**że.**
that
'Jan heard that Maria studied syntax but I didn't know that (she studied syntax).'

The behavior of Polish Focus sluicing is consistent with the structure Van Craenenbroeck and Lipták propose for Hungarian. Thus, the structure of (16a) is given in (16b).

(16) a. Wiem, że Maria studiowała składnię, ale nie wiedziałam, **że**
know that Maria studied syntax but not knew if
**fonologię.**
phonology
'I know that Maria studied syntax, but I didn't know that (she studied) phonology.'

b. ...

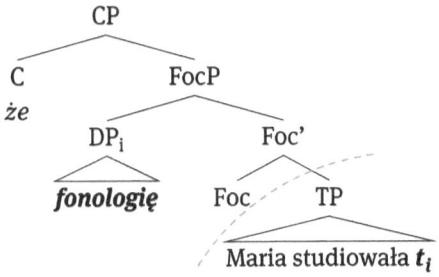

Further support for the structure in (16b) comes from the fact that sentence fragments can also be embedded in Polish (see Temmerman 2013; Valmala 2007; Weir

2014; Wurmbrand 2017 on the embeddability of fragments crosslinguistically), as shown in (17a–b).

(17) a. *Myślę, że **Jana**.*
  think that Jan.ACC
  'I think that Jan.'
 b. *Żałuję, że **Jana**.*
  regret that Jan.ACC
  'I regret that Jan.'

So can polarity particles, which are generally assumed to be heads of their own (Polarity) projections (see, for example, Authier 2013; Citko 2015, 2018, Gribanova 2017; Kazenin 2006; Laka 1990; López-Carretero 1995 on polarity and ellipsis).[9]

(18) a. *Myślę, że **tak/nie**.*
  think that yes/no
  'I think so/not.'

If (18) is type of stripping, where the term stripping refers to clausal ellipsis in which one constituent survives ellipsis (Hankamer 1979), Polish violates the Embedded Stripping Generalization of Wurmbrand 2017, given in (19).

(19) *Embedded Stripping Generalization*
 Stripping of embedded clauses is only possible when the embedded clause lacks a CP.
 (Wurmbrand 2017: 345)

I follow Merchant (2003) and Wurmbrand (2017) in treating stripping as TP ellipsis, which makes stripping, sluicing and sentence fragments part of the same family of elliptical constructions. Wurmbrand focuses on the contrasts of the kind given in (20a–b), which have been taken to show that stripping is impossible in embedded clauses.

(20) a. *Jane loves to study rocks, and **geography too**.*
 b. *\*Jane loves to study rocks, and John says that **geography too**.*
  (Wurmbrand 2017: 341-342, citing Lobeck 1995)

---

[9] If polarity particles head a different projection, their behavior does not bear directly on the issue of the Focus head licensing ellipsis.

What Wurmbrand discovered is that embedded stripping becomes possible when the complementizer is absent; note the contrast between the ungrammatical (20b) and the grammatical (21).

(21)     *Jane loves to study rocks, and John says **geography too**.*
        (Wurmbrand 2017: 344)

She provides a phase-theoretical account of this contrast, relying on the assumption that only complements of phase heads can be deleted. This means that when there is no complementizer, as in (22), there is no CP layer. This in turn means that FocP, the highest projection, is a phase, and its complement can be deleted. By contrast, in (23), which contains an overt complementizer, CP is a phase, which means sluicing (i. e., TP deletion) would be deletion of the complement of the complement of the phase head.

(22)    a.    Abby claimed (that) Ben would ask her out, but she didn't think **Bill** (too).
            (Merchant 2003: 4)
     b.    ...

          FocP                ← phase
       **Bill**    Foc'
           Foc    TP       ← complement of phase head deleted

(23)    a.    *\*Abby claimed Ben would ask her out, but she didn't think **that Bill** (too).*
            (Wurmbrand 2017: 344)
     b.    ...

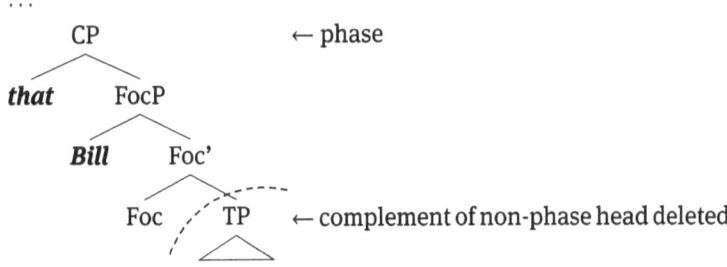

← phase

← complement of non-phase head deleted

Wurmbrand (2017) also noted that there is crosslinguistic variation with respect to stripping. In languages in which wh-movement targets [Spec, FocP] (i. e. Focus sluicing languages in Van Craenenbroek and Lipták's terminology), stripping is possible even if the complementizer is present. Her evidence comes from Hungarian and Spanish. Polish and Hungarian are alike in this respect, as shown in (24a–b).

(24) a. János meghívott valakit        és    azt       hiszem, hogy BÉLÁT.
        János PV.invited someone.ACC and that.ACC think   that Béla.ACC
        'János invited someone and I think it was Béla whom he invited.'
        (Van Craenenbroeck and Lipták 2006: 260)
    b. Jan kogoś            zaprosił. Myślę, że  Piotra.
        Jan someone.ACC invited     think that Piotr.ACC
        'Jan invited someone. I think it was Peter.'

This leads Wurmbrand to conclude that the Focus head is a phase head in Focus sluicing languages in spite of the presence of C. I agree with this conclusion, and turn to the question of *why* there should be crosslinguistic variation with respect to whether C or Foc head is a phase head.

## 3.4 Phasehood inheritance

I attribute the contrast between Focus sluicing languages like Polish or Hungarian and C sluicing languages like English to the fact that phasehood *itself* can be inherited by a Focus head from a C head, as shown in (25). This allows the complement of the lower (derived) phase head to be deleted without requiring the complementizer to be absent.

(25)    *Phasehood Inheritance*

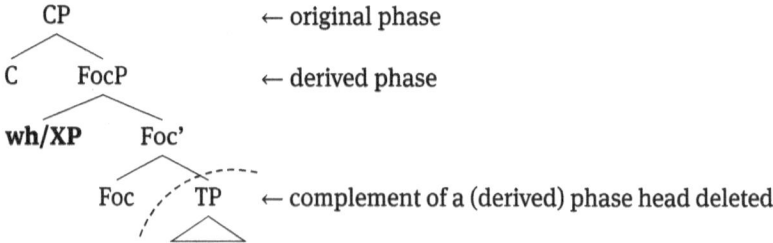

The idea that phasehood can be inherited is not novel. Den Dikken (2007) and Gallego (2010), for example, explore the consequences of head movement for phasehood (as also discussed in Citko 2014). For Den Dikken (2007), movement of a phase head α to a higher (non-phase) head ß makes ß the phase head, and causes α to lose its phasehood status.[10] Gallego (2010) proposes that in null subject languages T inherits phasehood from *v* if *v* moves to T.[11] For both Den Dikken and Gallego, phasehood is inherited upwards, which opens up the possibility that phasehood can be inherited downwards as well. The C to Focus head Phasehood Inheritance I am proposing here is one example of downward inheritance. Another one is Chomsky's (2015) account of the *that*-trace effect, which relies on T inheriting phasehood from C when C is null. Deal (2016: 439) also discusses the possibility of T inheriting a wh-feature from C, which is 'tantamount to inheritance of phasal status from C by T.' This is what allows C to delete. Consequently, the subject in [Spec, TP] is at the phase edge, since now TP is a phase. When *that* is present, deletion of C is impossible, which means that CP remains a phase, so the subject becomes inaccessible when the complement of C is spelled out.

The mechanism of Phasehood Inheritance I am suggesting here raises the question of how to constrain it (i. e., how to determine whether Phasehood Inheritance takes place or not, and how to determine which phase heads pass their phasal status to their complements, and which ones do not).[12] One way to think about Phasehood Inheritance is to treat it as an extension of Feature Inheritance, with Phasehood Inheritance being an extreme case of Feature Inheritance. If the original phase head (C in the case under consideration) does not have any uninterpretable features left, there is simply no reason for it to remain a phase.[13] If inheriting phasehood amounts to inheriting all uninterpretable features in one operation, inheriting phasehood is more economical than inheriting individual uninterpretable features separately.

So far, we have seen evidence that the Focus head licenses sluicing. We have not, however, seen any evidence yet that the same head triggers wh-movement.

---

**10** Den Dikken's (2007) characterization of Phase Extension is given in (i).

(i)    *Phase Extension*
Syntactic movement of the head H of a phase α up to the head X of the node ß dominating α extends the phase up from α to ß; α loses its phasehood in the process, and any constituent on the edge of α ends up in the domain of the derived phase ß as a result of Phase Extension.
(Den Dikken 2007: 1)

**11** In Gallego's system, *v* does not lose its phasehood status, and T also inherits φ-features from C. This 'double' inheritance (both from C and T) is what captures the mixed A/A-bar status of [Spec, TP] position in languages like Spanish or Catalan.
**12** I thank the anonymous reviewers for raising these questions.
**13** In Gallego's terms, being the locus of uninterpretable features is the definitional characteristic of phase heads, so if a phase head loses its uninterpretable features, it loses its raison d'être.

The evidence that it does comes from the following considerations. First, the moving wh-phrase can be pronounced in [Spec, FocP], following the overt complementizer (Lasnik and Saito 1984; Wiland 2009, 2010; Willim 1989, among others):

(26) Maria myśli, **że co**$_i$ Janek kupił **t**$_i$?
Maria thinks that what Janek bought
'What does Maria think that Janek bought?'
(Lasnik and Saito 1984: 238)

(27) a. Jan myślał, **że jaki samochód**$_i$ Paweł kupił swojej żonie **t**$_i$?
Jan thought that what car Paweł bought his wife
'What car did Jan think Paweł bought his wife?' **COMP WH**
b. *Jan myślał, **jaki samochód**$_i$ **że** Paweł kupił swojej żonie **t**$_i$?
Jan thought what car that Paweł bought his wife
'What car did Jan think Paweł bought his wife?' ***WH COMP**
(Wiland 2010: 338)

In multiple wh-questions, both wh-phrases follow the complementizer:[14]

(28) a. Jan myślał, **że co**$_i$ **komu**$_j$ Paweł kupił **t**$_j$ **t**$_i$?
Jan thought that what whom Paweł bought
'What did Jan think Paweł bought for whom?' **COMP WH WH**
b. *Jan myślał, **co**$_i$ **że komu**$_j$ Paweł kupił **t**$_j$ **t**$_i$?
Jan thought what that whom Paweł bought
'What did Jan think Paweł bought for whom?' ***WH COMP WH**
(Wiland 2010: 339)

Second, wh-words have to follow topics (Tajsner 2008; Wiland 2009):[15]

(29) a. **Marka** to **gdzie**$_i$ Ania spotkała **t**$_i$?
Marek.ACC TOP where Anna.NOM met
'As for Marc, where did Anna meet him?' **Top WH**
b. ***Gdzie**$_i$ **Marka** to Ania spotkała **t**$_i$?
where Marek.ACC TOP Anna.NOM met
'As for Marc, where did Anna meet him?' ***WH Top**
(Tajsner 2008: 359)

---

**14** This does not mean that they cannot front to the clause initial position.
**15** Wiland identifies the lower projection as ΣP.

Third, wh-phrases can be split with the nominal stranded in [Spec, FocP], as shown in (30a–b). This is an example of Left Branch Extraction, well-documented in the literature since Ross 1967.[16]

(30)  a.  ***Jaki**$_i$ chcesz, żeby [t$_i$ **samochód**]$_j$ Maria kupiła t$_j$?*
        what want  COMP  car        Maria bought
        'What kind of a car do you want Maria to buy?'
   b.  ***Ile**$_i$       Jan twierdzi, że  [t$_i$ **artykułów**]$_j$ Maria napisała t$_j$?*
        how.many Jan claims  that    articles     Maria wrote
        'How many articles does Jan know that Maria wrote?'

One of the reviewers raises the question of how the examples in (26)–(30) show that the Focus Phrase is a phase. These examples show that the specifier of Focus Phrase can be a landing site for moved wh-phrases in spite of the presence of an overt complementizer. The movement to [Spec, FocP] is driven by uninterpretable features. If phase heads are the loci of uninterpretable features, it follows that the Focus has to be a phase head.[17]

## 3.5 Sluicing in Polish relative clauses

The question I turn to now concerns the phasehood status of relative clauses in Polish. We saw above that Deal accounted for the absence of the *that*-trace effect in English relative clauses by treating relative TPs as phases. Polish, however, differs from English in that it does not exhibit the *that*-trace effect in either questions or relative clauses (Miechowicz-Mathiasen 2012; Szczegielniak 1999; Zabrocki 1984, but see, for example, Witkoś 1993, for a different view):[18,19]

---

[16] There is variation in judgements here. Wiland (2010) marks the following example as ungrammatical; I do not have any explanation for this variation.

(i)   *\*Jaki$_i$ powiedziałeś, że  t$_i$ samochód$_i$ Paweł kupił  swojej żonie t$_i$?*
     what said         that  car.ACC  Paweł bought his  wife
     (Wiland 2010: 343)

[17] The status of the examples in (26)–(30) is also compatible with the Focus head inheriting just the relevant uninterpretable feature from C (see, Germain 2017, for example, for an explicit proposal that uwh and EPP features driving wh-movement are inherited by the Focus head from C).
[18] The lack of the *that*-trace effect in Polish has also been taken to mean that the Polish complementizers *że* and *żeby* are true complementizers, rather than a reflex of T raised to C (Citko and Gračanin-Yuksek 2017; Pesetsky and Torrego 2001, contra Miechowicz-Mathiasen 2012).
[19] One of the reviewers wonders if the wh-relativizer and the complementizer can co-occur in (31b); the ungrammaticality of (i) shows that they cannot:

(31) a. ***Kto**$_i$ chcesz, **żeby** t$_i$ studiował językoznawstwo?*
 who want COMP studied linguistics
 'Who do you want to study linguistics?'
 b. *Studentki, **które**$_i$**/co** t$_i$ studiują językoznawstwo są mądre.*
 students who/COMP study linguistics are smart
 'The students who study linguistics are smart.'

The examples in (32a–d), obtained via Google search, provide further illustration that Polish allows the *that*-trace effect violations.

(32) a. ***Kto**$_i$ myślisz, **że** t$_i$ tu stoi i tego naucza?*
 who think that here stands and this teaches
 'Who do you think stands here and teaches this?'
 (https://www.przemianaumyslu.pl/badz-moja-walentynka, accessed 25 September, 2019)
 b. ***Kto**$_i$ chcesz, **żeby** t$_i$ został prezydentem?*
 who want COMP became president
 'Who do you want to become president?'
 (https://www.onet.pl/?utm_source=zapytaj_viasg&utm_medium=nitro&utm_campaign=zapytaj_nitro, accessed 25 September, 2019)
 c. ***Kto**$_i$ wydaje ci się, **że** t$_i$ kocha cię bardziej?*
 who seems you REFL that loves you more
 'Who seems to you to love you more?'
 (https://samequizy.pl/tata-czy-mama/, accessed 25 September, 2019)

Perhaps related is the fact the complementizer is obligatory in both wh-questions and relative clauses:

(33) a. ***Kto**$_i$ myślisz, ***(że)** t$_i$ studiuje językoznawstwo?*
 who think that studies linguistics
 'Who do you think studies linguistics?'
 b. *Te studentki, ***(które**$_i$**/co)** zatrudnili t$_i$ są mądre.*
 these students who/COMP hired are are smart
 'The students that they hired are smart.'

Given no differences between relative clauses and non-relative clauses with respect to the *that*-trace effect in Polish, there is no reason to treat relative TPs differ-

---

(i) **Studentki, **które**$_i$ co t$_i$ studiują językoznawstwo są mądre.*
 students who COMP study linguistics are smart
 'The students who study linguistics are smart.'

ently from non-relative ones. I take this to indicate that neither relative nor non-relative TPs are phases in Polish. Could, however, the opposite be the case? In other words, could the lack of the *that*-trace effect in both relative and non-relative clauses mean that both relative and non-relative TPs *are* phases? This, I believe, would be an unwelcome conclusion. For example, it would predict that sluicing should be ungrammatical, as it would involve deletion of an entire phase.

The question I turn to now is whether TPs can be sluiced in Polish relative clauses; given the conclusion we have just reached that relative TPs are not phases in Polish, it should be possible to sluice them, since we would not be sluicing an entire phase. And, indeed, Lipták and Aboh (2013) and Lipták (2015) have noted that sluicing is not universally banned in relative clauses, and that languages like Gungbe and Hungarian allow it, as shown in (34a–b), respectively:

(34) a. *Kòfí ná yrɔ́ mè   ɖé àmɔ̀n má     nyɔ́n mè   ɖĕ wè.*
       Kòfí FUT call person IND but   1SG.NEG know person REL FOC
       Lit. 'Kofi will call someone, but I don't know the person who.'
    b. *Ezért    tartunk    ott,  ahol.*
       this.for be.PRES.3PL there REL.where
       Lit. 'For this reason we are wherever we are.'
       (Lipták and Aboh 2013: 105)

However, Polish is different in this respect in that it disallows sluicing in relative clauses in the absence of an independent Focus movement. This is shown in (35a–b) for so-called light-headed relatives (in Citko's (2004) terminology).

(35) a. **Wiem, że ktoś    zna   składnię, ale nie znam tego, kto.*
       know that someone knows syntax   but not know DEM who
       'I know that someone knows syntax but I don't know the one who (does).'
    b. *Znam kogoś,   kto zna    składnię, ale nie znam nikogo, **kto***
       know someone who knows syntax    but not know anyone who
       **fonologię**.
       phonology
       'I know someone who knows syntax but I don't know anyone who (studies) phonology.'

We cannot appeal to TP being a phase in order to exclude the relative sluicing in (35a). There is, however, an alternative explanation, which is also phase-theoretical, and which does not rely on TPs being phases. It relies on the assumption, due to Rizzi (1997), that wh-pronouns in relative clauses occupy a higher position than wh-pronouns in wh-questions, as shown in (36b). Rizzi takes this position to be [Spec, ForceP].[20] If Focus Phrases are phases in Polish, the ungrammaticality of (35a) could be due to the fact that the entire phase (FocP) is deleted, as shown in (36b).[21]

(36)  a.  wh-questions

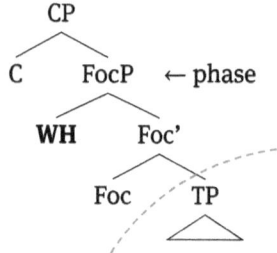

b.  relative clauses

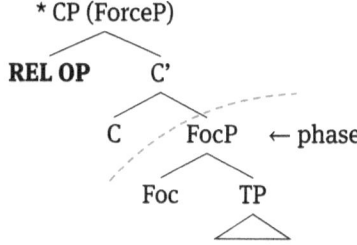

The upshot of the discussion in this section is that the same head, which I have taken to be the Focus head, licenses sluicing in both relative clauses and embedded questions. The differences that we see between relative and non-relative sluicing have an independent explanation (i. e., different landing sites for relative and interrogative wh-pronouns).

Let me conclude this section by mentioning another difference between relative and non-relative sluicing, which also has an independent explanation. It involves multiple sluicing: it is allowed in wh-questions but not in relative clauses, as shown by the contrast between (37a) and (37b) (see Grebenyova 2007, 2009; Marušič and Žaucer 2013; Szczegielniak 2008 on multiple sluicing in Slavic languages more generally):

---

**20** As we saw above, others (such as Lobeck 1995 or Merchant 2001), attribute the ungrammaticality of sluicing in relative clauses to the featural make-up of the head licensing ellipsis.
**21** One could wonder what prevents TP deletion in (36b). This would be deletion of a complement of a phase head. I take it to indicate that an empty Focus head with an empty specifier cannot license sluicing.

(37) a. *Każdy zaprosił kogoś     do tańca, ale nie pamiętam,* **kto kogo**.
   every invited  someone to dance but not remember who whom
   'Everyone invited someone to dance but I don't remember who whom.'
   (Grebenyova 2007: 54)
   b. *\*Każdy zaprosił kogoś     do tańca, ale nie znam tego,* **kto kogo**.
   every invited  someone to dance but not know DEM who whom
   'Everyone invited someone to dance but I don't know the one that invited whom.'

However, the ungrammaticality of (37b) has nothing to do with ellipsis, as its non-elliptical variant in (38) is equally degraded:[22]

(38) *\*Każdy zaprosił kogoś     do tańca, ale nie znam tego,* **kto kogo** *zaprosił*.
   every invited  someone to dance but not know DEM who whom invited
   Lit. 'Everyone invited someone to dance but I don't know the one who invited whom.'

What looks like multiple sluicing in relative clauses is only possible if the second remnant is *not* a wh-phrase, as shown in (39). This, however, is run-of-the-mill example of Focus sluicing.

(39) *Znam kogoś,    kto studiuje składnię, ale nie znam nikogo,* **kto**
   know someone who studies  syntax    but not know anyone who
   **fonologię**.
   phonology
   'I know someone that studies syntax but I don't know anyone that (studies) phonology.'

## 3.6 Conclusion

To conclude briefly, I have addressed the following three phase-theoretical issues in this paper: (i) the relationship between ellipsis and phasehood, (ii) crosslinguistic variation with respect to phasehood, and (iii) the mechanisms that affect phasehood. The view I have taken in this paper is that only complements of phase heads can be deleted. Furthermore, it is not always the case that the highest head

---

[22] See Citko and Gračanin-Yuksek (2016) for an account of why relative clauses with multiple wh-pronouns are ungrammatical. In short, they attribute it to a semantic mismatch. The nominal head (which is of type <e, t>) cannot combine with a CP which has undergone two instances of predicate abstraction, because such a CP is of type <e, <e,t>>.

in the extended projection is the phase head. More specifically, I have suggested that in so-called Focus sluicing languages, the Focus head inherits phasehood from the C head. This means that the Focus head, rather than the C head, licenses sluicing and triggers wh-movement. Furthermore, I have shown that in Focus sluicing languages like Polish, there is no reason to treat a relative TP as a phase.

# References

Abels, Klaus. 2003. *Successive cyclicity, anti-locality, and adposition stranding*. Storrs, CT: University of Connecticut PhD thesis.
Aelbrecht, Lobke. 2009. *You have the right to remain silent: the syntactic licensing of ellipsis*. Brussels: Catholic University of Brussels PhD thesis.
Authier, J.-Marc. 2013. Phase-edge features and the syntax of polarity particles. *Linguistic Inquiry* 44:345–389.
Błaszczak, Joanna. 2001. *Investigation into the interaction between the indefinites and negation*. Berlin: Akademie-Verlag.
Bošković, Željko. 2014. Now I'm a phase, now I'm not a phase: On the variability of phases with extraction and ellipsis. *Linguistic Inquiry* 45:27–90.
Bresnan, Joan. 1972. *Theory of complementation in English syntax*. Cambridge, MA: Massachusetts Institute of Technology PhD thesis.
Chomsky, Noam. 2015. Problems of projection: Extensions. In Elisa Di Domenico, Cornelia Hamann and Simona Matteini (eds.), *Structures, strategies and beyond: Studies in honour of Adriana Belletti*, 1–16. Amsterdam/Philadelphia: John Benjamins Publishing Company.
Citko, Barbara. 2004. On headed, headless, and light-headed relatives. *Natural Language and Linguistic Theory* 22:95–126.
Citko, Barbara. 2014. *Phase theory: An Introduction*. Cambridge: Cambridge University Press.
Citko, Barbara. 2015. The Gapping that Could. In Małgorzata Szajbel-Keck, Roslyn Burns and Darya Kavitskaya (eds.), *Formal Approaches to Slavic Linguistics #23: The Berkeley Meeting 2014*, 36–56. Ann Arbor, MI: Michigan Slavic Publications.
Citko, Barbara. 2018. On the relationship between backward gapping and right node raising. *Syntax* 21:1–36.
Citko, Barbara and Martina Gračanin-Yuksek. 2016. Multiple (coordinated) (free) relatives. *Natural Language and Linguistic Theory* 34:393–427.
Citko, Barbara and Martina Gračanin-Yuksek. 2017. On variation in COMP & WH structures. In Claire Halpert, Hadas Kotek and Coppe van Urk (eds.), *A Pesky set: Papers for David Pesetsky*, 203–212. Cambridge, MA: MIT Working Papers in Linguistics.
van Craenenbroeck, Jeroen and Anikó Lipták. 2006. The crosslinguistic syntax of sluicing: Evidence from Hungarian relatives. *Syntax* 9:248–274.
van Craenenbroeck, Jeroen and Anikó Lipták. 2013. What sluicing can do, what it can't, and in which language: On the cross-linguistic syntax of ellipsis. In Lisa Lai-Shen Cheng and Norbert Corver (eds.), *Diagnosing syntax*, 502–536. Oxford: Oxford University Press.
Deal, Amy Rose. 2016. Cyclicity and connectivity in Nez Perce relative clauses. *Linguistic Inquiry* 47:427–470.

Den Dikken, Marcel. 2007. Phase extension. Contours of a theory of the role of head movement in phrasal extraction. *Theoretical Linguistics* 33:1–41.

Douglas, Jamie. 2017. Unifying the that-trace and anti-that-trace effects. *Glossa: A journal of general linguistics*, 2 (1):60. 1-28.

Erlewine, Michael Yoshitaka. 2016. Anti-locality and optimality in Kaqchikel agent focus. *Natural Language and Linguistic Theory* 34 (2):429–479.

Gallego, Ángel J. 2007. Phase Theory, case and relative clauses. *Anuario del Seminario de Filología Vasca Julio de Urquijo. International Journal of Basque Linguistics and Philology* XLI-2:71–94.

Gallego, Ángel J. 2010. *Phase theory*. Amsterdam/Philadelphia: John Benjamins.

Gengel, Kirsten. 2007. *Focus and ellipsis: A generative analysis of pseudogapping and other elliptical structures*. Stuttgart: Stuttgart University PhD thesis.

Giannakidou, Anastasia. 2000. Negative ... concord? *Natural Language and Linguistic Theory* 18:457–523.

Germain, Allison. 2017. Non-nominative Subjects in Russian and Lithuanian: Case, argument Structure, and anaphor binding. Seattle, WA: University of Washington PhD thesis.

Grebenyova, Lydia. 2006. *Multiple interrogatives: Syntax, semantics and learnability*. College Park, MD: University of Maryland PhD thesis.

Grebenyova, Lydia. 2007. Sluicing in Slavic. *Journal of Slavic Linguistics* 15:49–80.

Grebenyova, Lydia. 2009. Sluicing and multiple wh-fronting. The Fifth Asian Generative Linguistics of the Old World Conference Proceedings. (GLOW in Asia).

Gribanova, Vera. 2017. Head movement and ellipsis in the expression of Russian polarity focus. *Natural Language and Linguistic Theory* 35:1079–1121.

Grohmann, Kleanthes K. 2000. Prolific peripheries: A radical view from the left. College Park, MD: University of Maryland PhD thesis.

Hankamer, Jorge. 1979. Deletion in coordinate structures. New York: Garland.

Kazenin, Konstantin. 2006. Polarity in Russian and typology of predicate ellipsis. Ms., University of Tubingen, Tubingen, Germany, and Moscow State University, Moscow.

Laka, Itziar. 1990. *Negation in syntax: On the nature of functional categories and projections*. Cambridge, MA: Massachusetts Institute of Technology PhD thesis.

Lasnik, Howard and Mamoru Saito. 1984. On the nature of proper government. *Linguistic Inquiry* 15:235–289.

Lipták, Anikó. 2015. Relative pronouns as sluicing remnants. In Katalin É. Kiss, Balázs Surányi and Éva Dékány (eds.) *Approaches to Hungarian: Volume 14. Papers from the 2013 Piliscsaba Conference*, 187–207.

Lipták, Anikó and Enoch O. Aboh. 2013. Sluicing inside relatives: The case of Gungbe. *Linguistics in the Netherlands* 30:102–118.

Lobeck, Anne C. 1995. *Ellipsis: functional heads, licensing, and identification*. New York: Oxford University Press.

López-Carretero, Luis. 1995. *Polarity and predicate anaphora*. Ithaca, NY: Cornell University PhD thesis.

Marušic, Franc and Rok Žaucer. 2013. A note on sluicing and island repair. In Steven Franks (ed.), *Formal approaches to Slavic linguistics: The Third Indiana Meeting 2012*, 176–189. Ann Arbor, MI: Michigan Slavic Publications.

Merchant, Jason. 2001. *The syntax of silence: Sluicing, islands, and the theory of ellipsis*. Oxford/New York: Oxford University Press.

Merchant, Jason. 2003. Remarks on stripping. Ms., University of Chicago.

Merchant, Jason. 2013. Polarity items under ellipsis. In Lisa Lai-Shen Cheng and Norbert Corver (eds.), *Diagnosing syntax*, 537–542. Oxford: Oxford University Press.

Merchant, Jason and Andrew Simpson. 2012. *Sluicing. Crosslinguistic Perspectives*. Oxford: Oxford University Press.

Miechowicz-Mathiasen, Katarzyna. 2012. Case, tense and finite clausal arguments in Polish. *Studies in Polish Linguistics* 7:63–81.

Perlmutter, David. 1971. *Deep and surface structure constraints in syntax*. New York: Holt, Rinehart and Winston.

Pereltsvaig, Asya. 2007. The universality of DP: A view from Russian. *Studia linguistica* 61 (1):59–94.

Pereltsvaig, Asya. 2013. Noun phrase structure in article-less Slavic languages: DP or not DP? *Language and Linguistics Compass* 7 (3):201–219.

Pesetsky, David. 2017. Complementizer-Trace Effects. In Martin Everaert and Henk van Riemsdijk (eds.) *The Wiley Blackwell Companion to Syntax*, Second Edition. 993–1026. New York: Wiley-Blackwell.

Pesetsky, David and Esther Torrego. 2001. T-to-C movement: Causes and consequences. In Michael Kenstowicz (ed.), *Ken Hale: A life in language*, 355–426. Cambridge, MA: MIT Press.

Przepiórkowski, Adam and Anna Kupść. 1999. Eventuality negation and negative concord. In Robert Borsley and Adam Przepiórkowski (eds.). *Slavic in Head-Driven Phrase Structure Grammar*, 211–246. Stanford, CA: CSLI Publications.

Rizzi, Luigi. 1990. *Relativized minimality*. Cambridge, MA: MIT Press.

Rizzi, Luigi. 1997. The fine structure of the left periphery. In Liliane Haegeman (ed.), Elements of grammar: A Handbook of generative syntax, 281–337. Dordrecht: Kluwer.

Ross, John Robert. 1967. Constraints on variables in syntax. Cambridge, MA: Massachusetts Institute of Technology PhD thesis.

Rouveret, Alain. 2012. VP ellipsis, phases and the syntax of morphology. *Natural Language and Linguistic Theory* 30:897–963.

Szczegielniak, Adam. 1999. That-t effects cross-linguistically and successive cyclic movement. In Karlos Arregi, Benjamin Bruening, Cornelia Krause and Vivian Lin (eds.), *Papers on morphology and syntax, Cycle One*, 369–393. Cambridge, MA: MIT Working Papers in Linguistics.

Szczegielniak, Adam. 2008. Islands in sluicing in Polish. In Natasha Abner and Jason Bishop (eds.), *Proceedings of the 27th West Coast Conference on Formal Linguistics*, 404–412. Somerville, MA: Cascadilla Proceedings Project.

Tajsner, Przemysław. 2008. *Aspects of the grammar of focus. A minimalist view*. Frankfurt am Main: Peter Lang.

Temmerman, Tanja. 2013. The syntax of Dutch embedded fragment answers: On the PF-theory of islands and the wh/sluicing correlation. *Natural Language and Linguistic Theory* 31:235–285.

Valmala, Vidal. 2007. The syntax of little things. Ms. (http://linguistics.huji.ac.il/IATL/23/Valmala.pdf).

Weir, Andrew. 2014. *Fragments and clausal ellipsis*. Amherst, MA: University of Massachusetts PhD thesis.

Wiland, Bartosz. 2009. *Aspects of order preservation in Polish and English*. Poznań: Adam Mickiewicz University PhD thesis.

Wiland, Bartosz. 2010. Overt evidence from Polish left branch extraction for punctuated paths.

*Linguistic Inquiry* 41:335–347.

Willim, Ewa. 1989. *On word order: A Government-binding study of English and Polish*. Kraków: Wydawnictwo Uniwersytetu Jagiellońskiego.

Witkoś, Jacek. 1993. *On certain aspects of phrasal movement in English and Polish*. Poznań: Adam Mickiewicz University PhD thesis.

Wurmbrand, Susi. 2017. Stripping and Topless Complements. *Linguistic Inquiry* 48:341–366.

Zabrocki, Tadeusz. 1984. On the nature of movement rules in English and Polish. In Jacek Fisiak (ed.), *Contrastive Linguistics: Prospects and problems*, 431–444. Berlin: De Gruyter Mouton.

Zeijlstra, Hedde. 2004. *Sentential negation and negative concord*. Amsterdam: University of Amsterdam PhD thesis.

## Part II: **Domain-internal phases**

Andrew Simpson and Saurov Syed
# 4 Parallels in the structure of phases in clausal and nominal domains

**Abstract:** It is commonly assumed that clauses are bi-phasal, consisting in a CP phase and a mid-level, internal phase vP/AspP. There is also a common view, since Abney 1987, Szabolcsi 1983, that clauses and nominal phrases are structured in similar ways. This chapter makes the claim that nominal phrases may be bi-phasal like clauses and examines the consequences of such a conclusion for recent general approaches to phases, in particular theories advocating the contextual determination of phases (e. g. Bošković 2014). The chapter presents arguments relating to blocking effects in Bangla/Bengali that nominal constituents in Bangla contain an internal QP phase as well as projecting a higher DP-level phase, motivated by patterns of extraction and argument ellipsis. Cross-linguistic variation with regard to the presence of mono- vs. bi-phasality are suggested to be due to differences in the amount of functional structure that languages grammaticalize in clausal and nominal domains. The chapter also probes ellipsis as a diagnostic for phasehood within nominals, and notes that ellipsis patterns in English and Hungarian (Ruda 2016) offer potential evidence for the presence of bi-phasal nominals in both these languages.

## 4.1 Introduction

It has long been suggested that clauses and nominal phrases are structured in similar ways (Abney 1987, Szabolcsi 1983). One important property ascribed to CPs in a Minimalist view of syntax is that they function as *phases* and also contain an internal *phase* – vP (Chomsky 2000). Given recent suggestions that DPs also occur as phases (Svenonius 2004, Bošković 2012, Hinzen 2012), it is natural to ask whether such nominal constituents might additionally contain an internal phase, paralleling the occurrence of a lower phasal unit within clauses. Drawing on work in Simpson and Syed (2016) and Syed and Simpson (2017), this paper presents arguments from word order patterns and other syntactic phenomena in Bangla nominal phrases which suggest that such constituents do indeed contain a mid-level internal phase projected above NP, and that a higher DP level of structure also projects as a phase. This results in the conclusion that the fully extended projection of noun phrases may contain two separate phases, in a way that resembles the occurrence of two phasal levels within clauses. The paper suggests that such proposals are not in conflict with the contextual approach to phases described in

Bošković (2014), which actually assumes that nominals are mono-phasal, and can in fact be shown to align with the premise in Bošković (2012, 2014) that languages may grammaticalize functional structure in the nominal and clausal domains to different degrees. The paper also presents novel ellipsis-related data from English and reference to similar patterns in Polish and Hungarian from Ruda (2016) which support the view that nominals in other languages are potentially bi-phasal domains.

The structure of the paper is as follows. Section 4.2 presents arguments given in Simpson and Syed (2016) that nominal constituents in Bangla contain an internal phase projected below possessors and demonstratives: QP. Section 4.3 motivates a DP analysis of nominal projections in Bangla, although the language lacks definite determiners, and shows that DPs in Bangla pattern as phases, as in other languages. Section 4.4 then considers the broader cross-linguistic consequences of the conclusion that DPs may have a bi-phasal structure and shows how such a conclusion can be reconciled with the influential approach to phases argued for in Bošković (2014, 2016), and Harwood (2015). Section 4.5 asks why the presence of nominal-internal phases may be harder to detect than clause-internal phases, and explores ellipsis as a diagnostic for phasehood within nominals in other languages. Finally, section 4.6 summarizes the results of the paper.

## 4.2 QPs as nominal-internal phases in Bangla (Simpson and Syed 2016)

In Bangla, the most neutral order of elements within nominal phrases is as seen in (1): Possessor > Demonstrative > Numeral > Classifier > Adjective(s) > Noun (Bhattacharya, 1999):

(1)   *Ram-er   ei    tin Te   notun tupi*
      Ram-GEN DEM 3   CLF new   hat
      'these three new hats of Ram's'

Other orders of these elements may, however, occur for certain interpretative effects. First, the phrasal sequence of adjectives and noun/NP regularly raises leftwards past the classifier and numerals to signal a definite interpretation (Bhattacharya 1999, Dayal 2012, Chacón 2012, Syed 2017), as shown in (2a/b).

# 4 Parallels in the structure of phases in clausal and nominal domains

(2) a.  tin Te  notun tupi           b.  [notun tupi]$_k$ tin Te  $t_k$
        3  CLF  new   hat                new    hat   3   CLF
        'three new hats'                 'the three new hats'

If a demonstrative is present, the [Adj N] constituent raises to a landing-site lower than the demonstrative but higher than the numeral, as shown in (3a/b):

(3) a.  ei    tin Te  notun tupi      b.  ei   [notun tupi]$_k$ tin Te  $t_k$
        DEM 3 CLF new  hat                 DEM  new    hat   3   CLF

When adjectives are heavily focused, a second kind of nominal-internal movement may take place to a higher position between possessors and demonstratives, which Syed (2017) identifies as a FocusPhrase/FocP.

(4)  Ram-er    [notun]$_m$ ei    tin Te   [$t_m$ tupi]
     Ram-GEN   new         DEM 3 CLF      hat
     'these three *new* hats of Ram's'

What is significant to note is that both types of leftwards displacement – definiteness-related NP movement and focus movement of AdjPs – may only take place when a low numeral is present and both are blocked when higher numerals occur, as shown in (5)–(8):

(5)  [notun tupi]$_k$ du To/tin Te/char Te  $t_k$
     new    hat       2  CLF/3 CLF/4  CLF
     'the 2/3/4 new hats'

(6)  *[notun tupi]$_k$ choy Ta/sat Ta/at Ta/nau Ta/doS Ta  $t_k$
     new    hat        6    CLF/7 CLF/8 CLF/9  CLF/10 CLF

(7)  [notun]$_k$ ei    du To/tin Te/char Te  [$t_k$ tupi]
     new         DEM 2 CLF/3 CLF/4    CLF    hat
     'these two/three/four *new* hats'

(8)  *[notun]$_k$ ei    choy Ta/sat Ta/at Ta  [$t_k$ tupi]
     new          DEM 6 CLF/7 CLF/8 CLF         hat

In Simpson and Syed (2016), we propose a structural account of the blocking effect of higher numerals which built on evidence that there is variation in the ways that numerals are merged into nominal projections. In a variety of works it has been argued that numerals may sometimes occur as phrasal constituents in specifier positions, and in other instances be merged as heads in the main projection line of nominal constituents (Danon 2012, Borer 2005, Bailyn 2004, Shlonsky 2004, Franks 1994, Pereltsvaig 2006). In Bangla, we suggest that the low numerals 1–4 occur as heads in $Q^0$, while higher numerals are projected as phrasal constituents in SpecQP, noting that such a structural difference in the position of low and high numerals allows for a straightforward account of the blocking patterns observed if it is additionally assumed that definitness-related NP-movement and focus AdjP-movement must proceed successive-cyclically through SpecQP. Higher numerals present in SpecQP will block this movement, while lower numerals in $Q^0$ will allow for it to occur, as schematized in (9a/b).

(9) a.

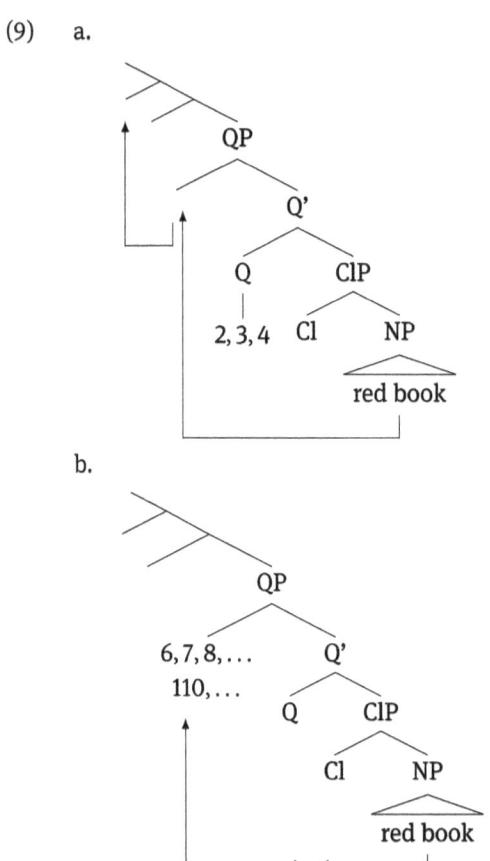

b.

In such a perspective, SpecQP functions as an escape hatch for movement to higher positions within nominal phrases, similar to other escape hatch phenomena such as the need for wh-phrases to move through lower SpecCP positions in order to exit a clause, and the requirement that elements within DPs pass through SpecDP in any movement to higher positions (McCloskey 2000, Szabolcsi 1983), as represented in (10).

(10)   [_CP WH_k ............ [_CP t_k [ C ......... t_k ......]]]

[ ...... XP_k ...... [_DP t_k D ...... t_k ......]]

In addition to high numerals, most quantifiers are found to block nominal-internal NP and AdjP movement in Bangla, and so can be assumed to occur in SpecQP. However, one quantifier *kOyek* 'some/a few' does allow for NP/AdjP movement to take place if it occurs in a reduced enclitic form *kO-*, as seen in (11) and (12). The full-form of this quantifier, *kOyek*, is therefore taken to be a phrasal constituent projected in SpecQP, while the reduced enclitic form *kO-* patterns like a head merged in $Q^0$, permitting movement to occur through the unoccupied SpecQP position.

(11)   *[_NP lal boi]_i [_QP kOyek [_ClP Ta t_i]]
         red book       some        CLF

(12)   [_NP lal boi]_i [_QP t_i kO  [_ClP Ta t_i]]
         red book       some        CLF
       'the few *red books*.'

The key properties of AdjP- and NP-movement within Bangla nominal constituents are consequently those listed in (13):

(13)   i.   AdjP-/NP-movement is caused by properties of focus and definiteness.
       ii.  AdjP-/NP-movement needs to pass through SpecQP.
       iii. AdjP-/NP-movement through SpecQP only takes place when an AdjP/NP constituent needs to reach a higher position, hence no raising of this type occurs in the absence of interpretations of focus or definiteness.
       iv.  SpecQP functions as an escape hatch for lower phrasal elements attracted by higher probes relating to focus and definiteness.

Focused AdjPs and NPs raising for definiteness-related reasons thus undergo obligatory successive cyclic movement through a lower position (SpecQP) with which there is no Agree relation involving focus/definiteness features solely in order to reach a higher position which does involve such a relation. In Simpson and Syed (2016), we argue that the only way such successive cyclic movement to/through a lower escape hatch can be analyzed is that raising to this intermediate position makes the moved element visible to a higher probe at the edge of a lower phase, allowing the higher probe to agree with the moved goal and attract it further. AdjP/NP-movement to SpecQP thus can be seen to occur as a way to avoid a violation of the Phase Impenetrability Condition/PIC (Chomsky 2000) – an element which needs to enter into an Agreement relation with a probe in a higher phase must first raise to the edge of a lower phase, and is otherwise inaccessible to the higher probe (Legate 2003, Bošković 2005). Such movement is technically facilitated via the presence of edge features on a phasal head and does not reflect any other necessary Agreement relation existing between the phasal head and the moved element. The conclusion which results from this is that: "QP is in fact a *nominal-internal phase*, forcing successive cyclic movement to occur through its specifier/edge when elements from within QP need to Agree with functional heads in a higher part of the noun phrase, and that phases may therefore be projected in embedded positions within nominal projections and not simply occur as the highest (DP) projection of a nominal constituent, as has often been assumed" (Simpson and Syed 2016:761).[1] The Bangla patterns of focus and definiteness-driven movement consequently provide novel evidence for the assumption that nominal expressions as well as clauses may contain internal phases, a fully natural expectation and prediction given other well-described structural parallels between CP and DP structure (Abney 1987, Szabolcsi 1983).[2]

---

[1] The analysis presented here assumes that QPs in Bangla only have a single specifier position. Simpson and Syed (2016:761) note that an alternative, multiple specifier analysis incorporating ideas in Bošković (2016) can be argued to lead to the same conclusion that QP is a phase. Bošković (2016) suggests that all phases permit multiple specifiers, but only the highest specifier position is visible to elements in a higher phase, and only elements in this position can therefore be extracted from phases. In Bangla nominals, when a higher numeral is merged into SpecQP and movement of an AdjP/NP subsequently occurs, this will result in the AdjP/NP coming to occupy a lower specifier position if Tucking In (Richards 2001) is assumed as a constraint on the establishment of multiple specifier positions, and in such a position it will not be visible to higher probes. Further movement of AdjPs/NPs will therefore be blocked when higher numerals occur, even if multiple specifier positions are in fact present with QP.

[2] If the blocking effect caused by higher numerals in Bangla indicates the underlying presence of a phase (QP), a natural question to ask is whether blocking and intervention effects can be used as a *general* diagnostic for phases, and *always* be taken to signal the presence of a phase. Here, we believe, the answer is 'no', because blocking/intervention effects may occur for (at least) two different reasons, and blocking/intervention effects will typically only reveal phasehood in one set of cases.

In patterns of 'structural blocking', an element X needs to move through a position W in order to reach a higher position, attracted by a probe Z. If another element occupies position W, as in (i), movement of X through position W is blocked and this makes extraction of X impossible. W serves as an escape hatch for movement, which in minimalist terms shows the need for movement to

A further, potential consequence of the conclusion that QP acts as a nominal-internal phase in Bangla is that if nominal phrases in Bangla project a higher, DP-level of structure, such constituents may be determined to be bi-phasal, with both an internal QP phase and a 'closing-off' (highest projection) DP phase. What needs to be investigated in this regard is therefore whether DPs are indeed projected in Bangla (a language without overt determiners), and whether there is also evidence that such constituents pattern as phases.

## 4.3 Bangla as a DP language

Bošković (2008:101) entertains a strong claim about nominal structures across languages, that languages without articles do not have DPs. This proposal builds on insights gained from the comparison of a broad range of syntactic properties in

---

and through the edge of a phase, to avoid violations of the PIC. Structural blocking and the need for successive cyclic movement functions as a useful diagnostic for phases.

(i)      ...Z...[$_{phase}$ W...X...]...

However, other occurrences of intervention effects which involve 'featural blocking' cannot be used in the same way as a diagnostic for the presence of phases. In instances of 'featural blocking', a probe Z cannot locate and agree with a potential goal X because another element W intervenes between Z and X, and features present on W cause the search by the probe to terminate at W and not search further down to X. If X can be moved/scrambled over W as in (ii), or if W is not present, as in (iii), this will allow for Z to Agree with X.

(ii)     ...Z...$X_k$......W......$t_k$....

(iii)    ...Z..................X....

Featural blocking occurs in classic cases of intervention effects such as those caused by the interference of focused phrases on wh-in-situ licensing in Korean, Japanese and Chinese, as well as in patterns involving the Person Case Constraint.

Structural blocking and featural blocking are significantly different in nature. With structural blocking, a goal needs to move through the structural position occupied by an intervener, and it is the physical presence of the latter which blocks movement, not any features which it bears – hence high numerals in Bangla do not carry features relating to definiteness which interfere with the relation between the probe and the goal NP when there is nominal-internal definiteness-related movement of NP constituents. In cases of featural blocking, by way of contrast, there is no need for a goal to move to the position occupied by an intervener, and the goal can be licensed without movement in its base position if no intervener is present. This indicates that there is no phasal boundary present between the goal and a higher probe, and when featural blocking does occur, it does not (necessarily) signal the presence of an underlying phase.

different languages, and results in the categorization of languages as being either DP languages (projecting D and DP), or NP languages (lacking a DP level of structure). As Bangla is a language which lacks overt determiners,[3] the strong claim considered in Bošković (2008) should lead to its analysis as an NP language without any DP level of structure. However, a closer consideration of other properties taken to characterize languages with articles shows that Bangla nominal syntax regularly aligns it with archetypal DP languages, rather than NP languages, and hence that Bangla nominals should be taken to project up to a DP level. Here we will review three core patterns which have been presented in Bošković (2008, 2009), Bošković and Gajewski (2011), and Despić (2013) as potential diagnostics that may be used for distinguishing DP from NP languages, all of which lead to the conclusion that Bangla is a language of the former type. For discussion of additional patterns that lead to the same conclusion, see Syed and Simpson (2017).

### 4.3.1 The majority reading of MOST

Bošković and Gajewski (2011) argue that only languages with articles allow a majority reading of MOST (words close to the meaning of English 'most'), and that NP languages only permit a relative reading of elements of MOST. English and German, for example, are both DP languages with overt determiners, and allow both a majority and a relative reading for MOST, as indicated in English (14):

(14)   *Most people going to pubs in Upton Snodsbury drink Bishop's Tipple.*
'More people drink Bishops' Tipple than any other beverage/beer in Upton Snodsbury pubs'. (Relative reading)
'More than half the people in Upton Snodsbury pubs drink Bishops' Tipple'. (Majority reading)

Bošković and Gajewski (2011) develop a syntactic analysis of the difference between DP and NP languages with regard to MOST and the interpretations it allows which suggests that a majority reading of MOST requires QR and adjunction to NP. Such adjunction is argued not to be available as an option in languages where NPs are arguments (NP languages), because adjunction to arguments is (taken to be) banned, following Chomsky (1986).

---

[3] Demonstratives are not assumed to be instances of the category D in Bangla, and occur lower down in nominal constituents than they do in English, to the right of possessors (which may co-occur with demonstratives) – see example (32) in section 4.3.3.

When Bangla is now considered, interestingly it patterns like a typical DP language and permits majority readings of MOST, as illustrated in (15). This distinguishes Bangla from other typical NP languages and makes Bangla look like a 'covert' DP language.

(15)  besirbhag lok    kal       parTi-te   beer khelo
      most      people yesterday party-LOC beer drank
      Available readings:
      (i) 'more people drank beer than any other beverage in the party yesterday' (relative reading)
      (ii) 'more than half the people drank beer at the party' (majority reading)

## 4.3.2 Neg(ative) raising

Neg-raising refers to a patterning in which the presence of negation in a higher clause can be interpreted as negating the content of a lower clause, possible with some verbs in some languages, but not with other verbs/languages, as described in Fillmore (1963), Horn (1971), Bošković and Gajewski (2011), among others. In English, for example, the co-occurrence of negation with the embedding verb 'believe' allows for negation to be understood as applying to the subordinate clause, as if 'not' had raised from an embedded position to the matrix, but this is not possible with the verb 'claim', as illustrated in (16) and (17):

(16)  a.  *Mary did not believe that Fred was smart.*   can mean:
      b.  *Mary believed that Fred was not smart.*
(17)  a.  *John did not claim that Mary was smart.*    cannot mean:
      b.  *John claimed that Mary was not smart.*

The presence of negation with neg-raising verbs also typically licenses lower clause negative polarity items, as seen in (18), in contrast to similar structures with non-neg-raising verbs, where embedded NPIs are not licensed (19):

(18)  *John didn't believe [that Mary would leave until tomorrow].*
(19)  **John didn't claim [that Mary would leave until tomorrow].*

Bošković (2008) finds that neg-raising only occurs in the class of DP languages, identified as such by the occurrence of articles:

(20) "Languages without articles disallow neg-raising, and languages with articles allow it."
Bošković (2008:104)

Such a distribution leads to the conclusion that languages with neg-raising phenomena should be classified as 'DP languages', even if no overt articles occur in these languages, and this is the situation found in Bangla. Typical neg-raising patterns occur in Bangla, showing again that it patterns like other DP languages, not NP languages. NPIs are licensed in lower clauses embedded by equivalents to the verb 'believe', but not other embedding verbs, as illustrated in (21) and (22).

(21) ami biSSas kOri na  je   ram kal        parTi-te kono khabar kheyeche
     I   belief  do  NEG that Ram yesterday party-at any  food  ate
     'I don't believe that Ram ate any food at the party yesterday'.

(22) *ami dekhi-ni je   ram kal        parTi-te  kono khabar kheyeche
     I   see-NEG  that Ram yesterday psrty-LOC any  food  ate

### 4.3.3 Binding and the position of possessors in nominal projections

Despić (2013) explores certain asymmetries found in DP and NP languages with regard to binding relations involving possessors in nominal projections. In DP languages such as English, possessors do not c-command out of the nominal projection, hence it is possible for a nominal possessor in a DP in subject position to be co-referential with an R-expression or a pronoun in object-of-verb position, as shown in (23) and (24). The lack of a Principle B or C violation is simply explained by the assumption that possessors are merged in DP-internal positions which block c-command of any elements external to the DP.

(23) [$_{DP}$ His$_i$ father] considers John$_i$ highly intelligent.

(24) [$_{DP}$ John$_i$'s father] considers him$_i$ highly intelligent.

In the NP language Serbo-Croatian, a different patterning is observed, and it is not possible for the possessor of a nominal phrase in subject position to be co-referential either with a pronoun or an R-expression in object position, as seen in (25) and (26).

(25) *[Kusturicin$_i$ najnoviji film] ga$_i$ je zaista razočarao.
     Kusturica's latest    film him is really disappointed
     'Kusturica$_i$'s latest film really disappointed him$_i$.'

(26)  *[Njegov$_i$ najnoviji film] je zaista razočarao   Kusturicu$_i$.
       his    latest   film is really disappointed Kusturica
       'His$_i$ latest film really disappointed Kusturica$_i$.'

The analysis Despić presents to account for the unacceptability of (25) and (26) suggests that possessors are adjoined to NPs in the NP language Serbo-Croatian (and there is no DP layer dominating NP), and that from such an adjoined position possessors c-command outside the NP, adopting May's (1985) proposal that an element not dominated by all segments of a constituent will c-command out of that constituent.

DP languages with possessors merged in internal specifier positions are consequently predicted to regularly allow co-reference between possessors and other DP-external pronouns and R-expressions in configurations such as (23) and (24), while NP languages with possessors merged in NP-adjoined positions are expected to disallow all similar attempts at co-reference, if no additional structure is projected above NP.

When parallel examples are constructed in Bangla, it is found that Bangla patterns entirely like English and other DP languages, and allows the kind of coreference relations seen in (23) and (24), involving pronouns and R-expressions. This is illustrated in (27) and (28):

(27)  [ritupOrno$_i$-r  SeS sinema Ta]  ta$_i$-ke  khub hOtaS   korlo.
       Rituporno-GEN last film   CLF he-ACC  very  disappoint did
       'Rituporno's last film really disappointed him'

(28)  [ta$_i$-r  SeS sinema Ta]  ritupOrno$_i$-ke  khub hOtaS   korlo.
       he-GEN last film   CLF Rituporno-ACC  very  disappoint did
       'His last film really disappointed Rituporno'

Possessors in Bangla thus seem to be merged in a high specifier position which is the leftmost position in nominal projections in Bangla, by assumption SpecDP.

In Serbo-Croatian, Bošković (2005) and Zlatić (1997) suggest that possessors and demonstratives are both *adjectival* in nature, and because of this such elements enjoy a greater freedom of ordering relative to adjectives than is found in DP languages, where possessors and demonstratives occupy fixed positions (SpecDP/D). Example (29) shows that possessors and demonstratives can either precede or follow other adjectives, a distribution which is accounted for if all such elements are NP adjuncts:

(29)  a.   *Jovanova/ova bivsa   kuca*
            Jovan's/this  former house

b. *bivsa Jovanova/ova kuca*
former Jovan's/this house
'Jovan's/this former house'

In Bangla, adjectives are merged in quite different positions from possessors and demonstratives. The former regularly occur between classifiers and nouns, while the latter can only be merged higher, to the left of numerals and classifiers.

(30) *du To choto sobuj chine fuldani*
2 CLF small green Chinese vase
'two small green Chinese vases'

(31) *amar/ei du To fuldani*
my/DEM 2 CLF vase
'my/these two vases'

A demonstrative and a possessor can in fact both be present, but must always follow a strict ordering, the possessor occurring to the left of the demonstrative, as shown in (32):

(32) a. *amar oi lal boi*      b. *\*oi amar lal boi*
my DEM red book           DEM my red book
'that red book of mine'

This fixed positioning of possessors and demonstratives in the leftmost portion of nominal phrases suggests these elements are merged into high functional projections, as in other DP languages, the highest of which can be taken to be DP, with possessors occurring in SpecDP.

A whole range of evidence thus converges on the conclusion that Bangla is a language in which nominals project up to a DP-level – when comparisons are made with other DP and NP languages, Bangla consistently patterns like the set of DP languages and not NP languages, despite not having any overt articles.[4] Bangla thus seems to show that the strong claim entertained in Bošković (2008) that only languages with articles project DPs cannot be fully maintained, and it

---

[4] A reviewer of the paper reminds us that the typological patterns distinguishing DP and NP languages catalogued in Bošković (2008) is based on a relatively small language sample of the world's languages, and so caution is necessary in utilizing such patterns to diagnose the presence of DP in other languages that do not have overt articles. We accept this point, but note that there is a very clear consistency in the way these patterns do indeed regularly point to Bangla being a 'covert' DP language. The conclusion that DPs are projected in Bangla therefore remains a strong, ongoing hypothesis which allows for a systematic account of a broad range of phenomena.

may also be possible for a DP level of structure to develop in languages which do not have definite or indefinite determiners. Such a conclusion is compatible with a weaker hypothesis considered in Bošković (2008) that *some* languages without articles may not project DPs. It also raises the question of how a DP level of structure might develop in the absence of articles providing overt evidence for D and DP. In Bangla, a plausible answer to this may be that the definiteness-related NP-movement within nominal projections discussed in section 4.2 provides robust overt evidence to speakers/learners that higher levels of structure exist in nominal phrases. Such patterns of nominal-internal movement may serve a function in signaling the presence of a level of structure above NP (including DP) which is similar to the actual occurrence of overt articles, and that either the grammaticalization of articles or the development of high, nominal-internal movement may give rise to the projection of DP within a language.[5]

Syed (2017) suggests that the patterns in Bangla support the assumption of a three-way typology of NP and DP languages, as described in (33):

(33)  *Three-way typology of 'NP' and 'DP' languages* (Syed 2017)
1. Languages without articles, which do not project DPs (Serbo-Croatian, Polish)
2. Languages with articles, which project DPs (English, German, Hungarian)
3. Languages without articles, which project DPs (Bangla)

To this typology, a fourth type might also possibly be added, following a recent claim in Börjars, Harries and Vincent (2016) that not all languages with articles actually do project DPs and that DPs may only develop some time after languages have fully grammaticalized determiners. Börjars et al. suggest that it is only when determiners come to be associated with a *fixed position* in nominals that DP functional structure comes into existence in languages which previously lacked DPs. Some languages may appear to have articles, but these elements do not cause the projection of a D position or a DP level of structure, due to their unfixed status. An

---

[5] A reviewer of the paper asks whether, in general, a phrase can be projected if its head position is not lexically filled with any element (feature set, morpheme etc), and is genuinely empty. With regard to the $D^0$ head of Bangla DPs, we assume that morphosyntactic features relating to definiteness may be present here, and serve to attract elements to SpecDP, hence $D^0$ is not fully void of content and essentially has the same kind of status as English $T^0$, which hosts tense-related features. We believe that the potential introduction of definiteness-related and tense features in $D^0$ and $T^0$ is made directly, without the need for any covert host morpheme, hence there is no need to assume that a 'covert article' or a 'covert auxiliary' occurs as a morphological container for such features.

example of such a language given by Börjars et al. is Old Norse, which had evolved a definiteness marker/definite determiner, but this element was: (a) optional, (b) not in complementary distribution with demonstratives and possessors, (c) not associated with a fixed position. Due to these properties, Börjars et al. claim that no D position was established by definite determiners in Old Norse and such elements were merged as optional adjuncts to NPs like other modifiers (see also Lander and Haegeman 2013 for a similar view of Old Norse). If such an interpretation of the patterns of Old Norse is indeed correct, the four-way typology of NP and DP languages in (34) can be assumed, in which overt articles are neither always necessary for the projection of DP in a language, nor a necessary guarantee that a DP level of structure does occur.

(34)   *A Four-way typology of 'NP' and 'DP' languages*

| Articles have developed | DPs are projected | Language |
|---|---|---|
| No | No | Serbo-Croatian |
| Yes | Yes | Modern English |
| No | Yes | Bangla |
| Yes | No | Old Norse |

## 4.3.4 DPs as phases in Bangla

Returning to the central issue of the occurrence of nominal phases in Bangla, if there is now reasonable evidence that DPs are indeed projected in Bangla, such constituents might simply be assumed to instantiate phases as the highest projection in the nominal domain, as in other languages (Svenonius 2004, Bošković 2012, Hinzen 2012 among many others). In support of such an assumption, there is also empirical evidence that DP constituents function as phases in Bangla, relating to patterns of ellipsis and extraction.

'Argument ellipsis' is the term used to refer to the omission of overt arguments which critically licenses interpretations of sloppy identity, as seen in Japanese (35) (unlike the occurrence of null pronominal elements/pro in languages such as Spanish and Italian, which do not permit sloppy identity readings – see Oku 1998, Saito 2004, Takahashi 2008 among others).

(35) a. *Taro-wa [zibun-no kodomo-ga eigo-o     sitteiru ito  itta.*
   Taro-TOP self-GEN  child-NOM English-ACC knows that said
   'Lit. Taro said that self's child knew English'.
 b. *Hanako-wa [_ furansugo-o isitteiru to    itta.*
   Hsnsko-TOP French-ACC    knows  that said

'Lit. Hanako said that _ knew French.' Şener and Takahashi (2009)
Strict: Hanako said that Taro's child knew French.
Sloppy: Hanako said that her own child knew French.

In Bošković (2014), it is suggested that only phases or the complements of phase heads may permit ellipsis, and that argument ellipsis can be made use of in the nominal domain as a diagnosis for the presence of a phase. In Bangla, an investigation into the interpretative properties of null arguments carried out in Simpson, Choudhury and Menon (2013) shows that argument ellipsis regularly occurs in the language, licensing typical interpretations of sloppy identity, as shown in (36):

(36) ram [$_{DP}$ nije-r    du To receptionist-ke] boklo,   kintu raj _
     Ram   self-GEN 2 CLF receptionist-ACC criticized but Raj
     proshongsha korlo.
     praise       did
     'Ram$_k$ criticized his$_k$ two receptionists, but Raj$_m$ praised (his$_m$ two receptionists).'

Patterns of argument ellipsis consequently provide support for the assumption that DPs occur as phases in Bangla.

A second patterning which also points towards the status of DPs as phases in Bangla involves extraction from DP constituents. If DPs are phases in Bangla, the PIC will require that any extraction from DPs must first reach and pass through the edge of the DP phase, in order for the element to become visible to a higher DP-external probe. If there is a single SpecDP position in the phasal edge and it is filled with an overt possessor, the expectation is that this should block extraction, and such a prediction is borne out. Example (37) shows that an NP can freely extract from a containing DP, stranding nominal-internal elements higher than the NP, such as numerals and classifiers. However, if the SpecDP position is occupied by a possessor phrase, as in (38), extraction is no longer possible, indicating that such movement has to pass through the SpecDP position. It should also be noted that the base sequence in (38) *Ram-er du To boi*, without any NP-extraction, allows for a non-specific indefinite partitive interpretation 'two of Ram's books', and so the extraction attempted in (38) is not ruled out by any constraint relating to specificity and a bar on extracting out of specific DPs.

(37) [$_{NP}$ boi]$_k$ ami [$_{DP}$ t$_k$ [$_{QP}$ t$_k$ du To t$_k$]] kinlam.
         book I                   2   CLF   bought
     'I bought two books.'

(38) *[$_{NP}$ boi]$_k$ ami [$_{DP}$ ram-er   [$_{QP}$ t$_k$ du To t$_k$]] kinlam.
          book I        Ram-GEN        2   CLF   bought

Such patterns show that SpecDP is a necessary escape hatch for extraction from DPs in Bangla, as in other languages (Szabolcsi 1983), forcing successive cyclic movement to occur through the DP phasal edge so as to avoid a violation of the PIC. This consequently provides further evidence that DP constituents in Bangla constitute phases as in other languages.

Putting the above conclusions together with those made earlier in section 4.2 now significantly results in the insight that Bangla nominal projections are *bi-phasal* constituents, containing both a mid-level phase QP and a higher level, 'closing-off' phase, DP. Nominal domains therefore potentially may consist in two cyclic phases, paralleling the bi-phasal structuring of clauses, in which an internal mid-level phase and a higher, closing off phase are both commonly assumed to occur. Such a basic parallelism between the phasal structuring of nominal and clausal projections is what might be predicted and expected given other extensive parallels in the structure of DPs and CPs that have regularly been highlighted in the literature since Abney (1987). Despite such a natural expectation, the more widespread view of phases assumed in the literature has been that there is actually an asymmetry between clauses and nominal projections, with only the former having a bi-phasal structure. In section 4.4, we consider a recent influential approach to phases, Bošković (2014), which assumes the existence of such an asymmetry and ask whether the conclusions of the current paper are compatible with this approach or not. Following this, in section 4.5 we ask why in general there may appear to be less abundant, clear evidence for the bi-phasal structure of nominals across languages, and highlight the potential value of ellipsis constructions as diagnoses for phasehood within nominal phrases.

## 4.4 Is there a real asymmetry in the phasal structure of clauses and nominals? Reconciling bi-phasality in Bangla nominals with Bošković (2014)

Bošković (2014) develops an interesting, new approach to the identification of phases, in which phases are not immutably fixed but contextually-determined by the amount of structure that is projected in any particular instance in a language. In the case of Serbo-Croatian nominal projections, it is argued that the frequent inextractability of complements of nouns may be explained if it is assumed that NPs serve as phases in Serbo-Croatian when no further layers of functional structure are projected. In such instances, complements of N need to raise to SpecNP to overcome the PIC and be visible to a higher probe triggering extraction from NP, but this movement is ruled out by the principle of antilocality (Abels 2003, Grohmann 2003). Consequently, attempts to extract the complements of nouns in Serbo-Croatian are regularly ungrammatical, as shown in (39).

(39) ?*Ovog studenta$_k$ sam pronašla [$_{NP}$ sliku t$_k$]
     this  student   am  found         picture

However, when numerals and other quantifiers are present, such elements are taken to project additional functional structure, a QP layer above NP, and, interestingly, this appears to allow for complements of N to be extracted out of nominal phrases, as illustrated in (40).

(40) Ovog studenta$_k$ sam pronašla [$_{QP}$ t$_k$ mnogo/deset sliku t$_k$]
     this  student   am  found              many/ten     picture
     'Of this student, I found many/ten pictures.'

Bošković suggests that QP is contextually determined as a phase in such cases, not NP, as QP is the highest layer of structure projected in the object in (40). Complements of N may legitimately raise to SpecQP at the phasal edge as this movement does not violate antilocality, and from SpecQP extraction can take place out of the nominal projection (Bošković 2014:36). In English, by way of contrast, it is found that the complements of nouns *can* be extracted:

(41) [Of which city]$_k$ did you witness [the destruction t$_k$]?

Bošković suggests that DP is the single phase projected in nominals in English. The complement of N can move from its base position to SpecDP, the edge of the phase, and then be attracted further. It is claimed that NPs should be concluded *not* to be phases in English, because if NP were to be a phase as well as DP, the complement of N should not be able to extract out of NP (due to antilocality) and then out of DP. The general claim made in Bošković (2014) is that it is only the highest level of structure in nominal projections that serves as a phase, and this may vary in its identity, depending on how much structure is projected in different instances.

The conclusions relating to nominal-internal phases which have been drawn from Bangla might seem to be at odds with this new perspective in Bošković (2014) that phases are contextually determined and nominal projections are monophasal constituents. Sections 4.2 and 4.3 have argued that QP serves as a phase in Bangla, and this occurs even in the presence of higher functional structure, when demonstratives, possessors, focused and definite-raised elements all signal the presence of higher nominal-internal functional projections. The addition of a DP level of structure then instantiates a higher phasal boundary, leading to the claim that Bangla nominals are regularly bi-phasal in their composition, which initially seems unexpected for the perspective developed in Bošković (2014). However, we believe that the Bangla patterns and the insights they provide are actually quite compatible with the broad position presented in Bošković (2014), and may also lead to a more generalized account of phasehood that does not distinguish nominal from verbal domains in any significant way. In Bošković's (2014) approach, clauses are viewed as patterning differently from nominal projections, and taken not to project just a single phase corresponding to the highest layer of structure, but both a mid-level phase, identified as AspP as well as a higher level phase, CP. Bošković suggests that AspP qualifies as a phase in virtue of being the highest layer of structure in the verbal domain, when it is projected, and that CP may be a phase 'because it is the highest projection in general.' It is added that '..the reader should bear in mind that full integration of CP into the current system is left for future research.' (Bošković 2014: 59). The asymmetry assumed in the phasal structure of clauses and nominals in Bošković (2014), with clauses being bi-phasal and nominals being mono-phasal domains is essentially the result of the patterns noted above in (39)–(41) – comparing Serbo-Croatian and English, NPs are concluded not to be phases in English because extraction of the complement of N is possible, unlike in Serbo-Croatian when QP is not projected over NP. Yet such a conclusion is no longer necessary if a slightly different view of the internal structure of English nominals is adopted. In Bošković (2014) it is assumed that nominal phrases in English consist only in a DP and NP level of structure, as represented in (42):

(42) English nominal structure (Bošković 2014): [$_{DP}$...[$_{NP}$...]]

However, supposing that English nominals were instead to contain an additional QP (or $n$P) projection between NP and DP, and this constituent were to be a phase, as in Bangla, it would be predicted that extraction of the complement of N should in fact be possible, as observed. The complement of N would be able to raise from its base position to the edge of the QP/$n$P phase, and from there to the edge of the DP phase, and then further out of DP, with no violations of the PIC or antilocality:

(43) Extraction of complement of N if English nominals contain an internal QP phase:
 *[Of which city]$_k$ did you witness [$_{DP}$ $t_k$ the [$_{QP}$ $t_k$ [$_{NP}$ destruction $t_k$]]?*

The generalizations about extraction of complements of N constituents in Serbo-Croatian and English are therefore consistent with (at least) *two* different possibilities:[6]

(44)  i.  NP is a phase in Serbo-Croatian but not English
ii. QPs (and NPs) may be phases in both Serbo-Croatian and English. QP is sometimes not projected in Serbo-Croatian (in which case NP is determined to be a phase), but may always occur in English when structure up to DP is created, even if no overt elements are present in Q or SpecQP.[7]

As claims have frequently been made in the literature that QP (or an equivalent projection such as #P) is regularly present in English nominal constituents (for example, Borer 2005), we suggest that the second possibility in (44) is equally as plausible as the first, and assuming (44ii) will not only allow for a fully consistent account of both English and Serbo-Croatian but have the additional advantages of: (a) reconciling the findings from Bangla with those in English and Serbo-Croatian, and (b) eliminating the odd asymmetry in assumptions about the projection of phases in clauses and nominal phrases – both domains may be biphasal in principle, as might naturally be expected, with cross-linguistic variation in the actual occurrence of phases being due to the diachronic development and synchronic projection of different amounts of functional structure in different languages – for example, a DP level of structure occurring in English, Bangla and other DP languages, but not in NP languages such as Serbo-Croatian. The broad hypothesis of phasehood in clauses and nominals which we believe is worth exploring and pursuing further is briefly as follows.

The highest projection present in any clause or nominal will always be (contextually) determined to be a phase. In the clausal domain, this will typically be some layer of CP, but potentially also lower categories in reduced clauses which exhibit evidence of successive cyclic movement through their edge (for example, the stranding of material in such positions). In the nominal domain, DP will regularly function as a phase in languages which have developed DPs, occurring as the highest projection in the extended nominal structure, whereas in NP languages,

---

[6] A reviewer of the paper notes that other alternative analyses have elsewhere been offered to the way that Slavic extraction patterns are analyzed in Bošković (2014), for example Fanselow and Féry (2013).
[7] In reduced English nominals with no DP or QP level of structure (for example: 'John became [$_{NP}$ king of England] in 1199.'), it may be assumed that NP as the highest level of structure present is determined as a phase, as in Serbo-Croatian.

which do not project up to a DP level, the highest projection present in a nominal phrase will function as a phase. In Serbo-Croatian, this will be QP if present, and otherwise NP, as in Bošković (2014). Additionally, in languages which have developed a substantial functional structure above the lexical core in nominals and clauses, an internal, mid-level phase will also be projected above this lower core, breaking down the computation of complex nominal/clausal projections into two phasal components, in line with Chomsky's proposal that cyclic spell-out and the chunking of clauses into phases functions to reduce processing/memory load. The patterns from Bangla indicate that the identity of this mid-level phase in nominal constituents can be QP. A possibility to be examined further is whether *n*P might also serve as an internal phase in DP languages when QP is not projected, overtly or covertly – perhaps in languages where numerals and quantifiers are merged as adjuncts to *n*P/NP rather than in dedicated functional projections. In the clausal domain, we follow the conclusions in Bošković (2014) and Harwood (2015) that AspP rather than vP may occur as the internal, mid-level phase, when present, in languages which have indeed developed AspP as a functional projection. Clauses and nominal phrases are thus taken to be fully alike in having the *potential* to project both an internal and a higher-level 'closing' phase, and there is no important difference in the two domains in this regard. Where variation in the projection of phasal constituents actually does occur, this will be due to the amount of functional structure that has been grammaticalized differently in each domain/language (the DP vs. NP language difference), and occurrences of variation in the actual use of functional structure in any instance where optionality in its projection is permitted, for example optionality in the projection of a QP layer in Serbo-Croatian nominals, as revealed by the extraction patterns in (39) and (40).[8]

---

[8] In both clauses and nominal constituents, both the mid- and higher-level phases can be taken to be contextually determined as phases, in virtue of being the highest projection present in a relevant domain in any particular instance. Bošković (2014) and Harwood (2015) argue that AspP (or *v*P) is contextually determined as a phase in the sub-IP verbal domain, and CP is assumed to be determined as a phase due to being the very highest projection present in a clause. In a parallel way, QP (or NP) will be contextually determined as a phase in the sub-DP nominal domain, and DP will regularly be determined as a phase (in DP languages) due to being the very highest projection present in nominal constituents. The contextual determination of phases can thus be taken to apply within clauses and nominals at two distinct points, when a certain amount of structure has been created – at an internal/mid-level stage, when material up to AspP/QP has been constructed, and again at a final, higher CP/DP level, when the construction of clausal and nominal projections has been completed.

## 4.5 Probing the cross-linguistic occurrence of internal phases in nominal constituents

If the hypothesis of a basic parallelism (vs. asymmetry) in the projection of phases in clausal and nominal domains is correct, or at least headed in the right direction, it is expected that evidence for internal phases in the nominal domain should potentially be available in all DP languages, and yet it is the clausal domain, not the nominal domain, which has regularly furnished empirical support for the existence of domain-internal phases during the last decade. One might naturally ask why this is so, and why it might perhaps be harder to notice the effects of nominal-internal phases than clause-internal phases. One possible reason for this is the simple observation that nominal phrases are very frequently much smaller constituents than clauses, hence movement-associated cyclicity effects indicative of phasal boundaries may be less immediately obvious within DPs as opposed to CPs. Quite generally, there is often less phrasal movement occurring within nominals, hence the potentially cyclic nature of movement and the effects of the PIC are less open to inspection inside DPs. However, where clear instances of successive cyclic movement within nominal constituents cannot be observed, *ellipsis* may be available as a tool to investigate the presence and identity of phases within the nominal domain, given suggestions in the literature that the possibility of eliding material indicates the underlying presence of a phase, for example Bošković (2014), Harwood (2015). Here we will now show how a brief examination of ellipsis within nominal phrases in English, and reference to recent work on Polish and Hungarian in Ruda (2016) offers further support for the assumption that internal phases may be projected in nominals as well as clauses.

First, considering English, one finds that ellipsis of the complement of phasal head D is possible, as illustrated in (45)–(48), where we take the D position to be instantiated by the determiner elements 'these' and 'each':

(45)   *John handed me two large boxes, and I put [each _] on a different table.*

(46)   *I like mangoes a lot. I bought [these _] yesterday.*

(47)   *I put those glasses in the cupboard. What shall I do with [these _]?*

(48)   *Those two nails are bent, so I'm going to use [these _].*

Interestingly, it is also possible to elide DP-internal material which follows numerals, which we suggest are merged in the head of a QP/#P projection which is the complement of D:

(49)   Where did you put the boxes?
       Most of them are in the garage. [These two_], I'm going to put in the cellar.

Whereas numerals license ellipsis of their complements, adjectives generally do not license ellipsis in English:

(50)   Where did you put the boxes?
       Most of them are in the garage. *[These two big _], I'm going to put in the cellar.

However, two special cases of ellipsis with adjectives need to be acknowledged as apparent exceptions to the generalization that material following adjectives cannot be omitted. The first of these is a set of conventionalized uses of adjectives with no following noun, for example in games and certain selling situations, where color terms have become regular substitutes for nouns (and players may not even know/ever use an overt noun for game pieces).

(51)   Gimme [two blue_] and [three red _].

The second set of exceptions is situations where heavy contrast on an adjective occurs, for example:

(52)   Sue bought **green** apples and I bought [**red** _].

Such cases may perhaps involve focus-raising of an adjective to some higher position prior to ellipsis of a constituent that is not just an NP. If the attempt is made to elide a noun following a contrastively focused adjective which remains in its base position following an overt demonstrative, this is unacceptable, as shown in (53), suggesting that cases of acceptable ellipsis such as (52) involve more than just simple NP deletion:

(53)   Joan bought these **green** apples and I bought those **red** *(ones).

In spontaneous, non-conventionalized, non-contrastive contexts, the broad observation is that numerals do license ellipsis of their complements, but adjectives do not:

(54)   Context: Looking for hidden Easter eggs:
       a.   Look! [Here are two _].
       b.   Look at [these two _]!
       c.   *Look! Here are [two big _].
       d.   *Look at [these two big _]!

Such patterns are fully consistent with the possibility that English, like Bangla, projects a nominal-internal phase QP/#P, instantiated by numerals, and the head of this phasal constituent, Q/# licenses ellipsis of its complement. A simple investigation of ellipsis phenomena within English DPs thus offers potential evidence that nominal constituents in English are also bi-phasal, as in Bangla, with DP and QP/#P respectively serving as the closing-off and internal phases in nominal phrases. It can also be noted that when an NP/$n$P is not overtly present in cases such as those considered here, this results from genuine ellipsis of the complement of Q/# and is not the use of any null pronominal substitute for NP, because readings of sloppy identity are possible when an NP is not expressed overtly, the signature property of ellipsis, and not possible with null pronominals:

(55)   John said he will sell [two of his cars] and Bill said he'll donate [three _].
       Possible sloppy interpretation: Bill$_k$ said he$_k$ will donate three of his$_k$ cars.

Finally, it can be observed that nominal-internal ellipsis phenomena which has recently been examined in other languages has also independently reached the conclusion that nominals in DP languages may be bi-phasal constituents, whereas those in NP languages are mono-phasal. Ruda (2016) contrasts patterns of ellipsis in Hungarian, a DP language, with those occurring in Polish, an NP language, and argues at length that differences in the morpho-syntactic realization of ellipsis in the two languages support the view that DPs in Hungarian consist in two phasal components, which Ruda actually identifies as DP and $n$P, whereas nominals in Polish simply project a single phasal constituent which is suggested to be $n$P.

(56)   Phases in Polish and Hungarian nominals (Ruda 2016):
       Polish: $n$P (an 'NP language')
       Hungarian: DP and $n$P (a 'DP language')

The investigation of ellipsis and its relation to the presence of phases in a language may thus lead to significant new insights into the distribution and identity of phases within nominal and other domains, and is likely to be an important area of study and debate in future work on the nature of phases in syntactic structure.

## 4.6 General conclusions and issues for further investigation

This examination of the occurrence of phases in the nominal domain in Bangla, and the extensions of the Bangla study in sections 4.4 and 4.5 have suggested a number of general conclusions relating to the cross-linguistic projection of phases which provoke further questions and encourage additional research in certain areas. In closing the paper, we highlight the main claims of the paper, in brief, and outline what we think the next steps should be in the ongoing minimalist study of phases.

### 4.6.1 Parallels in the structure of phases in clausal and nominal domains?

A principle, general claim of the paper has been that clauses and nominal phrases are alike in sharing the potential to project both an internal, mid-level phase and a higher-level phase, and that there is no important difference in the two domains in this regard. Whenever the necessary functional structure has been developed and is projected within a language and a syntactic domain, this will support a bi-phasal partition of CPs and DPs, and a broad parallelism in phasal structure in the two types of constituent rather than an imbalanced asymmetry. In this regard, the similar (potential) distribution of phases across nominal and clausal constituents is a further example of parallels in syntactic structure that have long been posited to be present in both domains (Abney 1987, Szabolcsi 1983 and much other work).

### 4.6.2 The identity of phases in clauses and nominals

Based on its comparison of Bangla with English and other work, the paper also identifies which categories are likely to occur/be determined as phases in nominal and clausal domains. Following Bošković (2014), it is assumed that the highest projection present in a domain will be contextually determined as a 'closing' phase. This will often be CP in the clausal domain, DP in DP languages, and a lower category in NP languages, either NP or QP if it is projected. Additionally, both clauses and nominals may project a mid-level internal phase, where relevant underlying syntactic structure is present. In CPs, this may be $v$P or AspP if projected, whereas in DPs there is evidence that it can be QP, if projected, and otherwise may be $n$P. Certainly more work needs to be carried out to substantiate the limits of variation in nominal-internal phases, just as has been initiated with investigations of clause-internal phases in Bošković (2014) and Harwood (2015).

### 4.6.3 Consequences for/integration with other recent approaches to phases

In section 4.5, we have attempted to show that the primary conclusions of the paper are *not* at odds with the fundamentals of the contextual determination approach to phases defended in Bošković (2014) and the claim that nominal phrases *may* contain a lower, internal phase in addition to a higher closing phase is actually quite compatible with this approach. The existence of two phasal levels in clauses was left as an unexplained oddity in Bošković (2014), but is here assumed to be a general structural feature of all phasal constituents of a certain size (CPs, DPs).

### 4.6.4 Might other categories also be bi-phasal, for example PPs?

In the hypothesis pursued here, if a lexical category projects complex, extended functional structure above a lexical core, it may be expected to be bi-phasal. Where such rigidly-ordered functional projections have not grammaticalized, however, a constituent will remain mono-phasal. PPs and other phrasal types might well have a bi-phasal structure in certain languages, but only if they have developed sufficient functional superstructure.

### 4.6.5 The use of ellipsis as a diagnostic to probe for the presence of phases

The potential use of ellipsis as a tool to reveal the occurrence of phases has been touched on in brief in sections 4.4 and 4.5, but there is clearly much more work to be done here, both with nominals and with clauses, extending cross-linguistic coverage of relevant data, and how it may support correlations between ellipsis and phases. What these correlations might actually be is also not yet fully agreed on and there are (at least) three different views of the ways that ellipsis has been suggested to link to phasehood. Different works have proposed that if a constituent can undergo ellipsis, it is (a) the complement of a phasal head, (b) either the complement of a phasal head or a phase itself, (c) itself a phase (and complements of phases *cannot* undergo ellipsis). At the present point in time, it is not fully clear which of these positions is correct, though here we have assumed and also provided evidence supporting (b), from Bošković (2014). In attempting to probe potential connections between ellipsis and the underlying presence of phases, a further complication needs to be borne in mind and carefully controlled for – when a constituent is phonetically null, this might either be the result of ellipsis, or the use of a null pronominal element (Hiraiwa 2016). Simply showing that a phrase or sub-part of a phrase can be phonetically null does not establish that this results from ellipsis and somehow signals the occurrence of a phase, and strict/sloppy reading tests of the type noted in section 4.4 and 4.5 need to be incorporated to confirm that ellipsis is genuinely taking place, not substitution of a constituent with a null pro-form (which may have no connection with the presence of phases).

### 4.6.6 Another potential diagnostic for phases: movement

Last of all, Chomsky (2005), Roberts (2010), and Fowlie (2013) have all put forward the suggestion that only phases can undergo movement, consequently proposing that if a constituent can undergo movement, this automatically identifies it as a phase. Such a diagnostic for phasehood has not been made use of or assessed here, but is a further potential mechanism to explore in tandem with ellipsis and successive cyclic movement effects. An important question which arises here is what level of convergence can one find in utilizing the different diagnostics to identify phases?[9] There is clearly much to investigate in the immediate future, but the relevant questions and challenges are all very interesting, and will hopefully lead on to a fuller understanding of the role of phases in syntactic computation.

## Bibliography

Abels, Klaus. 2003. Successive cyclicity, anti-locality, and adposition stranding. Storrs, Connecticut: University of Connecticut dissertation.

Abney, Steven. 1987. *The English noun phrase in its sentential aspect*. Boston: Massachusetts University of Technology dissertation.

Bailyn, John. 2004. The case of Q. In Olga Arnaudova, Wayles Browne, Maria-Luisa Rivero, Danijela Stojanovic (eds.), *Proceedings of the Formal Approaches to Slavic Linguistics 12*, 1–36. Ann Arbor: University of Michigan Press.

Bhattacharya, Tanmoy. 1999. *The Structure of the Bangla DP*. London: University of London dissertation.

Borer, Hagit. 2005. *In name only*. Vol. 1. Oxford: Oxford University Press.

Börjars, Kersti, Pauline Harries & Nigel Vincent. 2016. Growing syntax: the development of a DP in North Germanic. *Language* 92 (2):e1–e37.

---

[9] For useful discussion of additional diagnostics which may (sometimes) be used to analyze the presence of phases, see also Citko (2014:10).

Bošković, Željko. 2005. On the locality of left branch extraction and the structure of NP. *Studia Linguistica* 59:1–45.
Bošković, Željko. 2008. What will you have, DP or NP? In Emily Elfner and Martin Walkow (eds.), *Proceedings of the North East Linguistic Society* 37. 101–114. Amherst: BookSurge Publishing.
Bošković, Željko. 2009. More on the no-DP analysis of article-less languages. *Studia Linguistica* 63.187–203.
Bošković, Željko. 2012. Phases in DPs and NPs. In Àngel Gallego (ed.) *Phases: developing the framework*, Berlin: De Gruyter Mouton, 343–384.
Bošković, Željko. 2014. Now I'm a Phase, Now I'm Not a Phase: On the Variability of Phases with Extraction and Ellipsis. *Linguistic Inquiry* 45 (1):27–89.
Bošković, Željko. 2016. Getting really edgy: On the edge of the edge. *Linguistic Inquiry* 47 (1):1–33.
Bošković, Željko & Jon Gajewski. 2011. Semantic correlates of the NP/DP parameter. In Suzi Lima, Kevin Mullin & Brian Smith (eds.), *Proceedings of the thirty-ninth annual meeting of the North East Linguistic Society*, 121–134. Amherst: CreateSpace Independent Publishing Platform.
Chacón, Dustin. 2012. Head movement in the Bangla DP. *Journal of South Asian Linguistics* 4:3–24.
Chomsky, Noam. 1986. *Knowledge of language: its nature, origin, and use*. New York: Praeger.
Chomsky, Noam. 2000. Minimalist Inquiries. In Roger Martin, David Michaels, and Juan Uriagereka (eds.) *Step by step: essays on minimalist syntax in honor of Howard Lasnik*, 89-155. Cambridge, Mass: MIT Press.
Chomsky, Noam. 2005. On phases. In Robert Freidin, Carlos Otero, and Maria Luisa Zubizarreta (eds.) *Foundational issues in linguistic theory: essays in honor of Jean Roger Vergnaud*, 133–166. Cambridge, MA: MIT Press.
Citko, Barbara. 2014. *Phase theory. An Introduction*. Cambridge: Cambridge University Press.
Danon, Gabi. 2012. Two structures for numeral-noun constructions. *Lingua*, 1282–1307.
Dayal, Veneeta. 2012. What can South Asian Languages tell us about classifier systems? Conference presentation in Formal Approaches to South Asian Languages 2, Massachusetts University of Technology.
Despić, Miloje. 2013. Binding and the Structure of NP in Serbo-Croatian. *Linguistic inquiry* 44 (2):239–270.
Fanselow, Gisbert and Caroline Féry. 2013. A comparative perspective on intervention effects on left branch extractions in Slavic. In W. Sulym, M. Smolij, and C. Djakiw (eds.) *Non progredi est regredi [Not to go forward is to go back]*, 266–295 Lwiw: Pais.
Fillmore, Charles J. 1963. The position of embedding transformations in a grammar. *Word* 19:208–231.
Fowlie, Meaghan. 2013. Multiple multiple spellout. In Theresa Biberauer & Ian Roberts (eds.) *Challenges to Linearization*, 129–69. Berlin: Mouton de Gruyter.
Franks, Steven. 1994. Parametric properties of numeral phrases in Slavic. *Natural Language and Linguistics Theory* 12:597–674.
Grohmann, Kleanthes. 2003. *Prolific domains: on the anti-locality of movement dependencies*. Amsterdam: John Benjamins.
Harwood, William. 2015. Being progressive is just a phase: celebrating the uniqueness of progressive aspect under a phase-based analysis. *Natural Language and Linguistic Theory* 33:523–573.

Hinzen, Wolfram. 2012. Phases and semantics. In Ángel Gallego (ed.) *Phases: developing the framework*, 309–342. Berlin: Mouton De Gruyter.

Hiraiwa, Ken. 2016. NP-ellipsis: a comparative syntax of Japanese and Okinawan. *Natural language and linguistic theory* 34:1345–1387.

Horn, Laurence R. 1971. Negative transportation: Unsafe at any speed? In *Papers from the Seventh Regional Meeting of the Chicago Linguistic Society*, 120–133. Chicago: University of Chicago, Chicago Linguistic Society.

Lander, Eric and Liliane Haegeman. 2013. Old Norse as an NP language, with observations on the common Norse and Northwest Germanic Runic inscriptions. *Transactions of the Philological Society* 112:279–318.

Legate, Julie Anne. 2003. Some interface properties of the phase. *Linguistic Inquiry* 34:506–16.

May, Robert. 1985. *Logical Form: its structure and derivation*. Cambridge, Mass: MIT Press.

McCloskey, James. 2000. Quantifier Float and Wh-Movement in an Irish English. *Linguistic Inquiry* 31:57–84.

Oku, Satoshi. 1998. *A theory of selection and reconstruction in the minimalist perspective*. Storrs: Connecticut: University of Connecticut dissertation.

Pereltsvaig, Asya. 2006. Passing by cardinals: in support of head movement in nominals. In: James Lavine, Steve Franks, & Hana Filip (eds.) *Formal Approaches to Slavic Linguistics 14*, 277–292. Ann Arbor, MI: Michigan Slavic Publications.

Richards, Norvin. 2001. *Movement in language: interactions and architectures*. Oxford: Oxford University Press.

Roberts, Ian. 2010. A deletion analysis of null subjects. In Theresa Biberauer, Anders Holmberg, Ian Roberts, and Michele Sheehan (eds.) *Parametric variation: null subjects in minimalist theory*, 58–87. Cambridge: Cambridge University Press.

Ruda, Marta. 2016. NP ellipsis (effects) in Polish and Hungarian: FFs on Fs, Agree and Chain Reduction. *The Linguistic Review* 33 (4):649–677.

Saito, Mamoru. 2004. Notes on East Asian argument ellipsis. *Language Research* 43:203–27.

Şener, Serkan and Daiko Takahashi. 2009. *Argument ellipsis in Japanese and Turkish*. Ms, University of Connecticut and Tohoka University.

Shlonsky, Ur. 2004. The form of Semitic noun phrases. *Lingua*, 1465–1526.

Simpson, Andrew, Arunima Choudhury & Mythili Menon. 2013. Argument ellipsis and the licensing of covert nominals in Bangla, Hindi and Malayalam. *Lingua* 134:123–138.

Simpson, Andrew and Saurov Syed. 2016. Blocking effects of higher numerals in Bangla: a phase based approach. *Linguistic Inquiry* 47 (4):754–763.

Svenonius, Peter. 2004. On the Edge. In David Adger, Cecile Cat, & George Tsoulas (eds.) *Peripheries: Syntactic Edges and their Effects*, 259–287. Dordrecht: Kluwer.

Syed, Saurov & Andrew Simpson. 2017. On the DP/NP status of nominal projections in Bangla: Consequences for the theory of phases. *Glossa* 2 (68):1–24.

Syed, Saurov. 2017. The structure of noun phrases in Bengali: what it tells us about phases and the universality of DPs. Los Angeles, CA: University of Southern California dissertation.

Szabolcsi, Anna. 1983. The possessor that ran away from home. *The Linguistic Review* 3:89–102.

Takahashi, Daiko. 2008. Noun phrase ellipsis. In Shigeru Miyagawa & Mamoru Saito (eds.), *The Oxford Handbook of Japanese Linguistics*, 394–422. Oxford: Oxford University Press.

Zlatić, Larisa. 1997. *The structure of the Serbian Noun Phrase*. Austin: University of Texas at Austin dissertation.

Coppe van Urk
# 5 How to detect a phase

**Abstract:** This paper investigates the question of how we determine whether a particular phrase behaves like a phasal domain crosslinguistically. I present an overview of the morphophonological, syntactic, and semantic effects that should be associated with a phrase across languages if it hosts successive-cyclic movement. For both the clause and the verb phrase, I argue that the full range of such effects is attested, providing evidence for the parallelism of these domains (Chomsky 1986 et seq.). This overview then provides a set of predictions against which any candidate for a phasal domain can be tested. I examine PPs and DPs from this perspective and identify a number of missing effects.

**Keywords:** successive cyclicity, phases, movement, CP, *v*P, PP, DP

## Introduction

Since Chomsky (1973), much evidence has accrued for the idea that long-distance dependencies are successive-cyclic, and thus are decomposed into a series of shorter dependencies. However, different researchers have come to different conclusions about which domains evidence successive cyclicity effects. In some approaches, all phrases on the path of movement are implicated, but, in other theories, successive-cyclic dependencies are punctuated paths, because only some phrases constitute phases (e. g. CP and *v*P). Even in the context of a punctuated path approach, it has been questioned whether CP and *v*P have the same status (e. g. Rackowski and Richards 2005; Den Dikken 2009, 2010; Keine 2016), as well as whether PPs and DPs may also constitute phasal units. Finally, phase boundaries are routinely invoked in both morphological and syntactic analyses, to explain apparent domain restrictions (for instance, for heads such as *n*, *a*, or Appl).

This paper focuses on the issue of how to detect a phase, by asking the question of what the set of reflexes of intermediate movement is that is expected to be associated with a phase edge. I then investigate whether all such effects are found in some of the most influential phasal domains across languages. Focusing first on the clause and verb phrase, I demonstrate that the full range of morphophonological, syntactic, and semantic effects that should be associated with intermediate movement is indeed attested. The resulting picture provides clear evidence for at least two phasal boundaries in the clausal domain, one associated with the clause edge and one with the verbal domain (Chomsky 1986 et seq.). These domains display symmetry, in that they show the same range of successive cyclicity effects (contra, for instance, Rackowski and Richards 2005, Den Dikken 2009, 2010, and Keine 2016). Finally, I review the question of whether similar evidence can be found for the PP/DP domain, ultimately concluding that these too are phasal domains, even though some key effects appear to be absent. I provide independent explanations for the absence of multiple spell-out and semantic effects, but point out interactions with $\varphi$-agreement and stranding that should in principle be attested.

## 5.1 Featural effects on intervening nodes

I will start this paper by examining the question of what types of successive cyclicity effects should be visible on the intermediate material itself, such as the phase head. I adopt the assumption that an intermediate node that heads a locality domain hosts a feature relevant to extraction (1), responsible for triggering movement.

(1)
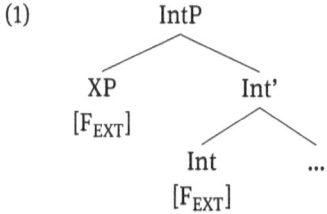

I identify three types of effects that we should expect if these features are present in a domain: extraction marking, parasitic agreement, and lexical choice phenomena. All three are evident at the edge of the clause and at the edge of the verb phrase.

### 5.1.1 Morphological form

The simplest way in which the presence of a feature can affect an intermediate head is through the morphological realization of an extraction feature, resulting in *extraction marking*. Such effects are commonly found at the CP edge, and at *v*P as well.

#### 5.1.1.1 Extraction marking at the CP edge

Extraction marking at the CP edge is perhaps one of the most commonly found reflexes of successive cyclicity. Irish complementizer alternations, for example, can be analyzed as reflecting the realization of extraction features (e. g. McCloskey 1979, 2001, 2002). In Irish, the declarative complementizer *go* alternates with extraction complementizer *aL*, depending on whether Ā-movement targets the left periphery (2a–b).[1]

(2) **Two different complementizers in Irish:**

    a. *Creidim* [CP ***gu**-r*    *inis sé bréag*].
        believe.1SG    C.DCL-PAST tell he lie
        'I believe that he told a lie.'

    b. *an fhilíocht* [CP ***a***    *chum*    *sí* \_\_]
        the poetry      C.EXT composed she
        'the poetry that she composed'
        (McCloskey 2002:185–186)

Importantly, all intervening complementizers on the path of long-distance movement must be *aL* (3), as expected if all intervening clauses are locality domains.

(3) **Extraction complementizer appears in intermediate clauses:**

     *an t-ainm* [CP ***a***    *hinnseadh dúinn* [CP ***a***    *bhí* \_\_ *ar an áit*]]
     the name     C.EXT was-told to-us    C.EXT was    on the place
     'the name that we were told was on the place'
     (McCloskey 2002:185)

Dinka also has an extraction marking pattern (Van Urk 2015). Dinka has a V2 effect at the clause edge that is found both in matrix and embedded clauses. In addition to this, the verb/auxiliary in V2 position carries a prefix with a dedicated extraction form found with Ā-movement. In long-distance dependencies, this extraction prefix must appear both at final and intermediate V2 positions (4a–b).

(4) **Extraction prefix in Dinka:**

    a. *Yè kɔ̂ɔc-kó$_i$*    *ø-yùu̱kù̱*    *ké tàak*    [CP *kè̱ ø-cí̱i*
        be people-which EXT.3-HAB.1P 3PL think.NF    C EXT.3-PRF.OV
        *Áyèn*    (*ké*) *càm*    *kè̱nè̱ kêek$_i$*]?
        Ayen.GEN 3PL eat.NF with 3PL
        'Which people do we think Ayen has eaten with?'

---

[1] There is also a complementizer *aN* that signals resumption. The terms *aN* and *aL* refer to the mutation effect triggered on the following verb, where N = nasalization and L = lenition. See McCloskey (2002) for detailed discussion of the distribution of these complementizers.

b.  *Ye kɔ́ɔc-kó*  ***ę́-kè*-*yá*  *ké tàak*  [CP
be people.CS-which.PL EXT.PST-3P-HAB.2SG 3PL think.NF
***ę́-kè*-*cı̨́i*  *Áyèn*  *ké gàam gàlàm]]?*
EXT.PST-3P-PRF.OV Ayen.GEN 3PL give.NF pen
'Which people did (s)he think that Ayen had given a pen to?'

In (4a), both the matrix and embedded auxiliary surface with a null prefix instead of the expected prefix in present tense declaratives, *à-*. In (4b), both auxiliaries appear with *ę́-* instead of the past tense variant *áa-*.

Other languages with extraction marking patterns include at least Asante Twi (Korsah and Murphy 2016), Chamorro (Chung 1982), Kîîtharaka (Abels and Muriungi 2008), Seereer (Baier 2014), and Wolof (Torrence 2005).

### 5.1.1.2 Extraction marking at *v*P edge

Extraction marking is found at the *v*P edge as well. Bennett et al. (2012) describe a *v*P-level extraction morpheme in Defaka (Ijoid). In Defaka, the morpheme *-kè* appears on all verbs crossed by movement (5a–b).

(5) **Defaka *-kè* appears on all intermediate verbs:**

    a.  *Bruce ndò Bòmá jírí-**kè***  [CP ___ *á  ésé-mà]*
        Bruce FOC Boma know-EXT  her see-NFUT
        'It is Bruce that Boma knows saw her.'

    b.  *áyá jíkà  ndò Bòmá ì bíè-**kè***  [CP *ì ísò* ___ *sónó-mà-**kè**]*
        new house FOC Boma I ask-EXT  I ISO  buy-NFUT-EXT
        'It is a new house that Boma asked me if I'm going to buy.'

Bennett et al. argue that this extraction morpheme is in the verb phrase and not in the left periphery, on the basis of the fact that extraction a local subject is not accompanied by extraction marking (6a). Subjects are generated at the *v*P edge and so do not need to undergo intermediate movement to escape this domain. The *-kè* morpheme is triggered by extraction of a local object or adjunct (6b–c).

(6) **Defaka *-kè* appears with non-subject extraction:**

    a.  *ì kò  Bòmá ésé-kà-rè*
        I FOC.SBJ Boma see-FUT-NEG
        'It is me that will not see Boma.'

    b.  *tárì  ndo Àmànyà ómgbìnyà sónó àmà-**kè*** ___ *kí́ á*  ꞌ*té?*
        who FOC Amaya  shirt  buy give-EXT  market P
        'Who did Amaya buy a shirt for at the market?'

c. [_PP_ *ándù kìkìà*] *ndò à  èbèrè rì  bòi-mà-**kè***
    canoe under FOC the dog   RE hide-NFUT-EXT
    'It is under the canoe that the dog is hiding.'
    (Defaka; Bennett et al. 2012:294,296)

In addition, long-distance movement of a subject does trigger the extraction morpheme in the higher clause, since a subject must still cross the matrix *v*P edge (7). This fact tells us that there is no independent restriction on using -*kè* with subject extraction.

(7) **Defaka -*kè* with long-distance subject movement:**
    *Bruce ndò Bòmá jírí-**kè***    [_CP_ __  *á   ésé-mà*]
    Bruce FOC Boma know-EXT         her see-NFUT
    'It is Bruce that Boma knows saw her.'
    (Defaka; Bennett et al. 2012:294,296)

A similar pattern at the *v*P edge is voice marking in Malay/Indonesian languages (e. g. Saddy 1991, 1992; Cole and Hermon 1998; Sato 2012). In these languages, extraction across a verb triggers obligatory deletion of the transitivity prefix *meN-* (8a), which is otherwise an optional morpheme (8b).

(8) ***MeN-* cannot appear on intermediate verbs:**
    a. *siapa Bill **(\*mem)**-beritahu ibunya*    [_CP_ *yang* __ ***(men)**-yintai*
       who   Bill (*meN)-tell   mother.his        that        (meN)-love
       *Fatimah]?*
       Fatimah
       'Who does Bill tell his mother that loves Fatimah?'
    b. *Ali **(mem)**-beri Fatimah hadiah  untuk hari lahirnya*
       Ali **(meng)**-give Fatimah present for   day  birth
       'Ali gave Fatimah a present for her birthday.'
       (Malay; Cole and Hermon 1998:231–232)

This prefix is usually analyzed as a *v*P-level voice or transitivity morpheme (Cole et al. 2008; Sato 2012; *cf.* Rackowski and Richards 2005). As in Defaka, extraction of a local subject does not trigger *meN*-deletion (9a), in contrast to an embedded subject (8), providing additional evidence that this effect is at the *v*P edge. In contrast, local object movement also requires *meN*-deletion.

(9) **No *MeN*- deletion with movement of subjects:**
   a. *siapa **(mem)**-beli    buku itu?*
      who   (meN)-bought book that
      'Who bought that book?'
   b. *apa Ali **(\*mem)**-beri pada Fatimah?*
      what Ali (\*meN)-gave to    Fatimah
      'What did Ali give to Fatimah?'
      (Malay; Cole and Hermon 1998:231)

Similar *v*P-level effects may be found at least in Tagalog (Rackowski and Richards 2005) and Asante Twi (Korsah and Murphy 2016).

### 5.1.2 Satisfaction of other features: φ-agreement and V2

Another way in which successive-cyclic movement might affect intermediate heads is through the satisfaction of independent features on the intermediate head. suppose an intermediate head Int carries other features in addition to the extraction feature, such as $F_2$ and $F_3$ in (10).

(10)
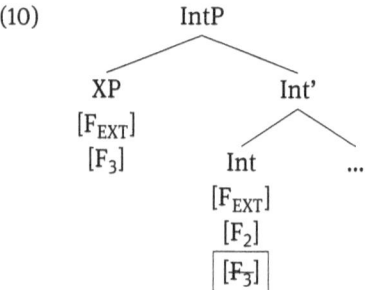

Since the moving XP ends up in a local relation with Int by virtue of the extraction feature, we might expect it to be capable of satisfying some of these unrelated features, if the XP happens to carry them as well, like $F_3$ in (10).

In fact, much work on probe-goal relations has argued that features can be satisfied parasitically in this fashion (e. g. Chomsky 2001; Bruening 2001; Kotek 2014; Deal 2014; Režać 2015; Van Urk 2015). Generalizing over this work, I will refer to this idea as Parasitic Agree (11).

(11)   **Parasitic Agree:**
       If a Probe on a certain head H has found a goal G, other probes on H can also enter into Agree/Attract relations with G.

If Agree relations can be parasitic on other Agree relations in this fashion, we expect extraction features to be detectable by the ability of intermediate dependencies to satisfy unrelated features, like φ-features. As I will show in this section, such effects are found in both the CP and *v*P domain.

### 5.1.2.1 φ-agreement at the CP edge

In a number of languages, long-distance movement may result in φ-agreement with the moving phrase at intermediate clause edges. Dinka provides one example. In Dinka, movement of a plural DP is reflected at intervening clause boundaries by the presence of a plural agreement prefix (12a–b).[2]

(12)   **Intermediate movement triggers φ-agreement:**
  a. **Yè kɔ̂ɔc-kó**   [CP Op ẹ̈-kè-yá       ké tàak     [CP ẹ̈
     be people.CS1-which    EXT.PST-PL-HAB.2SG 3PL think.NF   C
     ___ ẹ̈-kè-cîi       Áyèn      ké gâam  gàlàm]]?
     EXT.PST-PL-PRF.OV Ayen.GEN 3PL give.NF pen
     'Which people did (s)he think that Ayen had given a pen to?'
  b. **Wɔ̂ɔk yîi**   Bôl    ké luêeel [CP ẹ̈ ___ ẹ̈-kè-lɛ́ɛt
     we   HAB.OV Bol.GEN 3PL say.NF   C    EXT.PST-PL-insult.OV
     Áyèn     ké].
     Ayen.GEN 3PL
     'Us, Bol says Ayen was insulting.'

Van Urk (2015) provides an analysis of these φ-agreement patterns in terms of the notion of parasitic agreement. If the moving phrase already satisfies an extraction feature at the clause edge, this same relation may allow the intervening head to access φ-features.

Wolof also appears to have a pattern of φ-agreement at C (Torrence 2005, 2012). In particular, Torrence argues that Wolof has a complementizer that agrees in noun class with a moved *wh*-phrase. This agreeing complementizer may appear in intervening clauses (13a–b).[3]

---

[2] The morpheme found with singulars is always null. As discussed in Van Urk (2015), this can be attributed to the neutralization of person features as a result of anti-agreement. In non-movement contexts, the default singular morpheme is null.

[3] Torrence argues that such extractions involve silent *wh*-phrases, essentially null operators, obligatory in this construction as the result of a Doubly-Filled Comp Effect. See Torrence (2012) for detailed argumentation.

(13) **Agreeing complementizers in Wolof:**
  a. ***K*-*u*** *Isaa foog* [$_{CP}$ ***k*-*u*** *a bëgg*]?
     AGR-C Isaa think  AGR-C 2SG love
     'Who does Isaa think you love?'
  b. ***F*-*u*** *Isaa wax ne* [$_{CP}$ ***f*-*u*-*ma*** *jàng-e taalif y-a*]?
     AGR-C Isaa say FRC  AGR-C-1SG read-LOC poem DEF
     'Where did Isaa say that I read the poems?'
     (Torrence 2012:22)

### 5.1.2.2 φ-agreement at the *v*P edge

Similar interactions between successive-cyclic movement and agreement have been documented at the *v*P edge. Bruening (2001) observes that Ā-movement in Passamaquoddy can be accompanied by φ-agreement on intervening heads. Specifically, verbs on the path of movement may surface with agreeing participial endings (14a–b).[4]

(14) **Passamaquoddy verbs may agree with Ā-moving phrases:**
  a. ***Wen*-*ik*** *kisitahatom-on-**ik*** [$_{CP}$
     who-3PL decide.IO-2CONJ-PART.3PL
     *keti-naci-wikuwamkom-oc-**ik***]?
     IC.FUT-go.do-visit.AO-2CONJ-PART.3PL
     'Who all did you decide to go visit?'
  b. *Wot* **nit** ***pahtoliyas*** [$_{CP}$ *Mali elitahasi-c-**il*** [$_{CP}$ *eli*
     this that priest  Mary IC.think-3CONJ-PART.OBV  C
     *wen kisi-komutonom-ac-**il***]
     someone PERF-rob.AO-3CONJ-PART.OBV
     'This is the priest that Mary thinks someone robbed.'
     (Passamaquoddy; Bruening 2006:34)

Just as suggested here, Bruening (p. 209) analyzes this as parasitic agreement as a result of movement to *v*P, since the morphology is participial in nature. See also Den Dikken 2010 for discussion of the interaction of object agreement and movement in Hungarian.

As with extraction marking, the distribution of φ-agreement as a reflex of successive-cyclic movement is symmetrical: we can find examples of this effect both at the CP and *v*P edge.

---

[4] The suffix -*il* realizes agreement with a 3rd person obviative.

## 5.1.3 Lexical choice

Another way in which intermediate movement can affect the intermediate head is by having an effect on lexical choice. If intermediate movement is feature-driven, we may expect that flavors of the intermediate head can vary in whether they carry a featural trigger, as schematized in (15) and (16).

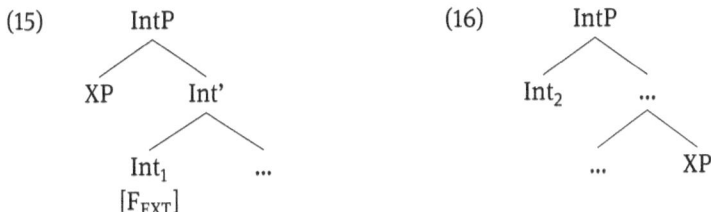

Such effects are distinct from extraction marking, because neither head necessarily realizes extraction morphology. In this section, I show that such effects are attested both at the CP and *v*P edge.

### 5.1.3.1 Lexical choice effects at the CP edge

It is well-known that the choice of complementizer may affect the availability of long-distance movement. In the simplest case, clauses headed by certain complementizers may block movement. For example, in Russian, movement is banned out of indicative clauses, but possible out of subjunctives (17a–b).[5]

(17) **Long-distance movement in Russian depends on complementizer:**
    a. *Kakuju knigu ty dumaeš' [$_{CP}$ **čto** Petr pročital ___]?
        which book you believe     that.IND Petr read
        'Which book do you believe that Petr read?'
    b. Kakuju knigu ty dumaeš' [$_{CP}$ **čtoby** Petr pročital ___]?
        which book you believe     that.SUBJ Petr read
        'Which book do you believe that Petr read?'
        (Müller and Sternefeld 1993)

This is a lexical choice effect, and not extraction marking, because neither complementizer realizes extraction morphology and there are other syntactic and semantic differences between the heads involved.

---

[5] On this analysis, the islandhood of finite CPs in some languages reflects the lack of an extraction feature on C. Another possibility is that some additional factors cause CPs to be islands in these languages, as is likely the case for other islands.

Another effect that can be analyzed as lexical choice is inversion. In a number of languages, the subject and auxiliary must invert if intermediate movement targets the CP edge (e. g. Kayne and Pollock 1978; Torrego 1984; Henry 1995). I illustrate with Belfast English (Henry 1995).

(18) **Inversion in Belfast English:**
    a.   *Who did John hope [$_{CP}$ **would** he see ___]?*
    b.   *What did Mary claim [$_{CP}$ **did** they steal ___]?*
        (Belfast English; Henry 1995:109)

A standard analysis of this pattern is to say the null C that hosts a featural trigger also happens to attract T.[6] This type of approach is essentially a lexical choice analysis, since inversion will only be obligatory if all other instances of C do not have a feature triggering movement and so would be blocked in the context of long-distance dependencies.

### 5.1.3.2 Lexical choice effects at the *v*P edge

There are again analogous effects in the *v*P domain. In Nupe, the choice of verb phrase correlates with extraction, as documented by Kandybowicz (2008). Specifically, extraction is blocked from verb phrases headed by perfect aspect (19a–b).

(19) **Movement out of perfect *v*Ps impossible in Nupe:**
    a.   Ke   Musa pa   ___ o?
           what Musa pound   o
           'What did Musa pound?'
    b.   Ke   Musa à   pa   ___ o?
           what Musa FUT pound   o
           'What will Musa pound?'
    c.   *Ke   Musa á   pa   ___ o?
           what Musa PRF pound   o
           'What has Musa pounded?'
           (Nupe; Kandybowicz 2008:288)

---

[6] It is worth noting that, in Romance languages, the auxiliary and verb invert together, so that inversion in these languages is not obviously the result of T-to-C movement. I set aside this issue here.

Evidence that this is a vP-level restriction comes from the fact that local subjects may freely extract, as well as high adverbs (20a–b). In contrast, like objects, low adverbs may not be extracted out a perfect verb phrase.

(20) **Subjects, high adverbs, not low adverbs may move in perfect:**
    a. ***Bagi** na \_\_\_ á nakàn ba na*
        man REL     PRF meat cut REL
        'the man that had cut the meat'
    b. ***Panyi lèé** \_\_\_ Musa á nakàn ba o.*
        before past   Musa PRF meat cut O
        'A LONG TIME AGO, Musa had cut the meat.'
    c. **\****Karayín** Musa á nakàn ba \_\_\_ o.*
        carefully Musa PRF meat cut   O
        'Musa had cut the meat CAREFULLY.'
        (Nupe; Kandybowicz 2008:291)

As predicted, such structural asymmetries disappear in long-distance extraction. If a higher vP is perfect, long-distance subject and object extraction are equally degraded (21a–b).

(21) **Long-distance movement across perfect vP banned:**
    a. **\****Nana** Musa á gan [$_{CP}$ gànán \_\_\_ pa eci o.*
        Nana Musa PRF say     COMP     pound yam O
        'Musa has said that NANA pounded the yam.'
    b. **\****Eci** Musa á gan [$_{CP}$ gànán Nana pa \_\_\_ o.*
        yam Musa PRF say     COMP Nana pound   O
        'Musa has said that Nana pounded THE YAM.'
        (Nupe; Kandybowicz 2008:295)

We can also find inversion effects at the vP edge, as pointed out by Cognola (2013) in work on the Germanic dialect Mòcheno, spoken in northern Italy. Mòcheno allows both OV and VO orders in the verb phrase:

(22) **Mòcheno allows VO and OV order:**
    a. *Gester hone [$_{vP}$ a puach **kaft**].*
        yesterday have-1SG   a book bought
        'Yesterday, I bought a book.'
    b. *Gester hone [$_{vP}$ **kaft** a puach].*
        yesterday have-1SG   bought a book
        'Yesterday, I bought a book.'
        (Mòcheno; Cognola 2008:81)

However, in the context of extraction, only VO syntax is possible (23a–b).[7]

(23) **Inversion in the *v*P with *wh*-movement in Mòcheno:**
    a. *En bem hòt-se* [*<sub>vP</sub> **kaft** de zaitung*]
       to whom has-she    bought the newspaper
       'Who has she bought a newspaper?'
    b. *\*En bem hòt-se* [*<sub>vP</sub> de zaitung* **kaft**]
       to whom has-she   the newspaper bought
       'Who has she bought a newspaper?'
    (Mòcheno; Cognola 2013:7)

This effect then is analogous to inversion in the CP domain and we can analyze it as a lexical choice effect. Suppose Mòcheno has two variants of *v*, one for OV and one for VO. If only the head that triggers VO is endowed with a featural trigger, we expect that OV verb phrases are islands, as shown in (23b).

In this section, I demonstrated that we can find at least three different types of reflexes of successive cyclicity that can be linked to the presence of features associated with extraction on intermediate heads: extraction marking, parasitic agreement, and lexical choice effects. These effects are equally distributed across the CP/*v*P domain, providing evidence that these are both phasal domains (e. g. Chomsky 1986 et seq.).

## 5.2 On the presence of intermediate copies

I now turn to evidence for the presence of intermediate copies, which should be detectable both at PF and LF. I start by examining the question of which PF effects should be attested and identify at least four types: intermediate copy realization, multiple spell-out, stranding and V2 satisfaction. As with featural effects, we can find instances of most reflexes at both the CP and *v*P edge.

### 5.2.1 Intermediate copy realization

The first way in which we expect the presence of intermediate copies of a moving phrase to be recoverable is if an intermediate copy can be realized. For example, if

---

[7] The inversion effect is also found with subject extraction. See Cognola (2008, 2013) for discussion.

there are independent constraints blocking the pronunciation of the highest copy, we might see a dislocated phrase surface in an intermediate position instead (24).

(24) **Intermediate copy realization:**
 [ ~~Copy~~ ... [IntP Copy ... ~~Copy~~ ... ]]

The first type of construction that seems to instantiate this is partial *wh*-movement, in which a *wh*-phrase surfaces in an intermediate position, although it behaves as if it has undergo movement to the scopal position. Fanselow (2006) and Abels (2012:sec. 3.3–3.4) point out that intermediate copy realization could also arise as the result of the interaction of intermediate movement with pied-piping. If a locality domain can be pied-piped by the final step of movement, the moving phrase should be realized in an intermediate position, since it can still undergo intermediate movement inside the locality domain a phasal domain. This situation is schematized in (25).

(25) **Wh-trapping:**
 [ [IntP Copy ... ~~Copy~~ ... ] ... [IntP Copy ... ~~Copy~~ ... ]]

I refer to such constructions as *wh-trapping*, and there are instances of this effect at the CP and *v*P edge.

### 5.2.1.1 Intermediate copy realization at the CP edge

Partial movement has been documented in a few languages, particularly for *wh*-phrases. Cole and Hermon (2000) describe a pattern along these lines for Malay. In Malay, *wh*-dependencies can be expressed with full *wh*-movement, partial movement, and *wh*- in situ (26a–c).

(26) **Wh-in situ and full and partial wh-movement in Malay:**
 a. **Siapa** Bill harap [CP ___ akan membeli baju untuknya]?
  who Bill hopes will buy clothes for.him
  'Who does Bill hope will buy clothes for him?'
 b. Ali memberitahu kamu tadi [CP **apa** Fatimah baca ___]?
  Ali told you just.now what Fatimah read
  'What did Ali tell you just now that Fatimah was reading?'
 c. Ali memberitahu kamu tadi [CP Fatimah baca **apa**]?
  Ali told you just.now Fatimah read what

'What did Ali tell you just now that Fatimah was reading?'
(Cole and Hermon 1998:224–225)

It is important to establish that such partial movement configurations reflect intermediate copy realization and not independent focus movement of an in situ *wh*-phrase inside the embedded clause (see, for instance, Zentz 2016). As Cole and Hermon point out, evidence for the intermediate copy analysis comes from the fact that this construction is sensitive both to islands above and below the pronunciation site, as evident in (27a–b).

(27)  **Partial *wh*-movement is sensitive to higher and lower islands:**
   a.  *Ali memberitahu kamu [CP **apa** Mary fikir   [CP dia suka [DP
       Ali told            you       what Mary think    he likes
       perempuan yang beli ___]]]?
       woman     that buy
       'What did Ali tell you that Mary thinks that he likes a woman who bought?'
   b.  *Kamu sayang [DP perempuan yang Ali fikir   [CP **apa** telah
       you  love         woman     that Ali thinks     what already
       makan ___]]?
       eat
       'Who do you love the woman who Ali thinks ate what?'
       (Cole and Hermon 2000:91–92)

These island effects follow from a full movement analysis, with intermediate spell-out. If this analysis is correct, partial *wh*-movement reveals intermediate movement in the embedded CP. See Fanselow (2006) for an overview of other languages that may allow similar partial *wh*-movement constructions.

Intermediate copy realization is also evident in languages that allow clausal pied-piping, which give rise to the *wh*-trapping configuration identified above. Imbabura Quechua and Basque are examples of languages with clausal pied-piping (e. g. Hermon 1985; Ortiz de Urbina 1989; Arregi 2003). In both (28a–b), the *wh*-phrase that triggers pied-piping must reside in a left-peripheral position inside the moved CP.

(28)  **Clausal pied-piping in Quechua and Basque:**
   a.  [CP **Ima-ta**  wawa    ___ miku-chun-taj] Maria muna-n?
       what-ACC child.NOM     eat-SUBJ-Q    Maria want-PR.3
       'What does Maria want that the child eat?'
       (Imbabura Quechua; Hermon 1985:151)

b.  [$_{CP}$ **Se**  idatzi  rabela Jonek]  pentzate su?
     what written has    Jon.ERG you-think
     'What do you think Jon wrote?'
     (Basque; Arregi 2003:118)

Such facts seem to demonstrate that the *wh*-phrase undergoes intermediate movement inside the CP. See also Heck (2008: sec. 2.3) for arguments that movement of infinitives in German relatives involves a similar configuration of clausal pied-piping.[8]

### 5.2.1.2 Intermediate copy realization at the *v*P edge

Let us now turn to the question of whether there are intermediate copy realization constructions at the *v*P edge. Manetta (2010) presents an analysis of Kashmiri and Hindi *wh*-dependencies which makes use of partial *wh*-movement to the edge of the verb phrase, analogous to the account of Malay discussed above. However, Dayal (2017) provides some critical discussion of this pattern. For *wh*-trapping, we can find counterparts at the *v*P edge. This may be surprising, because a crosslinguistic generalization that seems to govern pied-piping is that *v*Ps cannot be pied-piped (Cable 2007, 2010; Heck 2008, 2009). However, *wh*-trapping effects do seem to emerge when *wh*-movement co-occurs with an independent instance of VP-fronting, as shown by Cozier (2006) and Buell (2012). In such environments, we find evidence for intermediate movement to the *v*P edge.

Cozier (2006) describes an interaction between intermediate movement and predicate clefting in Trinidadian English that operates along these lines. Trinidadian English does not allow pied-piping of verbs in isolation. However, Trinidadian English possesses an independent operation of long-distance predicate clefting, as in the examples in (29a–b).

(29)  **Predicate clefting in Trinidadian English:**
   a. Is **walk** [that Tim did **walk**].
      'Tim really walked.'
   b. Is **talk** [he tell me [that she **talk** about Ricky]].
      (Trinidadian English; Cozier 2006:660,663)

---

[8] An interesting observation is that clausal pied-piping is typically restricted to nominalized or infinitival clauses, which may suggest that neither full CPs or *v*Ps can be pied-piped in isolation. This does not diminish the point, however, that we can see the effects of intermediate movement when pied-piping of a clause is possible.

Cozier argues that predicate clefting is phrasal movement, based on the observation that *v*P-internal adverbs to the left of the verb can be moved along (30a–b).[9]

(30)   **Predicate cleft pied-pipes material to the left:**
   a.   Is **briefly touch** [he did **touch** upon that matter].
        'He briefly touched upon that matter (as opposed to doing something else with that matter).'
   b.   Is **cleverly avoid** [he **avoid** the question].
        'He cleverly AVOIDED the question (as opposed to cleverly doing something else with the question, like answering it).'
        (Trinidadian English; Cozier 2006:666)

On this basis, Cozier proposes an analysis of predicate clefting as remnant *v*P-movement, with all other VP-internal material undergoing evacuating movements of the VP. As a result, only material at the *v*P edge, like a left-adjoined adverb, will surface in the fronted phrase.[10]

Importantly, *wh*-words that have undergone intermediate movement to the edge of the verb phrase can be pied-piped as well, as in (31a–c).

(31)   **Predicate cleft may pied-pipe *wh*-words:**
   a.   Is **what fix** [he did **fix** ___ yesterday]?
   b.   *Is **who talk** [___ **talking** about she]?
        (Trinidadian English; Cozier 2006:670,679)

Strikingly, this is possible even when the *wh*-phrase is undergoing long-distance movement from a lower clause and does not directly modify the clefted verb (32).

(32)   **Predicate cleft can pied-pipe *wh*-word from lower clause:**
        Is **who tell** [Tim **tell** you [that he give the car to ___]]?
        (Trinidadian English; Cozier 2006:681)

This is the same effect as the clausal pied-piping example discussed above. The *wh*-phrase undergoes intermediate movement to a position at the *v*P edge and pied-pipes the *v*P from this position. In this way, predicate clefting in Trinidadian English reveals the presence of a copy in an intermediate *v*P position.

---

**9** Note that these adverbs must originate in the lower verb phrase, because a reading in which they modify the cleft clause is semantically implausible.
**10** An alternative might be to adopt a distributed deletion analysis, but nothing hinges on the choice for our purposes.

A similar interaction of *v*P-fronting and pied-piping is found in Ewe (Buell 2012). Buell observes that a focus-fronted *v*P may be in a pied-piping configuration, as long as the *wh*-phrase is generated inside the *v*P.

(33)  **Objects but not subjects and high adjuncts can be pied-piped:**
    a.  [*ᵥP* **Núkà ɖù-ḿ**]    nè-lè?
          what eat-PROG 2SG-be.at
          'What are you eating?'
    b.  *[*ᵥP* **Àmékà dzó**] gé    lè?
          who    leave PROSP be.at
          'Who is about to leave?'
    c.  *[*ᵥP* **Núkàtà dzó-ḿ**]    nè-lè?
          why    leave-PROG 2SG-be.at
          'Why are you leaving?'
    (Ewe; Buell 2012:4,7)

As in Trinidadian English, even *wh*-phrases that have undergone long-distance movement from within an embedded clause can pied-pipe the *v*P.[11] In (34), it is the matrix verb that undergoes *v*P-fronting, but the *wh*-phrase originates in a lower clause.

(34)  **Movement of intermediate *v*P can pied-pipe *wh*-phrase:**
    [*ᵥP* **Núkà dí-ḿ**]    nè-lè    [*CP* bé  má-ɖà    ___]?
    what want-PROG 2SG-be.at    that 1SG.FUT-prepare
    'What do you want me to make?'
    (Ewe; Buell 2012:19)

Note that, as in Trinidadian English, this pattern of *v*P fronting involves at least one step of extraposition as well, in this case of the complement clause.

In this way, the Trinidadian English and Ewe patterns seem to provide evidence for the presence of intermediate copies at the verb phrase edge.

## 5.2.2 Multiple copy spell-out

Another effect that reveals the presence of a copy is multiple copy spell-out, or constructions in which intermediate copies are overtly realized alongside the highest copy. One example of this is *wh*-copying. In a number of languages, *wh*-movement can be accompanied by *wh*-copying, so that a copy of the *wh*-phrase

---

[11] Low adverbs do not seem to be included in the fronted *v*P in Ewe.

appears in all Spec-CP positions on the path of movement. Such constructions are found in German, Frisian, and Passamaquoddy, for example (35a–c).

(35) **Examples of *wh*-copying:**

a. ***Wen*** *glaubst du [$_{CP}$ **wen** sie getroffen hat]?*
who believe you     who she met     has
'Who do you believe she has met?'

(German; Felser 2004)

b. ***Wêr*** *tinke jo [$_{CP}$ **wêr**'t    Jan wennet]?*
where think you     where-c Jan lives
'Where do you think that Jan lives?'

(Frisian; Hiemstra 1986:99)

c. ***Tayuwe*** *kt-itom-ups [$_{CP}$ **tayuwe** apc    k-tol-i*
when     2-say-DUB     when    again 2-there-go
*malsanikuwam-ok]?*
store-LOC
'When did you say you're going to go to the store?'

(Passamaquoddy; Bruening 2006:26)

See Felser (2004) and Bruening (2006) for arguments that such constructions arise from movement.

*Wh*-copying is usually limited to *wh*-movement and relative clauses (see, for example, Pankau 2013), but not always. Baier (2014) describes a pattern of multiple copy spell-out with all Ā-dependencies in Seereer. As evident in (36a–b), intermediate copies at the clause edge in Seereer are spelled out as pronouns.

(36) **Pronoun copying in Seereer:**

a. ***Xar*** *foog-o        [$_{CP}$ yee **ten** Yande a-lay-u    [$_{CP}$ yee **ten** Jegaan*
what think-2SG.EXT    c   3SG Yande 3-say-EXT    c   3SG Jegaan
*a-ga'-u]]?*
3-see-EXT
'What do you think Yande said Jegaan saw?'

b. ***Aniin*** *foog-o        [$_{CP}$ yee **den** Yande a-lay-u    [$_{CP}$ yee **den***
who.PL think-2SG.EXT    c   3PL Yande 3-say-EXT    c   3PL
*Jegaan a-ga'-u]]?*
Jegaan 3-see-EXT
'Who all do you think Yande said Jegaan saw?'

(Seereer; Baier 2014)

A similar effect happens at the *v*P in Dinka. In Dinka, copies left at the *v*P edge by Ā-movement are spelled out as pronouns, in the same position as the V2 effect (37a–b).[12]

(37) **Movement in Dinka triggers pronoun copying at *v*P edge:**
    a.  *Bòl à-cḝ*   ***rọ̀ọọr*** *[CP cḛ̀*      *[vP **kêek** lâat]] tḭ̂iŋ.*
       Bol 3S-PRF men    PRF.3SG  3PL  insult.NF see.NF
       'Bol has seen the men he has insulted.'
    b.  *Yè **kɔ́ɔc-kó***     *[CP yíi*     Bôl    [vP **ké** luêeel [CP ḛ̀ cḭ́i*
       be people.CS1-which   HAB.OV Bol.GEN  3PL say.NF   C PRF.OV
       *Áyèn*     [vP **ké** tḭ̂iŋ]]]?*
       Ayen.GEN   3PL see.NF
       'Which people does Bol say Ayen has seen?'

See Baier (2014) and Van Urk (2018) for extensive arguments that this reflects multiple copy spell-out.

Although perhaps less widely attested in the verb phrase, multiple copy spell-out is then found at both domain edges. Again, there is no reason then to suppose a qualitative difference between CP and *v*P in how they interact with successive-cyclic movement.[13]

## 5.2.3 Stranding

A third reflex of successive-cyclic movement that reveals the presence of a copy in an intermediate position is stranding (e. g. McCloskey 2000; Barbiers 2002; Henry 2012), found in Spec-CP and Spec-*v*P.

Perhaps the most well-known case of stranding is *all*-stranding in West Ulster English, as first described by McCloskey (2000). McCloskey observes that complex *wh*-phrases such as *what all* may strand *all* at Spec-CP in West Ulster English (38a–c).

(38) ***All*-stranding in West Ulster English:**
    a.  ***What all*** *did he say [CP he wanted ___ ]?*

---

12 Note that copying is limited to plurals, as extensively discussed in Van Urk (2018).
13 I do not know of languages in which there is a multiple spell-out effect at the CP and *v*P edge at the same time. A common approach to multiple spell-out is to assume that there are special constraints on the edges that require realization, which prevent copy deletion (see Landau 2006, Van Urk 2018). In such a theory, it is not in principle surprising that the CP and *v*P edge might behave differently in the same language. See also Van Urk (2018) for discussion of this question in Dinka.

b. ***What** did he say [$_{CP}$ he wanted **all**]?*
c. ***What** did he say [$_{CP}$ **all** he wanted ___]?* (West Ulster English; Mc-Closkey 2000:61)

McCloskey argues that intermediate stranding in (38c) occurs in the intermediate Spec-CP, because the stranded *all* must follow material in the matrix verb phrase. This is demonstrated by the examples in (39a–c).[14]

(39) **Stranded *all* must follow matrix *v*P-material:**
 a. ***What all** did he say to him that he wanted to buy ___]?*
 b. *?**What** did he say to him [$_{CP}$ **all** that he wanted to buy ___]?*
 c. ****What** did he say **all** to him [$_{CP}$ that he wanted to buy ___]?*
 (West Ulster English; McCloskey 2000:63)

As McCloskey points out, these facts offer an argument for successive-cyclic movement through Spec-CP, under the assumption that *what all* moves as a unit to an intermediate position, followed by subextraction of *what*.

Similar stranding effects are found at the *v*P edge. Even in West Ulster varieties, Henry (2012) shows that there are grammars that allow stranding at the edge of *v*P as well. In South Derry English in fact, only *v*P-stranding is tolerated (40a–c).[15]

(40) **All-stranding only at *v*P in South Derry English:**
 a. ***What** did he [$_{vP}$ **all** do ___ on holiday]?*
 b. ***What** did he [$_{vP}$ **all** say [$_{CP}$ that he did ___ on holiday]]?*
 c. ****What** did he [$_{vP}$ say [$_{CP}$ **all** that he did ___ on holiday]]?*
 (Henry 2012:28)

Speakers of East Derry English allow stranding everywhere, both at the *v*P and CP edge (41a–c).

---

**14** That *all* is not stranded in a position in the verb phrase is evident in the contrast between *all*-stranding in the base position, which may precede a PP object (ia), and intermediate stranding, which cannot (ib). This contrast is unexpected if *all*-stranding takes place in an intermediate verb phrase position, but expected if intermediate *all* forms a constituent with the embedded CP.

(i) a. *?Who was talking **all** to the kids last night?*
 b. ****What** did he say **all** to his friends [$_{CP}$ that he wanted to buy]?*
 (West Ulster English; McCloskey 2000:63,74)

**15** Henry (2012) describes the different stranding varieties in geographical terms. Henry (2017) qualifies this and suggests that the different grammars described here may simply reflect variation within the same population.

(41) **_All_-stranding at _v_P and CP in East Derry English:**
   a. ***What** did he [$_{vP}$ **all** do ___ in Derry]?*
   b. ***What** did he say [$_{CP}$ **all** that he did ___ in Derry]?*
   c. ***What** did he [$_{vP}$ **all** say [$_{CP}$ that he did ___ in Derry]]?*
   (Henry 2012:31)

There are also instances of *all*-stranding at the *v*P edge in other languages.[16] As pointed out by Barbiers (2002) and Koopman (2010), a similar pattern is found in Dutch, with stranding of the quantifier *allemaal* (42a). In Dutch, this stranding must target an intermediate *v*P, as evident by the relative positioning of a higher verb and the complementizer (42b–c).

(42) **Stranded _allemaal_ in Dutch occurs at intermediate _v_P:**
   a. *Wat   heeft hij gezegd [$_{CP}$ dat  hij **allemaal** wil        hebben]?*
      what  has   he  said         that he  all              wants have.NF
      'What all has he said that he wants to have?'
   b. *Wat   heeft hij [$_{vP}$ **allemaal** gezegd [$_{CP}$ dat hij ___ wil        hebben]]?*
      what  has   he       all         said         that he        wants have.NF
      'What all has he said that he wants to have?'
   c. **Wat   heeft hij gezegd [$_{CP}$ **allemaal** dat hij ___ wil        hebben]?*
      what  has   he  said          all         that he        wants have.NF
      'What all has he said that he wants to have?'
   (Dutch; adapted from Koopman 2010:268)

In fact, Dutch allows stranding of other material in the same position, as Barbiers (2002) demonstrates. R-pronouns can strand a preposition at the *v*P edge as well, in any intermediate *v*P on the path of movement (43a–c).

(43) **Preposition stranding at intermediate _v_P in Dutch:**
   a. ***Waarmee**    had jij  dan gedacht [$_{CP}$ dat je   de vis ___ zou*
      where.with  had you  then thought         that you the fish     would
      *moeten       snijden]?*
      have.to.NF cut.NF
      'With what had you then thought that you would have to cut the fish?'

---

[16] As with multiple spell-out, the question arises why all stranding languages do not behave like East Derry English, with stranding at both the CP and *v*P edge. An open question here is what mechanism could restrict stranding to specific edges.

b. ***Waar*** *had jij dan gedacht [$_{CP}$ dat je de vis **mee** zou*
where had you then thought that you the fish with would
*moeten snijden]?*
have.to.NF cut.NF
'With what had you then thought that you would have to cut the fish?'

c. ***Waar*** *had jij dan [$_{vP}$ **mee** gedacht [$_{CP}$ dat je de vis ___ zou*
where had you then with thought that you the fish would
*moeten snijden]]?*
have.to.NF cut.NF
'With what had you then thought that you would have to cut the fish?'
(Dutch; adapted from Barbiers 2002:49)

The same facts obtain in the *wat-voor* split. The remnant DP can be pied-piped (44a), stranded in the base position (44b), or stranded at an intermediate *v*P edge (44c).

(44) **Stranding in *wat-voor* split:**

a. ***Wat voor bal*** *had jij dan gedacht [$_{CP}$ dat Ed ___ zou kopen]?*
what for ball had you then thought that Ed would buy.NF
'What kind of ball had you then thought that Ed would buy?'

b. ***Wat*** *had jij dan gedacht [$_{CP}$ dat Ed **voor bal** zou kopen]?*
what had you then thought that Ed for ball would buy.NF
'What kind of ball had you then thought that Ed would buy?'

c. ?***Wat*** *had jij dan [$_{vP}$ **voor bal** gedacht [$_{CP}$ dat Ed ___ zou*
what had you then for ball thought that Ed would
*kopen]]?*
buy.NF
'What kind of ball had you then thought that Ed would buy?'
(Dutch; adapted from Barbiers 2002:49)

A third pattern of stranding that shows symmetry between the CP and *v*P edge comes from Left Branch Extraction in Polish. Wiland (2010) points out that Left-Branch Extraction in Polish allows for the NP out of which extraction takes place to be stranded in intermediate positions, including the edge of *v*P and the edge of CP (45a–c).

(45) **Polish LBE may strand NP in intermediate positions:**

a. ***Jaki*** *Pawel [$_{vP}$ **samochód** kupil swojej żonie ___]?*
what Pawel car bought his wife
'What car did Pawel buy his wife?'

b. ?***Jaki*** *myślisz* [CP ***samochód*** *Pawel kupil swojej żonie___*]?
   what thought.2SG       car       Pawel bought his   wife
   'What car did you think Pawel bought his wife?'

c. %***Jaki*** *Maria* [vP ***samochód*** *myślala* [CP *że  Pawel kupil  swojej*
   what Maria       car        thought      that Pawel bought his
   *żonie___*]]?
   wife
   'What car did Mary think Pawel bought his wife?'
   (Polish; Wiland 2010)

The distribution of stranding phenomena then provides additional support for the notion of successive-cyclic movement and shows that there is symmetry between CP and *v*P in the possibility of stranding under intermediate movement.

### 5.2.4 V2 satisfaction

The final effect that I attribute to the presence of intermediate copies is V2 satisfaction in intermediate positions. If V2 effects are interpreted as requirement that an XP overtly occupies the specifier of a functional head, then an intermediate movement account predicts that the presence of an intermediate copy, despite undergoing deletion, may be diagnosable through its effect on V2. In an approach to V2 in which V2 is only about featural requirements, these facts may instead be attributed to the roles of features in intermediate movement. In any case, such effects should be attested.

Thiersch (1978) observes that extraction from embedded V2 clauses in German must satisfy the V2 requirement, resulting in overt V1 order (46a–b).

(46)   **Extraction satisfies V2 in German:**

   a. ***Wen***  *sagt Johan* [CP___ *sehe    er___*]?
      who.ACC says Johan         see.SBJ he
      'Who does Johan say that he is seeing?'

   b. *****Wen***  *sagt Johan* [CP *er sehe    ___*]?
      who.ACC says Johan      he see.SBJ
      'Who does Johan say that he is seeing?'
      (German; Thiersch 1978:135)

We can show that this is linked to intermediate movement, because movement in the matrix clause still requires V2 in the complement. The pairs in (47a–b) and (47c–d) demonstrate. In (47a–b), movement of a PP from an embedded clause requires V1. The pattern of grammaticality reverses with movement of the same

PP within the matrix clause: embedded V2 is now required and embedded V1 is impossible (47c–d).

(47) **V1 order due to extraction:**
    a.  In welche Schule sagte Leo [CP ___ sei  er gegangen]?
         to which school said Leo         is.SBJ he went
         'To which school did Leo say he went?'
    b.  *In welche Schule sagte Leo [CP **er** sei  gegangen]?
         to which school said Leo         he is.SBJ went
         'To which school did Leo say he went?'
    c.  *In welcher Sprache  sagte Leo [CP ___ sei  er gegangen]?
         in which  language said Leo         is.SBJ he went
         'In which language did say he went?'
    d.  In welcher Sprache  sagte Leo [CP **er** sei  gegangen]?
         in which  language said Leo         he is.SBJ went
         'In which language did say he went?'
         (German; Susi Wurmbrand, p. c.)

These facts provides evidence for a step of intermediate movement, with the copy satisfying V2.

Van Urk and Richards (2015) describe a similar pattern in the Nilotic language Dinka. Dinka requires V2 in embedded clauses. Intermediate movement must satisfy the V2 property of any clause it passes through, resulting in overt V1 order (48a–d).[17]

(48) **Long-distance movement and V2:**
    a.  Yè ŋà  yùukù  luêeel [CP ___ cé̱  cu̱ï̱in câam]?
         be who HAB.1PL say.NF      PRF food eat.NF
         'Who do we say [CP ___ has eaten food]?'
    b.  *Yè ŋà  yùukù  luêeel [CP **cu̱ï̱in** à-cí̱i̱    câam]?
         be who HAB.1PL say.NF   food 3SG-PRF.OV eat.NF
         'Who do we say [CP has eaten food]?'
    c.  Yè ŋó̱  yùukù  luêeel [CP ___ cí̱i̱  Bôl    câam]?
         be what HAB.1PL say.NF     PRF.OV Bol.GEN eat.NF
         'What do we say [CP Bol has eaten ___]?'

---

[17] In Dinka, we can also tell that an intermediate copy satisfies V2 in the embedded clause, because the moving phrase can trigger agreement on the highest verb/auxiliary in any clause it passes through, as discussed in section 5.1.2.1. This extraction marking effect is also evident in the alternation between cé̱, the unmarked form of the auxiliary, and cí̱i̱, which surfaces in the context of non-subject extraction.

d. *Yè ŋɔ́ yùukù̱ luêeel [CP **Bòl** à-cé̱ câam]?
   be what HAB.1PL say.NF    Bol 3SG-PRF eat.NF
   'What do we say [CP Bol has eaten ___]?'

Van Urk and Richards (2015; see also Van Urk 2015) show that an analogous V2 effect is found in the Dinka verb phrase. The Dinka verb phrase also has a V2 effect, so that the highest object must always appear initially, preceding the base position of the main verb, as with the ditransitive in (49a–d):

(49) **Dinka *v*P has V2 effect:**

   a. Yi̱in cé̱    [vP **Àyén** gàam  cáa].
      you PRF.SV   Ayen give.NF milk
      'You have given Ayen milk.'

   b. Yi̱in cé̱    [vP **cáa** gàam  Àyén].
      you PRF.SV   milk give.NF Ayen
      'You have given milk to Ayen.'

   c. *Yi̱in cé̱   [vP ___ gàam  cáa Àyén].
      you PRF.SV       give.NF milk Ayen
      'You have given Ayen milk.'

When an object is extracted from inside the verb phrase, however, the same effect as at the CP edge is observed. Intermediate movement satisfies *v*P V2, as demonstrated in (50a–d).

(50) **Object extraction satisfies V2:**

   a. Yè ŋɔ́  [CP cí̱i  môc     [vP ___ yi̱ɛ̌ɛn  Bòl]]?
      be what   PRF.OV man.GEN       give.NF Bol
      'What has the man given Bol?'

   b. *Yè ŋɔ́ [CP cí̱i  môc     [vP **Bòl** yi̱ɛ̌ɛn]]?
      be what   PRF.OV man.GEN       Bol give.NF
      'What has the man given Ayen?'

   c. Yè ŋà  [CP cí̱i  môc     [vP ___ yi̱ɛ̌ɛn  kítàap]]?
      be who    PRF.OV man.GEN       give.NF book
      'Who has the man given the book to?'

   d. *Yè ŋà [CP cí̱i  môc     [vP **kítàap** yi̱ɛ̌ɛn]]?
      be who    PRF.OV man.GEN       book give.NF
      'Who has the man given the book to?'

V2 effects are then also equally distributed across the CP and *v*P edge, offering additional evidence that these domains are parallel.

## 5.3 On the LF presence of intermediate copies

A movement approach to successive cyclicity also predicts that intermediate copies should influence LF representations. In this section, I show that the presence of intermediate copies can be detected in the consequences for the binding of pronouns and anaphors (Fox 1999), the availability of intermediate scope (e. g. Rullmann 1993; Fox 1999), and licensing of parasitic gaps (Nissenbaum 2000). As above, I demonstrate that these effects are symmetrically distributed across CP and vP edges.

### 5.3.1 Binding of pronouns and anaphors

One LF effect that intermediate copies should have is that they should make available additional positions for binding relations. For example, long-distance movement allows an anaphor contained in the moving phrase to be bound by an antecedent on the path of movement (51a–b), even though this antecedent would not be able to bind the anaphor in its base position.

(51) **Anaphors can be bound in intermediate positions:**
    a.   Which picture of herself$_{i/j}$ did Sam$_i$ say [Kim$_j$ likes ___]?
    b.   Which picture of herself$_{i/j}$ did you tell Sam$_i$ [Kim$_j$ likes ___]?

An example like (51a) can be accommodated both by assuming an intermediate copy in Spec-CP or Spec-vP, but (51b) provides evidence specifically for a CP edge position, since the intermediate position must at least be below the indirect object.

Fox (1999) constructs examples that specifically require an intermediate vP position through the interaction of anaphor binding and Condition C. As observed by Lebeaux (1998), not all material in a moved phrase needs to be interpreted in the base position. In an example like (52), the relative clause does not need to be interpreted in the lowest copy, as evidenced by the lack of a Condition C violation.

(52) **Relative clause does not need to be interpreted in base position:**
    [$_{DP}$ Which argument that John$_i$ made] did he$_i$ believe?

Fox demonstrates that we can use this property of relative clauses to provide evidence for intermediate copies, by constructing examples in which the requirements of Condition C compete with the requirements of variable binding (53a–b).

(53) **Relative clause must be interpreted in intermediate position:**
   a. *[$_{DP}$ Which of the papers that he$_i$ gave to Ms. Brown$_k$] did she$_k$ hope that every student$_i$ will revise ___?
   b. [$_{DP}$ Which of the papers that he$_i$ gave to Ms. Brown$_k$] did every student$_i$ hope that she$_k$ will revise ___?
   (Fox 1999:173)

The grammaticality of (53b) demonstrates that there is an intermediate copy of the moved phrase in which the relative clause can be interpreted, because both the overt position of the wh-phrase and the base position should yield a binding violation. The quantifier *every student* binds a pronoun in the relative clause, so that there must be a copy of the moved phrase below the quantifier. At the same time, the relative clause cannot be interpreted in the scope of the pronoun *she*, because a Condition C violation should result. Such cases then indicate that there must be an intermediate copy that can be interpreted, in between the position of the quantifier and the pronoun.

Fox (1999) uses such effects to argue for an intermediate landing site at the vP edge. He points out to contrasts such as (54a–b).

(54) **Relative clause interpreted at vP edge:**
   a. [$_{DP}$ Which of the papers that he$_i$ asked Ms. Brown$_k$ for] did every student$_i$ [$_{vP}$ get her$_k$ to grade ___]?
   b. *[$_{DP}$ Which of the papers that he$_i$ asked Ms. Brown$_k$ for] did she$_k$ [$_{vP}$ get every student$_i$ to grade ___]?
   (Fox 1999:174)

In the grammatical (54a), the only intermediate position that can satisfy both variable binding and Principle C is in between the subject quantifier and the object, thus providing evidence for a landing site for long-distance movement at the vP edge.

We can manipulate these examples to argue for an intermediate Spec-CP position. Consider the pair in (55a–b), where the only difference is in the matrix indirect object and the embedded subject.

(55) **Relative clause interpreted at CP edge:**
   a. [$_{DP}$ Which of the papers that he$_i$ asked Ms. Brown$_k$ for] did you tell every student$_i$ [$_{CP}$ she$_k$ liked ___]?
   b. *[$_{DP}$ Which of the papers that he$_i$ asked Ms. Brown$_k$ for] did you tell her$_k$ [$_{CP}$ every student$_i$ liked ___]?

The admissibility of (55a) suggests that there is an intermediate position between indirect objects and embedded subjects also, which I propose is Spec-CP.

The same picture as above then emerges from an examination of binding effects: Spec-CP and Spec-vP are implicated to the same degree as intermediate landing sites.[18]

### 5.3.2 Intermediate scope

Another semantic effect that should be associated with the presence of a copy is the availability of additional scope positions. Intermediate positions should create the possibility of intermediate scope relations.

*How many*-phrases have been shown to give rise to scope ambiguities (Kroch 1989; Rullmann 1993; Cresti 1995). For example, the *how many*-phrase in (56) can be interpreted above and below *want*, as indicated by the paraphrases in (56a–b).

(56) **Scope ambiguities with *how many*-phrases:**
*How many books does Chris want to buy ___?*
    a.  What is the number $n$ such that there are $n$ books that Chris wants to buy?
    b.  What is the number $n$ such that Chris wants to buy $n$ books?
       (Rullmann 1993:1)

Rullmann (1993) argues that *how many*-phrases may also take scope in an intermediate position, as demonstrated by the example in (57). In addition to wide and narrow scope, the intermediate reading paraphrased in (57c) is available as well (see also Fox 1999).

(57) **Intermediate reading of *how many*-phrase:**
*How many books did Mary say [John needs ___]?*
    a.  What is the number $n$ such that there are $n$ books which Mary says John needs?
    b.  What is the number $n$ such that Mary says John needs $n$ books?
    c.  What is the number $n$ such that Mary says that there are $n$ books which John needs?
       (Rullmann 1993:11)

---

[18] One question is whether we can find configurations similar to the grammatical examples in (54a) and (55a) which are inadmissible because of the absence of an intermediate position in between the relevant DPs. This is what we expect if long-distance movement follows a punctuated path, as Abels (2012) points out.

Following Rullmann, I propose that this intermediate reading is the result of interpreting the *how many*-phrase in the intermediate Spec-CP position.

We can construct similar examples that appear to demonstrate intermediate scope positions at a verb phrase edge. Consider an example like (58), with a modal above *require*. In addition to the wide and narrow scope readings, the intermediate reading in (58c) is available, in which the *how many*-phrase is interpreted in between the modal and *require*.

(58) **Intermediate reading of *how many*-phrase at *v*P edge:**
How many students could Kim be required to pass?
    a.  What is the number *n* such that there are *n* students that it is possible Kim is required to pass?
    b.  What is the number *n* such that it is possible that Kim is required to pass *n* students?
    c.  What is the number *n* such that it is possible that there are *n* students Kim is required to pass?

### 5.3.3 Parasitic gaps

Another LF effect is the distribution of parasitic gaps, a phenomenon that has been used to argue for intermediate copies at the *v*P edge, building on Nissenbaum (2000). Nissenbaum presents a theory of parasitic gap licensing that requires intermediate movement to the *v*P edge. Both intermediate successive-cyclic movement to *v*P and operator movement in a *v*P adjunct may create derived predicates, which can be conjoined:

(59) **Parasitic gap configuration in Nissenbaum (2000):**

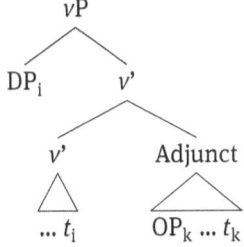

On the assumption that both intermediate movement and null operator movement result in λ-abstraction and so form open predicates, the *v*P and adjunct in

(59) can be combined to yield a conjoined predicate.[19] This conjoined predicate composes with the DP copy at the *v*P edge, leading to the appearance of a parasitic gap. If correct, parasitic gaps like (60) provide evidence for intermediate movement to the *v*P edge, assuming that the rationale clause is a *v*P adjunct.

(60)    **Parasitic gap at *v*P edge:**
        *What did he buy ___ [in order to read through ___]?*

There are also CP adjuncts that license parasitic gaps. As Engdahl (1983) notes, *if*-clauses permit parasitic gaps for some speakers (61a). These are possible even with extraction of the subject, providing evidence that these parasitic gaps are licensed outside the *v*P.

(61)    **Parasitic gaps in *if*-clauses:**
    a.  *This is the professor that Kim says that you must not say hello to ___ if you run into ___ .*
    b.  *This is the professor that Kim says that, if you run into ___, ___ won't say hello to you.*
        (modified from Engdahl 1983:11)

The semantic effects of copies can then be detected at the CP and *v*P edge. These facts provide evidence that the full range of effects that we expect to be associated with successive-cyclic movement are attested. In addition, a key conclusion that emerges from this discussion is that there are no empirical reasons to posit a qualitative asymmetry between CP and *v*P, since all the effects discussed can be detected in both domains (contra Rackowski and Richards 2005; Den Dikken 2009, 2010; Keine 2016).

## 5.4 Successive cyclicity in other domains

In this section, I examine how this taxonomy of successive cyclicity effects extends to other proposed phasal domains. I will look in particular at PP and DP. A key lesson that emerges from the overview given above is that, to a remarkable degree, the morphophonological, syntactic, and semantic effects that we expect

---

**19** It is important that the adjunct can be inserted in between the point of abstraction and the DP. In addition to this, more needs to be said about how such predicates can be conjoined. See Nissenbaum (2000) for details.

to be associated with successive cyclicity are attested. As a result, positing additional phase boundaries should be undertaken with care, because the full suite of these effects should in principle be associated with this boundary across languages.

In this section, I use this reasoning to scrutinize the phasal status of PP and DP domain. We will see that a more nuanced picture emerges. Some familiar effects in DPs and PPs are attested, such as extraction marking and lexical choice effects. In addition, there is some evidence for intermediate copy realization, in the interaction of PPs and DPs with pied-piping. However, a number of the other effects described are missing or difficult to detect. I provide independent explanations for the absence of LF effects as well as multiple spell-out, but identify at least interactions with $\varphi$-agreement and stranding as phenomena that should in principle be found.

## 5.4.1 Extraction marking in DPs and PPs

There appear to be extraction marking effects in the PP domain. In Jamaican Creole (Durrleman 2008), for example, the preposition *fi/fa* is sensitive to extraction. When the preposition is followed by an in-situ complement, it is realized as *fi* (62a). But when the complement has been extracted, the preposition must be realized as *fa* (62b).

(62) **Extraction marking on preposition in Jamaican Creole:**
  a. *Im bring aki* [$_{PP}$ **fi/\*fa** *piknidem*]
     3SG bring ackee for/for.EXT children
     '(S)he brought the ackee for the children.'
  b. *A huu im bring dat* [$_{PP}$ **\*fi/fa** ___ ]?
     A who 3SG bring that for/for.EXT
     'Who did (s)he bring that for?'
     (Jamaican Creole; Durrleman 2008)

A similar alternation is found with the preposition *nú/ná* in Fongbe (Da Cruz 1997).

(63) **Extraction marking on preposition in Fongbe:**
  a. *Kɔ̀kú sà mɔ̌tò ɔ́* [$_{PP}$ **nú/\*ná** *Àsíbá*].
     Koku sell car DET to/to.EXT Asiba
     'Koku sold the car to Asiba.'
  b. *Àsíbá wɛ̀ Kɔ̀kú sà mɔ̌tò ɔ́* [$_{PP}$ **\*nú/ná** ___ ].
     Asiba FOC Koku sell car DET to/to.EXT

'Asiba, Koku sold the car to.'
(Fongbe; Da Cruz 1997)

A worry about these facts is that it is possible to analyze this alternations as allomorphy (sensitive to whether an overt DP follows), since the gap site is necessarily immediately adjacent to the preposition. In addition, we could treat this pattern as lexical choice effect, in which these prepositions are instantiations of non-phasal and phasal variants of the same head (see also Abels 2003).

I do not know of extraction marking effects in the DP domain, such as a determiner that only appears in the context of extraction. There are a number of lexical choice phenomena, however. Jeoung (2018) describes a pattern along these lines in Indonesian-type languages. In Indonesian, the noun is optionally marked with the determiner suffix *-nya* before possessors (64a–b). In contexts of extraction, however, the determiner suffix is obligatory (64c).

(64) **Optional determiner suffix with possessors in Indonesian:**
    a. *Buku(-nya) dia biru, kalau buku(-nya) Desy kuning.*
        book-DEF 3SG blue but book-DEF Desy yellow
        'His book is blue, but Desy's book is yellow.'
    b. *Uang(-nya) orang kaya cepat di-keluar-kan.*
        money-DEF person rich quick PASS-exit-APPL
        'Rich people's money is quickly spent.'
    c. *Siapa yang adik baca buku-**nya**?*
        who REL younger.sibling read book-DET
        'Who is it that little brother is reading (her/his) book?'
        (Jeoung 2018:1,16)

Similarly, Uriagereka (1996) points out that Galician determiners have a clitic alternant that must be used in instances of extraction (65a–b).

(65) **Determiner clitic in Galician is used with extraction:**
    a. *(?)De quén liche-**los** [$_{DP}$ mellores poemas de amigo ___]?*
        of whom read.2SG-the best poems of friend
        'Who did you read the best poems of friendship by?'
    b. *\*De quén liches [$_{DP}$ **os** mellores poemas de amigo ___]?*
        of whom read.2SG the best poems of friend
        'Who did you read the best poems of friendship by?'
        (Uriagereka 1996:270–271)

In addition, there is a well-known correlation between the permissibility of Left-Branch Extraction and the presence of a D layer (Uriagereka 1988; Bošković 2005).[20]

(66) **LBE permitted in languages without overt determiners:**
    a. *Krasnuju ja kupil [NP ___ mašinu].*
        red          I bought       car
         'It is a red car that I bought.'
    b. *\*Red, I bought [DP a ___ car].*

## 5.4.2 Leftness effects

There is a class of effects that emerges with extraction out of PPs and DPs, leftness effects, that is reminiscent of V2 satisfaction. Specifically, in some languages, only items that may appear leftmost in PP/DP can undergo movement.

Van Riemsdijk (1978) points out, for example, that only elements that appear to the left of prepositions can extract out of PPs in Dutch. In Dutch, R-pronouns, a series of locative pronouns used to refer to inanimates, appear to the left of a preposition (67a), but not other DPs (67b).

(67) **R-pronouns appear on the left:**
    a. *Je kan [PP **daar**-op] rekenen.*
        you can    there-on count
         'You can count on it.'
    b. *Je kan [PP op **hem**] rekenen.*
        you can    on him count
         'You can count on him.'

In addition, only R-pronouns can undergo movement out of a PP (68a–b):

(68) **Only R-pronouns can move out of PPs:**
    a. *\***Wie** kan je [PP op ___] rekenen?*
        who can you    on      count

---

**20** The Specificity Effect might also be seen as a lexical choice effect (ia–b) (Fiengo and Higginbotham 1981).

(i) **Specific DPs are more resistant to extraction:**
    a. *Who did you see [DP a picture of ___]?*
    b. *??Who did you see [DP that picture of ___]?*

'Who can you count on?'
b. ***Waar** kan je* [$_{PP}$ ___ *op*] *rekenen?*
   where can you         on count
   'What can you count on?'

Bošković (2016) notes a similar effect in Left Branch Extraction in Serbo-Croatian. Although Left Branch Extraction of adjectives is generally permitted, it is blocked when a demonstrative is present, as in (69a–b).

(69) **LBE of adjectives is blocked with demonstrative:**
   a. *Ponosnog sam vidio* [$_{NP}$ ___ *oca*].
      proud    am seen            father
      'It is a proud father I saw.'
   b. **Ponosnog sam vidio* [$_{NP}$ *tog* ___ *oca*].
      proud    am seen    that       father
      'It is that proud father that I saw.'
      (Serbo-Croatian; Bošković 2016:3)

Bošković analyzes the ungrammaticality of (69b) as a leftness effect. Demonstratives are different from other DP-internal elements, like possessors, in that they must precede adjectives:

(70) **Demonstratives precede adjectives:**
   a. *ova skupa    slika*
      this expensive picture
      'this expensive picture'
   b. ?**skupa     ova slika*
      expensive this picture
      'this expensive picture'
      (Serbo-Croatian; Bošković 2016)

We can then explain why (69b) is bad. Adjectives can only undergo LBE when they are leftmost in the DP.

These facts provide evidence that PPs and DPs are phasal domains, in which only the edge is accessible. Leftness effects are reminiscent of V2 satisfaction in Dinka and German, in which the moving phrase also must be leftmost in the intermediate domain. A puzzle about leftness effects, however, is why elements that are not leftmost initially cannot undergo intermediate movement, as in CP and vP. One type of explanation that has often been pursued for this difference is to make use of a notion of anti-locality (e. g. Abels 2003).

## 5.4.3 Evidence for intermediate copies in DPs and PPs

Let me turn now to effects that imply the presence of intermediate copies, starting with overt evidence at DP and PP edges. There are no stranding or multiple spell-out effects in the DP or PP that I know of. However, when Ā-movement pied-pipes a DP or a PP, some languages show evidence of intermediate movement internal to the pied-piped phrase.

In Ch'ol, as demonstrated by Coon (2009), *wh*-possessors move internal to the DP. In ordinary DPs, possessors are strictly postnominal (71). A similar effect is found in a number of other Mayan languages.

(71) **Ch'ol has postnominal possessors:**
*Tyi yajl-i   [$_{DP}$ i-plato  **aj-Maria**]*
PRF fall-INTR   3s-plate CL-Maria
'Maria's plate fell.'
(Ch'ol; Coon 2009:166)

But when a possessor pied-pipes a DP, the *wh*-possessor must appear prenominally (72a–b).

(72) **Wh-possessor moves inside pied-piped DP:**
  a.  [$_{DP}$ **Maxki** *i-plato*] *tyi yajl-i?*
       who   3s-plate PRF fall-INTR
       'Whose plate fell?'
  b.  *[$_{DP}$ *I-plato* **maxki**] *tyi yajl-i?*
       3s-plate who   PRF fall-INTR
       'Whose plate fell?'
       (Ch'ol; Coon 2009:166)

These facts provide evidence for DP-internal intermediate movement.

We can find similar effects in the PP. In her work on Finnish, Huhmarniemi (2012) provides evidence for intermediate movement in a range of pied-piping configurations, including PPs. Finnish allows DPs to appear before and after prepositions (73a). However, a *wh*-phrase must appear leftmost when it pied-pipes a PP, as in (73b–c).

(73) **Wh-phrase moves inside pied-piped PP:**
  a.  *Pekka käveli  [$_{PP}$ kohti  **puistoa**].*
     Pekka walked   towards park.PAR
     'Pekka walked towards the park.'

b. [*PP* ***Mitä** kohti*] Pekka käveli?
   what towards Pekka walked
   'What did Pekka walk towards?'
c. [*PP* ***Mitä** yli*] Pekka käveli?
   what over Pekka walked
   'What did Pekka walk over?'
   (Huhmarniemi 2012:105,115)

These phenomena seem to offer evidence for intermediate movement within the DP and PP.

As for semantic effects associated with intermediate copies at the DP and PP edge, it is difficult to construct examples that test for the LF presence of copies in the DP and PP domain for independent reasons. Testing for the interaction of competing binding effects is difficult, because DPs and PPs out of which extraction takes place usually cannot contain other referential DPs. In addition, it is not clear that there are adjuncts that host parasitic gaps that attach directly to DP and PP. Similarly, scope reconstruction requires a node of the appropriate type for scope reconstruction and DP and PP may simply not provide such an attachment site.

We are left with the absence of parasitic agreement, multiple spell-out, and stranding. The absence of multiple spell-out is probably not surprising. Multiple spell-out has been linked to the presence of an EPP position or V2 effect (e. g. Landau 2006; Van Urk 2018), and it is not clear that such effects are found in the DP and PP domain.[21] In the *v*P domain, the only pattern of multiple spell-out, in Dinka, involves V2.

Parasitic agreement and stranding effects should in principle be attested, however. Although rare, some languages do allow agreement on prepositions, and so we might expect systems in which prepositional agreement is obligatory only in the context of extraction. In the DP domain, the same pattern could obtain with possessor agreement.[22] There should also be instances of stranding at DP and PP edges. Given the variation described for *all*-stranding in section 5.2.3, we would hope to find patterns of stranding at the PP edge at least.[23]

---

[21] I am not aware of V2-like patterns in DPs and PPs in any case. The question of whether there are EPP positions in DPs and PPs is harder to answer, because it is certainly possible to analyze some movements for basic word order as motivated by an EPP-like effect. But, as far as I know, such movements do not interact with extraction.

[22] It is possible that the Indonesian pattern described by Jeong (2018) could be analyzed in these terms.

[23] Stranding a DP-modifier at the DP edge may give rise to problems of ambiguity.

I leave the question of whether there are ultimately convincing explanations for the effects missing from DPs and PPs for future research. What I hope to have established, however, is that there is a suite of effects reliably associated with phasal domains, which should be investigated before positing an additional phase boundary. Invoking a novel phase boundary in a syntactic analysis is by no means a harmless move and makes predictions about the crosslinguistic profile of successive cyclicity that can and should be tested.

# Conclusion

This paper has investigated the question of how to detect a phase. The full range of effects that I have argued should at a minimum be associated with a phasal domain is summarized in Table 5.1.

Table 5.1: Reflexes of successive cyclicity at CP and vP.

|    |                               | CP                                   | vP                              |
|----|-------------------------------|--------------------------------------|---------------------------------|
|    | Effect on intermediate head   |                                      |                                 |
| 1. | Extraction marking            | Irish, Dinka, ...                    | Defaka, Malay, ...              |
| 2. | φ-agreement                   | Dinka, Wolof                         | Passamaquoddy                   |
| 3. | Lexical choice/inversion      | Russian, Belfast English, Spanish, ...| Nupe, Mòcheno                  |
|    | PF presence of copy           |                                      |                                 |
| 4. | Intermediate copy realization | Malay, Basque, Quechua               | Trinidadian English, Ewe        |
| 5. | Multiple copy spell-out       | German, Frisian, Seereer, ...        | Dinka                           |
| 6. | Stranding                     | West Ulster English, Polish          | West Ulster English, Dutch, Polish |
| 7. | V2                            | German, Dinka                        | Dinka                           |
|    | LF presence of copy           |                                      |                                 |
| 8. | Binding                       | English, ...                         | English, ...                    |
| 9. | Scope                         | English, ...                         | English, ...                    |
| 10.| Parasitic gaps                | English, ...                         | English, ...                    |

As I have demonstrated, the set of attested reflexes of successive cyclicity appears to match well crosslinguistically with the effects that should be associated with intermediate successive-cyclic movement. In addition to this, I have demonstrated that there is symmetry between the CP and vP in phasehood (contra, for instance, Rackowski and Richards 2005, Den Dikken 2009, 2010, and Keine 2016).

A more complicated picture emerges when this same taxonomy is investigated in the DP/PP domain. The larger lesson that emerges from this work is that positing a new phase boundary is not an innocuous exercise and should ideally be evaluated against the crosslinguistic expectations that come out of the overview in Table 5.1.

# References

Abels, Klaus. 2003. *Successive cyclicity, anti-locality, and adposition stranding*. Doctoral dissertation, UConn.
Abels, Klaus. 2012. *Phases: An essay on cyclicity in syntax*. Berlin: Mouton de Gruyter.
Abels, Klaus, and Peter Muriungi. 2008. The focus marker in Kîîtharaka: Syntax and semantics. *Lingua* 118:687–731.
Arregi, Karlos. 2003. Clausal pied-piping. *Natural Language Semantics* 11:115–143.
Baier, Nico. 2014. Spell-out, chains, and long distance *wh*-movement in Seereer. Paper presented at CLS 50, Chicago.
Barbiers, Sjef. 2002. Remnant stranding and the theory of movement. In *Dimensions of movement: From features to remnants*, ed. by Artemis Alexiadou, Elena Anagnostopoulou, Sjef Barbiers, and Hans-Martin Gaertner, 47–69. Amsterdam: John Benjamins.
Bennett, Will, Akinbiyi Akinlabi, and Bruce Connell. 2012. Two subject asymmetries in Defaka focus constructions. In *Proceedings of WCCFL 29*, ed. by Jaehoon Choi, E. Alan Hogue, Jeffrey Punske, Deniz Tat, Jessamyn Schertz, and Alex Trueman, 294–302. Somerville, MA: Cascadilla Proceedings Project.
Bošković, Željko. 2005. On the locality of left branch extraction and the structure of NP. *Studia Linguistica* 59:1–45.
Bošković, Željko. 2016. Getting really edgy: On the edge of the edge. *Linguistic Inquiry* 47:1–33.
Bruening, Benjamin. 2001. *Syntax at the edge: Cross-clausal phenomena and the syntax of Passamaquoddy*. Doctoral dissertation, MIT.
Bruening, Benjamin. 2006. Differences between *wh*-scope marking and *wh*-copy constructions in Passamaquoddy. *Linguistic Inquiry* 37:25–49.
Buell, Leston. 2012. A first look at Ewe VP fronting and derivation by phase. LingBuzz, lingbuzz/001486.
Cable, Seth. 2007. *The grammar of Q: Q-particles and the nature of Wh-fronting, as revealed by the Wh-questions of Tlingit*. Doctoral dissertation, MIT.
Cable, Seth. 2010. *The grammar of Q: Q-particles, wh-movement, and pied-piping*. Oxford: Oxford University Press.
Chomsky, Noam. 1973. Conditions on transformations. In *A festschrift for Morris Halle*, ed. by Stephen Anderson and Paul Kiparsky, 232–286. New York: Holt, Rinehart & Winston.
Chomsky, Noam. 1977. On *wh*-movement. In *Formal syntax*, ed. by Adrian Akmajian, Peter Culicover, and Thomas Wasow, 71–132. New York: Academic Press.
Chomsky, Noam. 1986. *Barriers*. Cambridge, MA: MIT Press.
Chomsky, Noam. 1995. *The minimalist program*. Cambridge, MA: MIT Press.

Chomsky, Noam. 2000. Minimalist inquiries: The framework. In *Step by step: Essays on minimalist syntax in honor of Howard Lasnik*, ed. by R. Martin, D. Michaels, and J. Uriagereka, 89–155. Cambridge, MA: MIT Press.
Chomsky, Noam. 2001. Derivation by phase. In *Ken Hale: A life in language*, ed. by M. Kenstowicz, 1–52. Cambridge, MA: MIT Press.
Chomsky, Noam. 2008. On phases. In *Foundational issues in linguistic theory: Essays in honor of Jean-Roger Vergnaud*, ed. by Robert Freidin, Carlos P. Otero, and Maria Luisa Zubizarreta, 133–166. Cambridge, MA: MIT Press.
Chomsky, Noam. 2013. Problems of projection. *Lingua* 130:33–49.
Chung, Sandra. 1982. Unbounded dependencies in Chamorro grammar. *Linguistic Inquiry* 13:39–77.
Cognola, Federica. 2008. OV/VO syntax in Mòcheno declarative clauses. *Rivista di Grammatica Generativa* 33:79–93.
Cognola, Federica. 2013. *Wh*-long extraction in Mòcheno and the derivation of OV word order in West Germanic. Paper presented at the 28th Comparative Germanic Workshop.
Cole, Peter, and Gabriella Hermon. 1998. The typology of WH movement: WH questions in Malay. *Syntax* 1:221–258.
Cole, Peter, and Gabriella Hermon. 2000. Partial wh-movement: Evidence from Malay. In *Wh-scope marking*, ed. by Uli Lutz, Gereon Müller, and Arnim von Stechow, 101–130. Amsterdam: John Benjamins.
Cole, Peter, Gabriella Hermon, and Yanti. 2008. Voice in Malay/Indonesian. *Lingua* 118:1500–1553.
Coon, Jessica. 2009. Interrogative possessors and the problem with pied-piping in Chol. *Linguistic Inquiry* 40:165–75.
Cozier, Franz. 2006. The co-occurrence of predicate clefting and *wh*-questions in Trinidad Dialectal English. *Natural Language & Linguistic Theory* 24:655–688.
Cresti, Diana. 1995. Extraction and reconstruction. *Natural Language Semantics* 3:79–122.
Da Cruz, Maxime. 1997. Serial verb constructions and null arguments in Fòn. In *Object positions in Benue-Kwa*, ed. by Rose-Marie Déchaine and Victor Manfredi, 31–45. The Hague: HAG.
Dayal, Veneeta. 2017. Does Hindi-Urdu have feature-driven *wh*-movement to Spec, vP? *Linguistic Inquiry* 48:159–72.
Deal, Amy Rose. 2014. Properties of probes: Evidence from Nez Perce complementizer agreement. Presentation at NELS 45, MIT.
den Dikken, Marcel. 2009. Arguments for successive-cyclic movement through Spec-CP: A critical review. *Linguistic Variation Yearbook* 9:89–126.
den Dikken, Marcel. 2010. On the nature and distribution of successive cyclicity. Manuscript, CUNY Graduate Center.
Durrleman, Stephanie. 2008. *The syntax of Jamaican Creole*. Amsterdam: John Benjamins.
Engdahl, Elisabet. 1983. Parasitic gaps. *Linguistics and Philosophy* 6:5–34.
Fanselow, Gisbert. 2006. Partial *wh*-movement. In *The Blackwell Companion to Syntax*, ed. by Martin Everaert and Henk van Riemsdijk, 437–492. Blackwell.
Felser, Claudia. 2004. *Wh*-copying, phases, and successive cyclicity. *Lingua* 114:543–574.
Fiengo, Robert, and James Higginbotham. 1981. Opacity in NP. *Linguistic Analysis* 7:395–421.
Fox, Danny. 1999. Reconstruction, binding theory, and the interpretation of chains. *Linguistic Inquiry* 30:157–196.
Heck, Fabian. 2008. On pied-piping: *Wh*-movement and beyond. Berlin: Walter de Gruyter.
Heck, Fabian. 2009. On certain properties of pied-piping. *Linguistic Inquiry* 40:75–111.

Henry, Alison. 1995. *Belfast English and Standard English: Dialect variation and parameter setting*. Oxford: Oxford University Press.
Henry, Alison. 2012. Phase edges, quantifier float and the nature of (micro-)variation. *Iberia* 4:23–39.
Henry, Alison. 2017. *Explaining syntactic variation*. Ling-Lunch, Queen Mary University of London.
Hermon, Gabriela. 1985. *Syntactic modularity*. Foris.
Hiemstra, Inge. 1986. Some aspects of *wh*-questions in Frisian. *North-Western European Language Evolution* 8:97–110.
Huhmarniemi, Saara. 2012. *Finnish Ā-movement: Edges and islands*. Doctoral dissertation, University of Helsinki.
Jeoung, Helen. 2018. Possessors move through the edge, too. *Glossa* 3(1): 135. 1–35.
Kandybowicz, Jason. 2008. On edge features and perfect extraction. In *Proceedings of the 26th West Coast Conference on Formal Linguistics*, ed. by Charles B. Chang and Hannah J. Haynie, 288–296. Somerville, MA: Cascadilla Proceedings Project.
Kayne, Richard, and Jean-Yves Pollock. 1978. Stylistic inversion, successive cyclicity, and Move NP in French. *Linguistic Inquiry* 9:595–622.
Keine, Stefan. 2016. *Probes and their horizons*. Doctoral dissertation, UMass Amherst.
Koopman, Hilda. 2010. On Dutch *allemaal* and West Ulster English *all*. In *Structure preserved: Studies in syntax for Jan Koster*, ed. by Jan-Wouter Zwart and Mark de Vries, 267–276. Amsterdam: John Benjamins.
Korsah, Sampson, and Andrew Murphy. 2016. What can tone tell us about successive-cyclic movement? Evidence from Asante Twi. In *Proceedings of NELS 46*, ed. by Christopher Hammerly and Brandon Prickett, 227–240. GLSA Amherst.
Kotek, Hadas. 2014. *Wh*-fronting in a two-probe system. *Natural Language & Linguistic Theory* 32:1105–1143.
Kroch, Anthony. 1989. Amount quantification, referentiality, and long *wh*-movement. Manuscript, University of Pennsylvania.
Landau, Idan. 2006. Chain resolution in Hebrew V(P) fronting. *Syntax* 9:32–66.
Lebeaux, David. 1998. *Where does binding theory apply?* Technical report. Princeton, NJ: NEC Research Institute.
Manetta, Emily. 2010. *Wh*-expletives in Hindi-Urdu: The *v*P phase. *Linguistic Inquiry* 41:1–34.
McCloskey, Jim. 1979. *Transformational syntax and model-theoretic semantics: A case study in Modern Irish*. Dordrecht, The Netherlands: Reidel.
McCloskey, Jim. 2000. Quantifier float and *wh*-movement in an Irish English. *Linguistic Inquiry* 31:57–84.
McCloskey, Jim. 2001. The morphosyntax of *wh*-extraction in Irish. *Journal of Linguistics* 37:67–100.
McCloskey, Jim. 2002. Resumption, successive cyclicity, and the locality of operations. In *Derivation and explanation in the Minimalist Program*, ed. by Samuel David Epstein and T. Daniel Seely, 184–226. Blackwell.
Müller, Gereon, and Wolfgang Sternefeld. 1993. Improper movement and unambiguous binding. *Linguistic Inquiry* 24:461–507.
Nissenbaum, Jon. 2000. *Investigations of covert phrase movement*. Doctoral dissertation, MIT.
Ortiz de Urbina, Jon. 1989. *Parameters in the grammar of Basque: A GB approach to Basque syntax*. Dordrecht: Foris.
Pankau, Andreas. 2013. *Replacing copies: The syntax of wh-copies in German*. Doctoral

dissertation, Utrecht University.
Rackowski, Andrea, and Norvin Richards. 2005. Phase edge and extraction: A Tagalog case study. *Linguistic Inquiry* 36:565–599.
Režać, Milan. 2015. Case and licensing: Evidence from ECM+DOC. *Linguistic Inquiry* 44:299–319.
van Riemsdijk, Henk. 1978. *A case study in syntactic markedness: The binding nature of prepositional phrases*. Peter de Ridder Press.
Rullmann, Hotze. 1993. Scope ambiguities in *how many*-questions. Paper presented at the 1993 LSA meeting.
Saddy, Douglas. 1991. *Wh*-scope mechanisms in Bahasa Indonesia. In *MIT Working Papers in Linguistics 15*, ed. by Lisa Cheng and Hamida Demirdache, 183–218. Cambridge, MA: MITWPL.
Saddy, Douglas. 1992. A versus A-bar movement and WH fronting in Bahasa Indonesia. Manuscript, University of Queensland, Australia.
Sato, Yosuke. 2012. Successive cyclicity at the syntax-morphology interface: Evidence from Standard Indonesian and Kendal Javanese. *Studia Linguistica* 66:32–57.
Thiersch, Craig. 1978. *Topics in German syntax*. Doctoral dissertation, MIT.
Torrego, Esther. 1984. On inversion in Spanish and some of its effects. *Linguistic Inquiry* 15:103–129.
Torrence, Harold. 2005. *On the distribution of complementizers in Wolof*. Doctoral dissertation, UCLA.
Torrence, Harold. 2012. The morpho-syntax of silent *wh*-expressions in Wolof. *Natural Language & Linguistic Theory* 30:1147–1184.
Uriagereka, Juan. 1988. *On government*. PhD diss., University of Connecticut.
Uriagereka, Juan. 1996. Determiner clitic placement. In *Current issues in comparative grammar*, ed. by Robert Freidin, 257–294, Kluwer, Dordrecht.
van Urk, Coppe. 2015. *A uniform syntax for phrasal movement: A Dinka Bor case study*. Doctoral dissertation, MIT.
van Urk, Coppe. 2018. Pronoun copying in Dinka Bor and the Copy Theory of Movement. *Natural Language & Linguistic Theory* 36:937–990.
van Urk, Coppe, and Norvin Richards. 2015. Two components of long-distance extraction: Successive cyclicity in Dinka. *Linguistic Inquiry* 46:113–155.
Wiland, Bartosz. 2010. Overt evidence from Left-Branch Extraction in Polish for punctuated paths. *Linguistic Inquiry* 41:335–347.
Zentz, Jason. 2016. *Forming wh-questions in Shona: A comparative Bantu perspective*. Doctoral dissertation, Yale University.

---

Part III: **Phases and labeling**

Željko Bošković
# 6 On the Coordinate Structure Constraint, across-the-board-movement, phases, and labeling

**Abstract:** The paper deduces a modified version of the ban on extraction out of conjuncts (CSC) based on the claim that conjuncts are phases which also captures the across-the-board-movement (ATB) exception and a number of other cases where extraction from conjuncts is shown to be possible in violation of the CSC (left-branch extraction in Serbo-Croatian, *r*-pronouns in Dutch, V-2 movement in German, clitic doubling in Dutch and Romance, quantifier-float in Japanese, article-incorporation in Galician, and object shift in English). Based on these cases, the paper shows that the CSC holds only for successive-cyclic movement out of conjuncts, as in *$Who_i$ did you see $[t_i$ friends of $t_i]$ and Sue*: elements that are base-generated at the edge of a conjunct or move there independently of successive-cyclic movement can extract. It is also shown that ATB can license an additional extraction from a conjunct in violation of the CSC. The discussion in the paper also leads to establishment of a new type of ATB, where movement must take place out of each conjunct though it is not the same element that is extracted from the conjuncts but different elements. Additionally, the paper shows that unlabeled elements do not count as interveners, a rather natural generalization given the nature of intervention effects, where features of the intervener matter (projecting features requires projecting a label). The discussion also sheds light on the ban on local wh-movement from SpecTP to SpecCP which is argued to require a return to split IP: it is shown that subjects undergoing wh-movement cannot move to the highest projection in the split IP even when the next step of movement is not SpecCP.

## 6.1 Introduction

Islandhood has been in the center of theorizing in generative grammar ever since Ross (1967). In spite of numerous works on islands, one island in particular has resisted a satisfactory account, which holds for both the GB tradition and the Min-

---

**Acknowledgement:** For helpful comments and suggestions, I thank the audiences at WCCFL 36, FASL 27 (Stanford), Generative Perspectives on the Syntax and Acquisition of Japanese 2 (Tokyo), Current Issues in Comparative Syntax (National University of Singapore), the participants of my 2017 UConn seminar, two anonymous reviewers, Jairo Nunes, and Sandra Stjepanović.

https://doi.org/10.1515/9781501510199-006

imalist Program, namely the Coordinate Structure Constraint (CSC). The CSC was traditionally assumed to have two parts, one banning extraction of conjuncts, and the other extraction out of conjuncts. It has, however, been shown that the two should be divorced (Grosu 1973, Postal 1998, Oda 2017, Bošković to appear b), the main argument being that there are languages which are sensitive to only one part of the CSC (see especially Oda 2017). I will also separate the two parts of the CSC, focusing on the ban on extraction from conjuncts, given in (1) (I will refer to it as the CSC) and illustrated by (2)–(3).

(1) Extraction out of conjuncts is disallowed.

(2) *Who$_i$ did you see [enemies of t$_i$] and John?

(3) *Who$_i$ do you think [Mary likes t$_i$] and [Jane hates Peter]?

The CSC is inextricably connected to the across-the-board-movement (ATB) exception: Extraction from a conjunct is possible if it takes place from each conjunct.

(4) Who$_i$ did you see [friends of t$_i$] and [enemies of t$_i$]?

ATB is what makes accounting for the CSC particularly difficult. CSC was a rare island that was not accounted for in Chomsky (1986). It appears that capturing it within the *Barriers* system would have been easy. All that was needed was to assume that conjuncts are barriers (which they are) and that adjunction to conjuncts is prohibited. However, (4) would then raise a massive problem. Given the cumulative nature of crossing barriers, if (2) is unacceptable because it involves movement that crosses a barrier, (4) should be even worse since it involves two such movements. I suspect this is the reason why Chomsky didn't attempt to analyze the CSC within *Barriers*. In fact, it appears that the ATB exception is bound to raise its head in any attempt to extend existing accounts of islands to the CSC.[1]

---

[1] A rare exception that analyzes both the CSC and ATB is Takahashi (1994), which can be considered a predecessor of this work. (I refer here to the spirit of Takahashi's analysis, since its implementation is quite different; note also that under Takahashi's [but not the current] analysis the CSC holds only for A'-movement). The same holds for Sag et al's (1985) account, which, though implemented in a different framework, is even closer to the analysis given below in its spirit. However, we will see that the current analysis predicts extraction from conjuncts to be possible in a number of contexts, none of which are allowed under Sag et al (1985).

Still, Sag et al (1985) and Takahashi (1994) are important predecessors of the current work in that, like the account given below, they invoke Coordination-of-Likes in the account of the CSC. However, as will become obvious below, the current work significantly differs from these works both theoretically (in terms of implementation and theoretical consequences) and empirically (in terms of the empirical predictions the accounts make and the resulting empirical coverage).

The goal of this paper is to provide an account of the CSC that will also capture the ATB exception. Importantly, the account will leave room for extraction from conjuncts to take place even in the absence of ATB in well-defined contexts, which will be shown to indeed be possible with a variety of constructions, namely left-branch extraction in Serbo-Croatian, r-pronouns in Dutch, V-2 movement in German, clitic doubling in Dutch and Romance, quantifier-float in Japanese, article-incorporation in Galician, and object shift in English. The proposed analysis will also be shown to account for an exception to the CSC from Postal (1998). The predictions of the analysis will also reveal new cases of ATB where movement must take place out of each conjunct though it is not the same element that is extracted out of the conjuncts, as in traditional ATB, but different elements.

The account also has a number of theoretical consequences. It crucially appeals to phases and Chomsky's (2013) labeling approach, which allows unlabeled elements during the derivation. To the extent that it is successful, it thus provides evidence for these theoretical mechanisms. It also provides an argument for Nunes's (2004) sideward-movement approach to ATB (a locality condition on sideward movement is also established) and a particular contextual approach to phases (based on the claim that conjuncts are phases). Perhaps the most important theoretical consequence of the proposed analysis concerns the notion of interveners. It is well-known that traces do not count as interveners (Chomsky 1995): turning an intervener into a trace voids intervention effects. This paper shows that it is not just traces that do not count as interveners, but also elements that have a trace at their edge: turning the edge of an intervener into a trace also voids intervention effects. The paper shows that this otherwise puzzling effect can be captured naturally in the labeling system, which in turn provides evidence for it. The effect in question, to be established below, is given in (5).

(5)     Unlabeled elements do not count as interveners.

The labeling system does not merely allow for an easy statement of this effect, but also captures it in a natural way. The notion of intervention is picky, it depends on the nature of the intervener.[2] For Rizzi (1990), this involved the A/A' distinction; recent works state it in terms of featural properties of the interveners. Labeling plays a crucial role here. Consider a case where X and Y merge, and the resulting object ? functions as an intervener. For an intervention effect to occur, either X or Y must have the relevant feature that is involved in the intervention and pass this feature to ? by labeling it. In other words, if X has the relevant feature, then X

---

[2] I am putting aside occasional exceptions, like wh-movement from Romance DPs, which is subject to the poss-agent-theme hierarchy (Torrego 1987, Ticio 2003, among others).

must project and label ?. What this boils down to is that labeling is necessary for ? to function as an intervener, which means that unlabeled elements should not function as interveners. In other words, since intervention is feature-sensitive, the intervener must have the relevant feature. This is trivially not possible with unlabeled elements (due to the lack of projection the relevant feature is not projected either).

The proposed analysis of the CSC will also be shown to shed light on the ban on local wh-movement from SpecTP to SpecCP, attested in many languages, by enabling us to pinpoint the culprit for this ban.

The gist of the analysis is the following: Conjuncts are phases. As a result, any movement out of a conjunct must proceed via its edge. In Chomsky (2013), successive-cyclic movement via a conjunct edge delabels the conjunct, i.e. it changes its category. The intuition is then that if movement takes place only out of one conjunct, a violation of the Coordination-of-Likes requirement ensues, the violation being remedied if movement takes place out of each conjunct, as with ATB. While the basic idea is quite straightforward, we will see that it has important theoretical and empirical consequences for a number of phenomena. Significantly, we will see that it predicts that in a number of (non-ATB) environments extraction out of conjuncts should be possible, which will be shown to be borne out.

Section 6.2 will give the relevant background. The account of the CSC, as well as ATB and a number of previously unnoticed exceptions, is given in sections 6.3-6.4. Sections 6.5-6.6 discuss the phasehood of conjuncts and an intervening factor regarding subject questions, which concerns the ban on SpecTP-to-SpecCP movement. Section 6.7 discusses intervention effects with extraction from conjuncts which will also involve establishing the generalization that unlabeled elements do not count as interveners and examining cases of ATB that involve movement of different elements from the conjuncts. Another new case where the CSC is violated is also noted. Section 6.8 examines a CSC exception from Postal (1998).

## 6.2 Phases, labels, and Coordination-of-Likes

The first ingredient of the account proposed below is the phase theory, the crucial mechanism being the Phase-Impenetrability Condition (PIC), which forces movement to proceed via phasal edges.

The second ingredient is the well-known Coordination-of-Likes requirement (CL), which requires conjuncts to be parallel in their categorial status. (CL goes back to Chomsky 1957; see also Schachter 1977, Williams 1978, Sag et al 1985, Bowers 1993, Beavers & Sag 2004, Chaves 2006, among others.)[3]

The last ingredient is Chomsky's (2013) labeling system, where labeling is not forced as part of Merge. Chomsky proposes a labeling algorithm where when a head and a phrase merge, the head projects (providing the label for the resulting object). When two phrases merge, there are two ways to implement projection/labeling: through feature-sharing or traces, traces being ignored for labeling.[4] (6) illustrates the former: when *which book* merges with interrogative CP, both the wh-phrase and the CP have the Q-feature; what is projected (determining the label of the resulting object) is the Q-feature. (This is reminiscent of Spec-Head agreement.)

(6)   I wonder [$_{CP}$ which book$_i$ [$_{C'}$ C [John bought t$_i$]]].

As for non-feature-sharing phrase-phrase merger, Chomsky (2013) crucially assumes that successive-cyclic movement does not involve feature-sharing (which essentially follows Bošković 1997a, 2002, 2007, 2008). Successive-cyclic movement cases like (7) are then relevant. There is no feature-sharing between *that* and the wh-phrase which passes through its edge. Since labeling via feature-sharing is not an option, the embedded clause cannot be labeled when *what* moves to its edge (indicated by ? in [8]). When v is merged, *what* moves. The element merged with *that*-CP being a trace, it is ignored for labeling (see fn 4), hence ? is labeled as CP after *what* moves.

(7)   What$_i$ do you think [$_{CP}$ t'$_i$ [$_{C'}$ that [John bought t$_i$]]]?

(8)   v [$_{VP}$ think [$_?$ what [$_{CP}$ that [John bought t$_i$]]]]

This is the general treatment of successive-cyclic movement in the labeling framework.

---

**3** The references also explain away a number of reported counterexamples to CL. A comprehensive discussion of CL is beyond the scope of this paper. I simply adopt CL and the phase theory here. To the extent that the proposed account is successful it can in fact be interpreted as providing evidence for these mechanisms.

**4** A trace is taken to be invisible to the labeling algorithm since it is part of a discontinuous element (a chain), where the element to be labeled does not dominate every occurrence of the moving element (Chomsky 2013 argues that traces do not function as interveners for the same reason).

## 6.3 Deducing the CSC

The above mechanisms rather straightforwardly deduce the CSC. Consider (9).

(9)   *Who$_i$ did you see [enemies of t$_i$] and John?

Movement from the conjunct must proceed successive-cyclically through its edge. As shown in (10), this movement, which involves merger of *who* and the conjunct DP, yields an unlabeled object, as is always the case with successive-cyclic movement. Importantly, as a result of this movement, the conjuncts differ in their categorial status: the second conjunct is a DP while the first conjunct is ? (it is unlabeled). This configuration is ruled out by CL, which requires that conjuncts be parallel in their categorial status. (I assume that CL is checked at the point when ConjP is formed, hence it is not affected by later movement outside of ConjP.)

(10)   [$_{ConjP}$ [$_?$ who$_i$ [$_{DP}$ enemies of t$_i$]] and [$_{DP}$ John]]

The crucial ingredient of the account is that successive-cyclic movement changes the category of the element it targets in the labeling framework, which induces a CL violation.

I will argue below that conjuncts are phases, which follows from a contextual approach to phases. As a result, the phasal/labeling account of (2) extends to other cases that have motivated positing (1), like (3). In other words, it deduces the CSC.

Not only does the account deduce the CSC, it also captures the ATB exception. Consider (11).

(11)   Who$_i$ did you see [friends of t$_i$] and [enemies of t$_i$]?

Here, successive-cyclic movement takes place to the edge of both conjuncts, delabeling them. Since both conjuncts are ? (i.e. unlabeled), CL is not violated. ([12] shows the stage of the derivation when CL applies, which is when ConjP is formed).

(12)   [$_{ConjP}$ [$_?$ who$_i$ [$_{DP}$ friends of t$_i$]] and [$_?$ who$_i$ [$_{DP}$ enemies of t$_i$]]]

The phasal/labeling system thus provides a rather straightforward deduction of the CSC, which also captures the ATB exception. In fact, no additional assumptions were needed. Movement from a conjunct must proceed via the conjunct edge. This delabels the conjunct, yielding a CL violation unless movement also takes place from the other conjunct. Both conjuncts are then delabeled, so that there is no CL violation.[5]

I emphasize here an important feature of the above account. As noted above, in typical accounts of islands, like Chomsky (1986), island violations are cumulative: the more islands are crossed the worse the sentence gets. Treating conjuncts as islands (as barriers which cannot be adjoined to in Chomsky 1986) then has the effect that ATB example (11) should be even worse than CSC violations like (9) since (9) involves one extraction from a conjunct island and (11) involves two such extractions. The phasal/labeling account, on the other hand, easily captures the ATB improvement.

## 6.4 Non-ATB exceptions

Deductions of principles often have the effect that they don't fully overlap with the deduced principles in that they allow "violations" of the relevant principles in well-defined configurations. In such cases, their success should be evaluated with respect to whether such "violations" are indeed attested.

The current deduction of the CSC in fact predicts that the CSC can be violated in well-defined configurations. Since the deduction is based on movement out of a conjunct delabeling the conjunct, it predicts such movement to be possible if the relevant element is base-generated at the conjunct edge, and can otherwise stay there, which indicates that it undergoes feature-sharing at the conjunct edge. Such movement in violation of the CSC is indeed possible. One relevant case involves possessor-extraction in Serbo-Croatian (SC), which I turn to next.

### 6.4.1 CSC-violating extraction of base-generated Specs

SC possessors have been argued to be base-generated at the edge of the traditional NP (TNP) based on the fact that they extract and bind out of their TNP, as (13) shows for the latter (see Bošković 2012, 2013a, Despić 2011, 2013, among others). They also undergo agreement in Φ-features and case.[6]

---

[5] The moving element does not actually delabel the element it merges with. Movement creates another structural layer on top of it—it is this new structural layer that lacks a label (I will be using the term delabeling for this situation for ease of exposition).
[6] The precise identity of the projection where the possessor is located is not important. I use the neutral term TNP, which stands for whatever is the highest projection in the nominal domain (see

(13) [Kusturicin$_j$ najnoviji film] ga$_{i/*j}$ je zaista
Kusturica's.NOM.MASC.SG latest movie.NOM.MASC.SG him is really
razočarao.
disappointed
'Kusturica's latest movie really disappointed him.'
(Despić 2013)

SC normally disallows extraction from conjuncts, as in (14), where the genitive complement of N is extracted. Crucially, as (15) shows, such extraction is allowed with possessors.

(14) *Fizike$_i$ je on [studenta t$_i$] i [Ivanovu sestru] vidio.
physics.GEN is he student.ACC and Ivan's.ACC sister.ACC seen
'He saw a student of physics and Ivan's sister.'

(15) ?Markovog$_i$ je on [t$_i$ prijatelja] i [Ivanovu
Marko's.ACC.MASC.SG is he friend.ACC.MASC.SG and Ivan's.ACC.FEM.SG
sestru] vidio.
sister.ACC.FEM.SG seen
'He saw Marko's friend and Ivan's sister.'

In (15), the possessor is base-generated at the conjunct edge, undergoing feature-sharing, so that the conjunct is labeled (I assume that labeling occurs as soon as it is possible, see Bošković 2015, Shlonsky 2015, Rizzi 2016, Saito 2016).[7] In contrast, in (14) the moving element needs to undergo successive-cyclic movement to the conjunct edge, which delabels the conjunct, yielding a CL violation.

What is important here is that (15) is a counterexample to the CSC since it involves extraction from a conjunct but its grammaticality is captured under the proposed account of the CSC.

## 6.4.2 CSC-violating head-movement

Under the above account, a base-generated phasal edge is expected to be extractable from conjuncts, in violation of the traditional CSC. This holds not only for the Spec of a phase, but also its head, given that both are located at the phasal edge. One relevant case of this kind is provided by article-to-V incorporation in

---

Bošković 2012, Despić 2011 for the structure of constructions like [13] in SC, as well as languages like English that do not show the binding effect in question).

7 Nothing would change if labeling occurs at the phasal level, as in Chomsky (2013), given that the projection where the possessor is located, which is the highest projection in the nominal domain, is a phase (see Bošković 2014).

Galician, illustrated by (16).

(16)   Vimo=lo$_j$   [$_{DP}$[$_{D'}$ t$_j$ [$_{NP}$ Kremlin]]]
       (we)saw=the         Kremlin
       (Uriagereka 1988)

Importantly, article-incorporation is possible out of a conjunct.

(17)   Vistede=lo$_j$   [$_{DP}$ t$_j$ [$_{NP}$ amigo de Xan]] e-mais [a Diego] onte.
       (you)saw=the           friend of Xan   and   Diego   yesterday

Movement from the conjunct does not create a labeling problem for CL here: the conjunct from which article-incorporation takes place is labeled as DP before the incorporation, given that when a head and a phrase merge the head projects. Consequently, there is no CL violation in (17), hence its grammaticality is captured.

(17) appears to differ regarding the possibility of a CSC violation with head-movement from (18), which involves T-to-C movement from a conjunct.

(18)   *Should John buy a car and Peter might sell a house?

Under the proposed analysis, locality can always be satisfied with traditional CSC violations; however, satisfying it induces a CL violation. We have seen that there is no CL violation with head-movement from the conjunct in (17), and the same reasoning should extend to (18). I therefore suggest that (18) is ruled out by independent factors.

This is indeed the case under Chomsky's (2008) C-T association analysis, where C and T share features. As Bošković (2016a) notes, this means that when there is a Q-feature in C, there is also a Q-feature in T. We then have both Cq and Tq in (18). Now, English has a requirement that in matrix clauses Tq moves to Cq: the association requires actual movement here. The problem is that the Tq of the second conjunct did not undergo this movement. The difference between (17) and (18) is then that the CSC-violating head-movement in (17) is in principle optional, which enables us to leave the relevant head in place in one conjunct, moving it only in the other, while in (18) it is obligatory: this independently prohibits failing to do it in one conjunct. The point here is that the CSC test for head-movement is conductable only with head-movement that is in principle optional.

## 6.4.3 CSC-violating extraction of Specs created by movement

The above account, which allows extraction from conjuncts under well-defined conditions, enables us to explain a number of additional CSC violations. Notice first that the account extends to Specs created by movement, but crucially only when the relevant element can stay in the Spec, i. e. if it moves there independently of successive-cyclic movement, which indicates it undergoes feature-sharing. In other words, the account only blocks successive-cyclic movement from a conjunct, since such movement delabels the conjunct (see Bošković 2018 for a labeling account of the ban on movement from moved elements, which allows such movement in the same contexts as the current account does for the CSC).

This enables us to explain some otherwise puzzling CSC violations in German, in a way which also sheds light on the nature of the SOV order in German. Consider (19).

(19) *Die Suppe$_i$ wird der Hans [t$_i$ essen] und [sich hinlegen].*
the soup will the Hans eat and self down.lie
'The soup, Hans will eat and lie down.'
(Johnson 2002)

(20) gives the structure of (19) before movement from ConjP. Assuming movement of the object to SpecvP in German to be obligatory due to its SOV nature (Kayne 1994, Zwart 1993), the object does not move to the edge of the vP phase in (20) for reasons of successive-cyclicity. We are dealing here with regular movement where the moving element can stay in the position in question, which means that it involves feature-sharing, which enables labeling. Consequently, this movement does not create the labeling problem that successive-cyclic movement creates: while successive-cyclic movement through the edge of a conjunct delabels it, the movement under consideration does not do that, allowing further movement out of the conjunct.[8]

(20) *wird der Hans [$_{ConjP}$[$_{vP}$ Die Suppe$_i$ essen [$_{VP}$ t$_i$]] und [$_{vP}$ sich hinlegen]]]*
will the Hans the soup eat and self down.lie

Note also that the analysis provides evidence for the movement account of the SOV order in German.

Another relevant case concerns *r*-pronouns in Dutch. They are exceptional in that they must precede a preposition (21), although Dutch adpositions are otherwise always prepositional (22).

(21) a. *daar op/van*
there on/of
b. **op daar/*van daar*

---

**8** Since German allows subjects to remain in-situ the second conjunct is also labeled as vP at the point when ConjP is formed, before subject movement.

(22) a. *op/van deze tafel*
       on/of this table
    b. **deze tafel op/van*

This is analyzed as involving *r*-pronoun movement to SpecPP (or a higher position in extended PP). The fact that *daar* must move to SpecPP (21) and can stay in SpecPP (23) provides evidence that its movement to SpecPP does not occur for reasons of successive-cyclicity–it is independent of it.

(23) a. *[$_{PP}$ Daar op]$_i$ heb ik boeken t$_i$ gelegd.*
       there on have I books put
    b. *Ik heb boeken [$_{PP}$ daar op] gelegd.*

We then seem to have another testing case here. There is, however, an interfering factor. There are strong restrictions on P-stranding in Dutch and German which in fact make it impossible to test the CSC here in German. Den Besten & Webelhuth (1990) note that P-stranding in German is possible only if the P is adjacent to the verb/its trace (see [24]; *von* 'of' is adjacent to the verb or its trace in [24a,b,d] but not [24c]). Since, as shown in section 6.7, for independent reasons only extraction from the first conjunct is in principle allowed under the current analysis, this makes it impossible to test *r*-pronoun extraction from coordinated PPs in German.

(24) a. *Er hat da$_i$ noch nicht [das Vorwort [t$_i$ von t$_i$]] gelesen.*
       he has it yet not the foreword of read
    b. *Er hat da$_i$ [das Vorwort t$_j$]$_k$ noch nicht [t$_i$ von t$_i$]$_j$ t$_k$ gelesen.*
    c. **Da$_i$ hat er [t$_i$ von] noch nicht das Vorwort gelesen.*
    d. *[$_{VP}$ t$_k$ t$_j$ gelesen]$_m$ hat er da$_i$ [das Vorwort]$_k$ noch nicht [$_{PP}$ t$_i$ von]$_j$ t$_m$*
       (den Besten & Webelhuth 1990)

However, at least for some speakers P-stranding in Dutch is less restrictive, allowing us to test the CSC.

(25) gives the initial paradigm. (25a) involves a regular PP, with a P-DP order, and (25b) a PP with an *r*-pronoun, which moves out of it.

(25) a. *Ik heb boeken [op deze tafel] gelegd.*
       I have book on this table put
    b. *Ik heb daar boeken op gelegd.*
       I have there books on put

I now turn to coordinated PPs. Importantly, *r*-pronoun movement is possible from coordinated PPs.[9]

(26)  a.  *Ik heb daar$_i$ boeken [$_{PP}$ t$_i$ op t$_i$] en [$_{PP}$ op deze tafel] gelegd.*
          I have there books           on and      on this table put
      b.  ?*Daar heb ik boeken [$_{PP}$ t$_i$ op t$_i$] en [$_{PP}$ op deze tafel] gelegd.*
          (Paula Fenger, p. c.)

The current approach readily captures these CSC violations. Before extraction from the coordinated PPs, the *r*-pronoun undergoes regular obligatory movement to SpecPP. Its extraction from the coordination then does not create the problem successive-cyclic movement creates: while successive-cyclic movement through the conjunct edge delabels the conjunct, *r*-pronoun movement does not do it.

Clitic doubling provides additional evidence. Van Craenenbroeck and van Koppen (2008) note that Wambeek Dutch allows clitic doubling of a conjunct, in violation of the CSC (27). This is not a quirk of Wambeek Dutch: Spanish (28) and Brazilian Portuguese ([29], Minas Gerais dialect, which allows clitic doubling) also allow it.

(27)  *Ik paus da* **se** *[zaailn en waailn] dui suimen wel*
      I think that they.CL they.STRONG and we.STRONG there together PRT
      *oitgeruiken.*
      out.come
      'I think that they and we will solve that together.'
      (Van Craenenbroeck and van Koppen 2008:208)

---

[9] Such cases require particular prosody. In (26a), there needs to be an intonational break after first *op* or *daar* should be stressed; (26b) requires an intonational break after *op*. I assume this is necessary due to non-V-adjacency of the stranded P. It is actually possible that the correct generalization regarding P-stranding in Dutch/German is that stranded Ps must be either adjacent to a verb or followed by an intonational-phrase boundary, which is reflected in the presence of a pause ([24d], where the P is not V-adjacent, fits this generalization). Any differences between Dutch and German regarding P-stranding may then be due to differences in intonational phrasing/the requirement in question (in work in preparation I argue for a prosody-based account, where these Dutch/German data are analyzed within a broader crosslinguistic context regarding the possibility of dropping the host of phonologically weak elements). At any rate, what is particularly interesting here is that extraction is unacceptable from the second conjunct, as in (i), although in that case the stranded P is V-adjacent. As discussed below, this is exactly what the current analysis predicts.

(i)  *\*Ik heb daar boeken op deze tafel en op gelegd.*
     I have there books  on this table and on put

(28) Yo la     vi  a María y   a Juan.
     I  her.CL saw María   and Juan
     'I saw Mary and Juan.'
     (Gabriel Martínez Vera, p. c.)

(29) Que Deus te       ilumine    você e  sua família.
     that God  2SG.ACC illuminate you  and your family
     'May God illuminate you and your family.'
     (Machado-Rocha 2016:88)

Many have argued for the big-DP account, where the clitic and the double are base-generated together, with the clitic moving away (e. g. Uriagereka 1995, Cecchetto 2000, Kayne 2002, Boeckx 2003, Belletti 2005). Runić (2014) provides strong evidence for it. She shows the big-DP is preserved in some languages, where the clitic and the double cannot be split (30). These languages then minimally differ from those in (27)–(29) in that the clitic doesn't move out of the big-DP; more importantly, they provide evidence that the clitic and the double indeed form a constituent at one point in the derivation.

(30) a. *Je l' me          čekaš    mene?
        AUX Q me.CL.ACC wait.2SG me.ACC
     b. Je l' me mene čekaš?
        'Are you waiting for me?'
        (Prizren-Timok Serbian)

From this perspective, (27)–(29) are not surprising: since the clitic and the doubled conjunct are generated as a single DP, conjunct clitic doubling can be easily captured under the current account. The account can actually help us determine more precisely the structure of the big-DP, which is otherwise not easy to do since we are dealing with a pre-movement structure. To be able to extract, the clitic must be located at the edge of the big-DP, either as its Spec (in which case [27]–[29] parallel CSC violations with SC possessors [15]) or its head (in which case they parallel CSC violations with Galician article-incorporation [17]).

Clitic doubling thus provides another case of extraction that violates the CSC which is captured under the current deduction of the CSC.

Consider also Japanese numeral constructions:

(31) a. John-wa [hon-o    san satsu] katta.
        John-TOP book-ACC 3   CL     bought
        'John bought three books.'
     b. Hon-o John-wa san-satsu katta.

Following Watanabe (2006), I assume that *hon-o* moves to the edge of the bracketed TNP (I will refer to it as ClasP). The NP can move outside of ClasP, as in (31b). Importantly, the movement is also possible from coordinations:

(32)  Ringo-o$_i$  Taro-wa  [$t_i$ san ko] to  [banana-o  ni hon] tabeta.
      apple-ACC Taro-TOP  3  CL  and banana-ACC 2 CL  ate
      'Taro ate three apples and two bananas.'
      (Satoshi Oku, p. c.)

(32) represents another case of movement from conjuncts that is captured under the proposed analysis.

Consider now extraction from conjuncts with English ECM.

(33)  ?I've believed John$_i$ for a long time now [$t_i$ to be a liar] and [Peter to be trustworthy].

(33) is somewhat degraded though clearly better than typical CSC violations like (2)–(3). I interpret this as indicating the CSC is not violated in (33), putting aside the reason for its residual awkwardness (it may have to do with the presence of the adverbial in only one conjunct, but see Bošković [to appear b] for an alternative account where the CSC effect is only partially voided in [33]). Lasnik (1999) argues object shift is optional in English. The first conjunct subject in (33) must have undergone object shift since it precedes a matrix adverbial. This is then another case of movement from a conjunct.[10]

As noted above, Lasnik (1999) argues that object shift is optional here. This means that the infinitival subject can remain in the Spec of the infinitive, which means that movement to the Spec of ECM infinitives is independent of successive-cyclicity. In other words, it results in labeling. Both infinitival conjuncts are then labeled, enabling extraction of the infinitival subject in violation of the CSC.

(15), (17), (19), (26), (27)–(29), (32), and (33) all involve acceptable extractions from a conjunct, in violation of the traditional CSC ban in (1). They are, however, captured under the proposed account of (1), which also captures ATB exceptions like (11). The account then does not actually deduce the CSC ban in (1), but a modified version of it which allows extraction from conjuncts under well-defined conditions. In particular, the account confines the CSC effect to successive-cyclic movement from conjuncts. The labeling framework enables us to make a principled distinction between successive-cyclic movement on one

---

**10** I assume we are dealing here with coordination of two infinitives (but see Bošković 1997a). Johnson (2002) also notes the CSC can be violated under ECM movement based on *I made Sally$_i$ out [[$t_i$ to be honest] and [Mark to be trustworthy]]*.

hand, and obligatory movement (i. e. movement that can be the final landing site) and base-generation on the other hand, since they have a different effect on labeling. What we have seen above is that we find exactly this cut with extraction from conjuncts, which enables the labeling system to account for the ban on extraction from conjuncts in a way that also captures the exceptions to this ban.[11]

## 6.5 Conjuncts as phases

Conjuncts are traditionally assumed to be islands. In the phasal system, it is natural to assume that they are phases, given that phases have a potential for inducing locality violations.[12] The islandhood-phasehood connection has an interesting consequence: since each conjunct is an island even if the relevant phrase is otherwise not an island, this means that each conjunct should be a phase even when the relevant phrase otherwise would not be a phase. The assumption, which I show below follows from a contextual approach to phases, is motivated by examples like (34). (34) appears to involve coordination of IPs, which is not a phase in Chomsky (2000). In the current system, wh-movement needs to proceed via the conjunct edge here, which means the conjunct needs to be a phase. Successive-cyclic movement to the edge of the conjunct delabels it, inducing a CL violation.[13]

(34)  *I wonder what$_i$ Betsy purchased t$_i$ and Sally advertised it.

In the current approach, if phrases that are not phases when they are not coordinated are also not phases when coordinated it would in principle be possible to extract from such non-phasal conjuncts. However, it turns out that under Bošković's

---

[11] Johnson (2009) gives an account of gapping involving ATB VP-fronting with movement of the subject out of only one conjunct. If subjects in their base-position can be involved in labeling in English (a possibility in Chomsky 2015, though not Chomsky 2013, see also fn 18), Johnson's analysis can be accommodated in the current system and would represent another case of an acceptable CSC "violation".

[12] I do not mean to suggest that phases in general are islands, just that phases have the potential to induce locality violations, which can then capture islandhood.

[13] Under the natural assumption that A'-Specs are higher than A-Specs when a phrase has both (see Abels 2007, Bošković 2018), wh-movement will proceed via the outmost conjunct edge in (34). There is actually no need to assume this. Under Bošković's (2016b) approach to the PIC, where only the outmost Spec of a phase is accessible from the outside, *who* is anyway inaccessible outside of the conjunct phase unless it moves through the outmost Spec (above *Betsy*). (There is no issue regarding the possibility of multiple Specs for the relevant IP in (34) given the standard assumption that phase heads in general can have multiple Specs [see Bošković 2007] if this IP is a phase by virtue of being a conjunct, as argued here).

(2014) approach to phases, the coordinated IPs in (34) are anyway phases (even though the embedded IP is not a phase in *I wonder what Betsy purchased*); there is no need to stipulate that conjuncts are always phases, independently of whether the coordinated phrases are phases on their own.

While Chomsky (2000) assumes that a particular phrase is a phase or not regardless of its syntactic context (CP is always a phase and IP is never a phase), many have argued for various contextual approaches where the phasal status of $\alpha$ depends on the syntactic context where it occurs (as Bošković 2014 notes, this follows the spirit of *Barriers*, where we cannot determine whether CP is a barrier or not without knowing its syntactic context—CP is sometimes a barrier and sometimes not, depending on its structural position). Focusing on IP, Bošković (2014, 2015, 2016a) and Wurmbrand (2013) argue that the highest clausal projection is a phase, which makes IP a phase when not dominated by CP. However, it appears that the relevant IP would still not be a phase in (34), since it is dominated by CP. This is actually not the case in Bošković (2014).

Bošković (2014) argues that the highest projection in the extended domain of a lexical head and the highest clausal projection function as phases (i. e. the highest phrase in a phasal domain functions as a phase, phasal domains being the domains of lexical heads and the clause[14]). This makes vP (the highest projection in the V-domain) and CP (the highest projection in the clausal domain) phases in (35), as in Chomsky (2000). However, in contrast to Chomsky (2000), if V takes an IP complement in (35) this IP will be a phase as the highest projection in the clausal domain.

(35)    [$_{vP}$ [$_{VP}$ [$_{CP}$ [$_{IP}$

Consider how this system applies to coordinations, i. e. how the presence of ConjP affects it. The issue here is that ConjP disrupts domain projection for the clausal phasal domain. In contrast to (35), CP does not immediately dominate IP in (36). ConjP separates CP and IP into separate domains, making IP the highest phrase in its phasal domain, just like when V takes an IP complement. (More generally, merger of [a projection of] the Conj head with a conjunct closes the extended domain of the conjunct in Bošković's 2014 system, making the highest projection of the conjunct a phase; see also Oda 2019.)

(36)    [$_{vP}$ [$_{VP}$ [$_{CP}$ [$_{ConjP}$ [$_{IP}$

---

**14** See Bošković (2014:74–75) regarding how this is implemented without look-ahead.

The presence of ConjP then affects the phasal status of IP in Bošković (2014), making it a phase (this actually holds for all conjuncts). In other words, coordination makes coordinated IPs phases, which is exactly the effect we saw at work in (34). The gist of the discussion here is that IP is a phase if it is not immediately dominated by CP, as argued independently in Wurmbrand (2013) and Bošković (2014, 2015, 2016a). Though the cases discussed in these works do not involve coordination, ConjP has the same effect in that the relevant IP is not immediately dominated by CP, which makes it a phase.

We may also be in a position to capture the claim from Oda (2017) and Bošković (to appear b) that both conjuncts and ConjP are islands,[15] which means phases given the above discussion. In Bošković (2014), the clausal domain and the domains of lexical heads are phasal domains, the highest phrase in these domains being a phase. ConjP does not naturally belong to either of these domains. Now, Epstein and Seely (2002) argue that each phrase is a phase (see also Boeckx 2007, Müller 2010). Suppose we combine that view and Bošković (2014) in a way that each phrase has the potential to be a phase; however, the phasehood is voided if the phrase belongs to a phasal domain and is not the highest projection within the domain. Under this view, ConjP, which, as noted above, does not belong to Bošković's (2014) phasal domains, would then be a phase (since its potential phasehood would not be voided by virtue of not being the highest phrase in a phasal domain). Both ConjP and the conjuncts are then phases. Since this paper focuses on extraction from conjuncts I will put the phasehood of ConjP aside below.[16]

## 6.6 Subject questions

This section discusses an interfering factor which arises with subject wh-extraction in IP&IP coordinations (I use the term IP neutrally, similar to TNP). Consider (37) (which differs from [33], where the subject *John* undergoes object shift).

(37)   *I wonder who$_i$ [t$_i$ left] and [Mary disappeared].

---

[15] Their motivation is attempting to capture both parts of the traditional CSC.
[16] Phasehood does not necessarily equate with islandhood. However, Bošković (2016c) argues that a double-phase configuration, where a phase dominates a phase, creates islandhood. Given that both ConjP and conjuncts are phases, coordination would then always bring in islandhood, resulting in a locality effect (unless the effect is voided in one of the ways discussed here and Bošković 2016c, to appear b).

It appears that on the IP&IP derivation (where what is coordinated is the embedded clause IPs, the wh-CP being outside of the coordination), (37) involves extraction of a conjunct edge that is created by obligatory movement (to SpecIP), which should not cause a labeling problem. Why is then (37) unacceptable?

This brings us to the puzzle of *who left*, where apparently there is no movement to SpecIP although English otherwise requires it (see Bošković 2016a, Messick 2020). There are a number of accounts of *who left*. There are strong arguments against accounts where *who* stays in SpecIP. E. g., (38)–(39) indicate that *wh-the-hell* phrases are only possible with wh-movement. (40) then shows that the wh-phrase is not located in SpecIP.

(38)  *What the hell did John buy?*

(39)  *\*Who bought what the hell?*

(40)  *Who the hell arrested Mary?*

Further, in contrast to (42), (41) is unambiguous. Since (42) shows that an object quantifier can scope over a quantifier in SpecIP, as Mizuguchi (2014) notes, *who* in (41) should not be located in SpecIP.

(41)  *Who loves everyone?*      (who>everyone;\*everyone>who)

(42)  *Someone loves everyone.*  (someone >everyone;everyone>someone)

Particularly important are West Ulster English (WUE) (43)–(44), which show not only that subject questions involve movement to SpecCP but also that the movement does not proceed via SpecIP.

(43)  *Who$_i$ was arrested all t$_i$ in Duke Street?*

(44)  *\*They$_i$ were arrested all t$_i$ last night.*
      (McCloskey 2000)

In contrast to standard English, WUE allows Quantifier(Q)-float under wh-movement. Still, in spite of allowing (43), like standard English WUE disallows (44). McCloskey (2000) observes that given that Q-float is disallowed from SpecIP in (44), *all* cannot be floated under movement to SpecIP in (43). He then concludes that *who* moves here directly to SpecCP, without moving via SpecIP.

This is an issue that has been discussed for many languages, e. g. Italian, Kaqchikel, Kinande. There are well-known arguments from these languages that subject movement to SpecIP cannot feed movement to SpecCP, as assumed under the previously standard treatment of *who left* (what makes *who left* puzzling is that movement to SpecIP is otherwise obligatory in English, which means the EPP requirement is voided here).¹⁷

This is exactly the problem with (37). Movement of *who* to SpecIP is needed due to the coordination structure independently of whatever is going on in *who left*. Given that conjuncts are phases, this movement is required by the PIC. Consequently, even if the way of voiding the EPP requirement (whatever it is) in *who left* is also available in (37), movement of *who* to SpecIP is independently needed in (37) because of the coordination structure (i. e. the PIC). Whatever is responsible for the impossibility of subject SpecIP-to-SpecCP movement (see below) will then block (37). (Another issue is that, as discussed above, the I of the second conjunct in (37) is Iq, due to C-I association; what we have in (37) is then a wh-question (not a yes-no question) where there is no wh-phrase/wh-trace in the IPq of the second conjunct, which may cause a problem—the issue here being whether IPwh-q must contain a wh-phrase/wh-trace.)¹⁸

---

**17** See Messick (2020) and Bošković (2016a) for different labeling accounts within Chomsky's (2013) and Chomsky's (2015) approach respectively.
**18** Consider also (i), which involves ATB subject movement from both conjuncts (which is not shown) and wh-movement from the first conjunct.

(i)   *Who$_i$ did John hire t$_i$ and fire Mary?

There are several ways of analyzing (i) due to uncertainty regarding how several relevant issues should be treated (the open questions are the level of coordinaton, whether such examples involve object shift before wh-movement and whether this movement lands in a position higher than the subject base-position, whether the base-merger of the subject results in labeling...) I give here one way of analyzing (i) involving a particular set of assumptions regarding these issues. Suppose that objects undergoing wh-movement undergo object shift on the way up, and that the object-shift position is higher than the subject base-position, as argued in Bošković (1997b) (and as was the case in the system that assumed that object shift targets AgroP; with the elimination of AgroP, this means that object shift targets a SpecvP above the subject base-position [the subject SpecvP can be created via tucking-in after the object SpecvP is created; see also Abels 2007]). Assuming that (i) involves vP-level coordination and that subjects in their base-position cannot undergo labeling, as in Chomsky (2013), the first conjunct in (i) is labeled, as shown in (ii) (since object shift results in labeling, like movement to SpecIP), while the second conjunct is not (before subject movement to SpecIP, which is what matters hence I ignore labeling that occurs after the relevant movements. Note also that, as discussed in Lasnik 1999, object shift is not limited to DP arguments in English.).

(ii)  *Who$_i$ did John$_j$ [$_{vP}$ t$_i$ t$_j$ hire t$_i$] and [$_?$ t$_j$ fire Mary]?

There is an alternative account, where movement of a wh-phrase via the edge of vP is always considered true successive-cyclic movement, hence it would not involve labeling. Under this assumption, we would need to assume that the subject can undergo feature-sharing with its sister

Also relevant is (45):

(45) Who can leave and must work harder?

There are many arguments that the traditional IP domain contains more than just TP–there is additional structure between vP and the phrase whose Spec the subject occupies (see Belletti 1990, Cinque 1999, Bošković 2001 regarding intermediate V-movement, Bobaljik & Jonas 1996 regarding multiple subject positions, and Bošković 2004 regarding Q-float). In fact, sentential adverbs can intervene even between the subject and modals/auxiliaries in English, which also indicates that the subject is located in the Spec of a projection that is higher than the projection where modals/auxiliaries are located. Within Pollock-style split IP, Bošković (1997a) and Watanabe (1993) place the subject in (46) in SpecAgrsP and the modal in T (Kayne 1989 also proposes such an analysis).[19]

(46) John probably can play the guitar.

Given that bar-level coordination is disallowed, constructions like (47), where the subject is outside of the coordination but the modal is not, also provide evidence that the subject and the modal are not located in the same projection, the modal being lower than the phrase whose Spec the subject occupies.

(47) John [travels to Rome tomorrow] and [will fly for Paris on Sunday].

Assuming the Bošković/Watanabe analysis (the exact labels of the relevant projections do not really matter), (45) can then be analyzed as involving TP coordination (see [48] below), with the subject moving from SpecTP directly to SpecCP (after forming an ATB dependency), the ban on local subject wh-movement being implemented as a ban on movement from SpecAgrsP to SpecCP (see also the discussion below), which does not occur in (45)/(48). (I will refer to the subject not passing through SpecAgrsP, which otherwise has to be filled, when moving

---

vP in the base-position, which means that the second conjunct in (i) would be labeled. Since the first conjunct is not, due to its "hosting" successive-cyclic movement, (i) then still violates CL.

**19** (46) and (ia) are unacceptable in French but so is (ib) (see Belletti 1990, Bošković 2000; [ib] is acceptable in English), which indicates that there is more to the difference between English and French here than just V-movement.

(i) a. *Jean probablement vendra ces livres.
      Jean probably     will.sell these books
   b. *Probablement, Jean vendra ces livres.

to SpecCP as the *who left* effect).[20] The ban in question is then tied to agreement, i. e. the agreeing SpecAgrsP subject position where lexical subjects are located. SpecAgrsP is where the subject is located in the second conjunct of (37), which must then involve AgrsP-level coordination (given CL), (37) being ruled out as discussed above (due to the PIC/*who left* effect). Note also that in (45), which involves TP coordination, the subject will move to the edge of the conjunct because the conjunct is a phase although otherwise such movement is not necessary, the traditional EPP requirement, which is anyway voided in subject questions, holding for the highest position in split IP (AgrsP). (48) gives the structure for (45) and (49) for (37) (coordinated phrases are given in bold).

(48)  [$_{CP}$ Who$_i$ [$_{AgrsP}$ [$_{TP}$ t$_i$ can leave] and [$_{TP}$ t$_i$ must work harder]]]?

(49)  *I wonder [$_{CP}$ who$_i$ [**$_{AgrsP}$** t$_i$ [$_{TP}$ left]] and [**$_{AgrsP}$** Mary [$_{TP}$ disappeared]]].

Under the proposed analysis, (37) is ruled out independently of the CSC (due to the PIC/*who left* effect). Consequently, we would expect that it would not become acceptable with ATB, as long as the second conjunct has an overt subject so that it is forced to be an AgrsP. The expectation is borne out. Consider (50), where *who* undergoes ATB movement from both conjuncts.

(50)  *I wonder who$_i$ [t$_i$ left] and [Mary kissed t$_i$].

The second conjunct must be an AgrsP due to the presence of a lexical subject, which then forces the first conjunct to be an AgrsP too. However, if the first conjunct is an AgrsP, movement of *who* to the conjunct edge, which is necessary since the conjunct is a phase, results in a violation, as discussed above (for two reasons actually: due to the *who left* effect and because of CL, given that the first conjunct is then labeled while the second conjunct, whose outmost edge is targetted by successive-cyclic movement [not shown above], is not).

Consider also (51).

(51)  *I wonder who$_i$ [John saw t$_i$] and [t$_i$ kissed Mary].

It is not clear whether the *who left* effect would arise here. The coordination here has to be on the AgrsP-level due to the presence of a lexical subject in the first conjunct. Below I will adopt Nunes's (2004) sideward-movement analysis of ATB.

---

**20** In fact, under the approaches to antilocality in Bošković (2016a) and Erlewine (2016), in [$_{CP}$ [$_{AgrsP}$ [$_{TP}$]]] antilocality bans movement to SpecCP from SpecAgrsP but not from SpecTP. Furthermore, the presence of ConjP in AgrsP&AgrsP cooordinations doesn't change anything under Bošković's (2016a) approach (see also [52] below).

Under that analysis, *who* moves to SpecAgrsP of the second conjunct and then gets remerged into the object position of the first conjunct. While I have assumed above that what is behind the *who left* effect is a ban on movement from SpecAgrsP to SpecCP, if what is responsible for the *who left* effect is actually that a subject undergoing wh-movement cannot move to SpecAgrsP, movement of *who* to the SpecAgrsP of the second conjunct will still be blocked in (51). On the other hand, if what is responsible for the *who left* effect is indeed movement from SpecAgrsP to SpecCP, the issue will not arise (due to sideward movement of *who* into the first conjunct, there is no SpecAgrsP-to-SpecCP movement in [51]).[21] Anyway, (51) is still ruled by CL: the first conjunct is targeted by successive-cyclic movement, which is not the case with the second conjunct. This yields a CL violation due to a labeling conflict.[22]

An interesting contrast in (52)–(53), noted by Qilin Tian, can help us pinpoint the culprit for the *who left* effect. This contrast also indicates that infinitives have split IP (AgrsP+TP), with the presence of *Peter* in the second conjunct forcing this conjunct to be an AgrsP—the first conjunct then also must be an AgrsP.

(52) *Who$_i$ did you believe for a long time now [t$_i$ to be a liar] and [Peter to be trustworthy]?

(53) ?I've believed John$_i$ for a long time now [t$_i$ to be a liar] and [Peter to be trustworthy].

As discussed above (cf. [33]), *John* in (53) undergoes feature-sharing movement to the Spec of the infinitive (SpecAgrsP), which results in labeling. It then moves to the matrix SpecvP (the adverb modifies the matrix clause), which violates the CSC but conforms with its deduction proposed above. If movement of subject wh-phrases quite generally cannot proceed through AgrsP, that derivation is not an

---

**21** Note that if what is responsible for the *who left* effect is SpecAgrsP-to-SpecCP movement, the unacceptability of *Who$_i$ did he say [$_{CP}$[$_{AgrsP}$ t$_i$ left] and [$_{AgrsP}$ she arrived]] shows that the ban should not be limited to movement to +wh-SpecCP but SpecCP in general (the first conjunct must be an AgrsP given that the second conjunct is an AgrsP due to the presence of a lexical subject and movement to SpecAgrsP of the first conjunct is forced independently of the EPP by the PIC, conjuncts being phases, an issue that would not arise in *who$_i$ did he say t$_i$ left*, where wh-movement via SpecAgrsP is not forced for reasons discussed above).
**22** Note also the improvement of (51) in (i).

(i) I wonder who$_i$ [John saw t$_i$] and [Peter thinks t$_i$ kissed Mary]

Here the outmost edge of both conjuncts is targeted by successive-cyclic movement so that no problem regarding CL arises.

option in (52); (52) can then be accounted for in the same way as (37)/(49) (the disallowed movement to SpecAgrsP is required by the PIC, conjuncts being phases). Since, in contrast to *who* in (37)/(49), after moving to SpecAgrsP (of the infinitive) *who* in (52) does not move directly to SpecCP, the unacceptability of (52) then indicates that what is responsible for the *who left* effect is that subjects undergoing wh-movement cannot move to SpecAgrsP; i. e., the culprit is the movement of the wh-moving subject to SpecAgrsP, not its movement from SpecAgrsP to SpecCP.

Extraction from coordinated clauses thus enables us to pinpoint the culprit for the *who left* effect, also providing evidence for split IP.

## 6.7 Intervention effects

### 6.7.1 Intervention effects and ATB-movement

We have seen that movement from a conjunct in violation of the CSC is possible exactly where expected under the current account. E. g. SC possessors, which are base-generated at the TNP-edge, can extract.

(54) ?*Markovog$_i$*    je on [t$_i$ *prijatelja*]    i    [*Ivanovu*
Marko's.ACC.MASC.SG is he  friend.ACC.MASC.SG and Ivan's.ACC.FEM.SG
*sestru*]    *vidio.*
sister.ACC.FEM.SG seen
'He saw Marko's friend and Ivan's sister.'

However, such movement is possible only from the first conjunct, as shown by the unacceptability of (55), involving possessor-extraction from the second conjunct. In fact, the CSC-violating movements discussed above are all possible only from the first conjunct.[23]

---

**23** See fn 9 regarding *r*-pronouns. (i)–(ii) show this for clitic doubling and Japanese Q-float.

(i) *\*Que Deus **te**    ilumine    ele e    **você**.*
that God 2SG.ACC illuminate he and you
'May God illuminate him and you.'
(BP, Machado-Rocha, p. c.)

(ii) *\*Banana-o    Taro-wa [ringo-o    san ko] to    [t$_i$ ni hon] tabeta.*
banana-ACC Taro-TOP apple-ACC 3    CL and    2 CL  ate
'Taro ate three apples and two bananas.'
(Satoshi Oku, p. c.)

(55) *Ivanovu$_i$ je on [Markovog prijatelja] i [t$_i$
Ivan's.ACC.MASC.SG is he Marko's.ACC friend.ACC and
sestru] vidio.
sister.ACC.FEM.SG seen

There should be no CSC violation here; if the CSC were to ban possessor-extraction from conjuncts in SC it would also rule out (54). Given the well-established fact that the first conjunct is higher than the second conjunct, following Johnson (2002) I sugggest that (55) involves an intervention effect. The first conjunct causes an intervention effect, blocking movement from the second conjunct.[24]

There is independent evidence for this. It is well-known that traces void intervention effects (56). Thus, A-movement across an experiencer is disallowed in Italian (57), an intervention effect involving A-movement across an A-Spec. The effect is voided if the intervener is a trace (58).

(56) Traces do not count as interveners.
(Chomsky 1995, Bošković 2011, among others)

(57) *Gianni$_i$ sembra a Maria [t$_i$ essere stanco].
Gianni seems to Maria to.be ill

(58) A Maria$_j$, Gianni$_i$ sembra t$_j$ [t$_i$ essere stanco].

Traces also void islandhood. Thus, Bošković (2013b) argues for (59), observing that turning the head of an island into a trace voids islandhood. Galician (60)–(61) illustrate this. (60) is ruled out because it involves extraction from an adjunct. The effect is voided by article-incorporation in (61), given (59).

(59) Traces do not head islands.

(60) *de que semana$_j$ traballastedes [$_{DP}$ o [Luns t$_j$]]?
of which week worked the Monday
'Of which week did you guys work the Monday?'

---

[24] We may not actually be dealing here with a relativized-minimality but a PIC effect. If ConjP is a phase, extraction from ConjP must proceed via SpecConjP. Assuming Richards' (2001) tucking-in, a phrase moving from the second conjunct must move to a lower SpecConjP, tucking in under the first conjunct. If only the outmost edge of a phase with multiple edges is accessible from the outside due to the PIC, as Bošković (2016b) argues, the element in the lower SpecConjP then cannot move out of ConjP due to the PIC. Nevertheless, for ease of exposition I will simply use the term intervention effect for the configuration in question. (At any rate, the way the effect is treated below when it comes to exceptions to it would not change regardless of whether it is seen as a PIC or a relativized-minimality effect [note that Rackowski & Richards 2005 treat it in terms of classical intervention].)

(61) de que semana$_j$ traballastede=lo$_i$ [$_{DP}$ [$_{D'}$ [t$_i$ [Luns    t$_j$]]]?
     of which week    worked=the                  Monday

Returning to (55), evidence that (55) indeed involves an intervention effect is provided by the fact that it becomes acceptable if the first conjunct is a trace.
   SC allows extraction of conjuncts (see e. g. Stjepanović 2014).

(62) ?Knjige$_i$ je Marko [t$_i$ i   filmove] kupio.
     books is Marko       and movies bought
     'Marko bought books and movies.'

Crucially, Stjepanović (to appear) notes that if the first conjunct is a trace, extraction from the second conjunct is possible. Compare her examples (63)/(64). In (64), the first conjunct stays in situ, blocking extraction from the lower conjunct. In (63), the first conjunct is a trace (it undergoes movement), which enables extraction from the second conjunct (see below for what happens with the conjunction).

(63) Koja serija$_i$ se i   čiji$_j$   tebi    [$_{ConjP}$ t$_i$ [t$_j$ film]] dopadaju?
     which series self and whose you.DAT              movie please
     'Which series and whose movie are pleasing to you?'

(64) *I  čiji$_j$  se tebi    [$_{ConjP}$ koja  serija [t$_j$ film]] dopadaju?
     and whose self you.DAT        which series      movie please
     'Which series and whose movie are pleasing to you?'

These facts parallel (57): turning an intervener into a trace voids intervention. The presence of a typical intervention-voiding effect provides evidence that the impossibility of extraction from the second conjunct in (55) indeed involves an intervention effect.
   The reader may have noticed that extraction from the second conjunct carries the conjunction with it in (63). The reason is that, as Stjepanović (2014) shows, the conjunction is a proclitic which proclicitizes to the element following it, so that any movement of that element carries it along. Oda (2017) and Stjepanović (2014) in fact argue that conjunction-cliticization is a prerequisite for conjunct extraction. Thus, conjunct extraction is also possible in Japanese, where the conjunction is an enclitic, and is in fact carried along under movement of the first conjunct.

(65) ?Kyoodai$_i$=to        kanojo-wa [t$_i$ Toodai]-ni        akogareteiru.
     Kyoto.University=and she-TOP      Tokyo.University-DAT admire
     'She admires Kyoto University and Tokyo University.'
     (Oda 2017)

Oda (2017) and Stjepanović (2014) analyze this in terms of (59): ConjP is an island but its islandhood is voided in SC/Japanese because the head of ConjP is a trace, due to movement of the conjunction head.[25]

I then conclude that the reason why possessor-extraction is normally disallowed from the second conjunct (i. e. the reason for the contrast in [54]–[55]) is an intervention effect: The first conjunct intervenes for extraction from the second conjunct; the effect is voided if the intervener is a trace.

A question now arises. Given that the first conjunct induces an intervention effect for extraction from the second conjunct, why doesn't the effect arise in ATB-constructions, where it appears that there is movement from each conjunct, which means movement from the second conjunct crosses the first conjunct. Since the goal of this paper is to account not only for the CSC but also ATB, the question cannot be put aside. What is then the difference between (55), where the first conjunct induces an intervention effect, and ATB example in (11), where this is apparently not the case?

Note first that in (63), where extraction from the second conjunct is possible, the intervener is a trace. This is not the case in ATB (11): there is a trace in (11) (see [67]) but the trace is the edge of the conjunct, the conjunct itself is not a trace. We will see below that this may actually be relevant. Pending that discussion, I focus on another difference between (11) and (63), which is the fact that it is the same element that is extracted from the conjuncts in (11), the defining property of ATB. There is an approach to ATB which easily resolves the intervention issue, namely Nunes (2004).

Nunes proposes a unified account of parasitic gaps (PG) and ATB involving sideward movement, where XP participating in a PG/ATB construction is merged within the adjunct/second conjunct, then re-merged in a non-c-commanding position that corresponds to the other gap of PG/ATB constructions. (66) shows this for the former. *What* is merged in the adjunct object position, then in the matrix object position, undergoing movement from there. Two chains are then formed,

---

**25** Stjepanović provides evidence that the second conjunct in (62)–(63) moves to lower Spec-ConjP, with the conjunction procliticizing to it. She unifies (63) with SC (i), which Bošković (2005, 2013b) and Talić (2019) analyze as involving AP-movement to SpecPP, followed by procliticization of the P to the adjective. Further movement of the adjective then carries the P along (the PP is an island, but its islandhood is voided through [59]).

(i)     [U veliku]$_i$ je on ušao    [t$_i$ sobu].
       in big    is on entered    room
       'He entered a big room.'

both of which are headed by moved *what*, with the lower copy of each chain deleted in PF.

(66)    *What$_i$ did [John file* ~~*what$_i$*~~*] [without reading* ~~*what$_i$*~~*]?*

The analysis straightforwardly extends to ATB (11)/(67). *Who* is merged in its θ-position in the second conjunct, moving to the edge of the conjunct (which is a phase).[26] It is then re-merged in its θ-position in the first conjunct, moving to its edge. Movement to the edge of the conjuncts delabels them, so that CL is obeyed.[27] Crucially, there has never been movement from the second conjunct that crosses the first conjunct. The intervention problem with such movement that arises in (55) then does not arise here. The sideward-movement analysis thus straightforwardly resolves the intervention issue, which can be interpreted as an argument for it.

(67)    *Who$_i$ did you see [t$_i$ friends of t$_i$] and [t$_i$ enemies of t$_i$]?*

## 6.7.2 ATB cover up

Under the above analysis, we may expect the possibility of interaction between ATB and an independent movement that violates the CSC where the CSC violation would be covered up by a separate ATB dependency on top of it, i. e. where an ATB dependency formed with extraction from two conjuncts would sneak in a separate extraction in violation of the CSC. Abstractly, we would have (68), where ATB extraction and non-ATB extraction are mixed and the relevant elements are at conjunct edges, getting there as a result of successive-cyclic movement (which means that they undergo further movement that is not shown below).

(68)    [$_{ConjP}$ [ATB$_i$ non-ATB$_j$...t$_i$ t$_j$] and [ATB$_i$...t$_i$]]

Both conjuncts are then unlabeled, and there is no crossing of the first conjunct due to ATB involving sideward movement. Although both elements are extracted from ConjP, no CSC violation should arise under the current analysis, in contrast

---

[26] There are islandhood effects within the second conjunct, which indicate that there must be movement to the edge of this conjunct, before remerger/sideward movement. The current analysis may actually explain why this movement, which delabels the second conjunct, takes place: without it, a CL violation would occur.

[27] Note that the copy of *who* at the edge of the second conjunct does not count as a trace (hence is not ignored for labeling) at this point of the derivation since there is no higher copy of *who* that c-commands it (the relevant chain is formed only later, after movement out of ConjP).

to the traditional CSC approach, where non-ATB extraction in (68) would violate the CSC. Since both elements are extracted from ConjP an independent locality violation is bound to arise in English, but not in SC, where it is possible to have both wh-phrases move to the same clause, as in (69)–(70), SC being a multiple wh-fronting language. What is important here is that (70), which involves a traditional CSC violation (with extraction of "which car") combined with ATB (of "who"), is better than (69), where the CSC violation (with extraction of "which car") is not combined with ATB. Under the traditional CSC approach, both examples involve a CSC violation (we will see below that [70] involves an additional violation, which then means that [70] should actually be worse than [69] under the traditional CSC analysis). This is not the case under the current analysis, where the CSC is not violated in both of these examples. In particular, although (70) violates the traditional CSC, it does not violate the CSC under its deduction proposed here, since the CSC-"violating" extraction is covered up by an ATB dependency, as discussed above regarding (68) (which is the structure of [70] before movement from ConjP). (69), on the other hand, does violate the CSC even under the current approach. While the judgments are obviously subtle due to the complexity of the examples, (70) is indeed better than (69).

(69) *Koja kola$_i$ je [ubijedio Petra da kupi t$_i$] i [umalo nagovorio Ivana
 which car is persuaded Petar that buys and almost convinced Ivan
 da proda kuću]?
 that sells house
 'Which car did he persuade Petar to buy and almost convinced Ivan to sell the house?'

(70) ??Koga$_j$ je koja kola$_i$ [ubijedio t$_j$ da kupi t$_i$] i [umalo nagovorio t$_j$
 who is which car persuaded that buys and almost convinced
 da proda kuću]?
 that sells house
 'Who did he persuade to buy which car and almost convinced to sell the house?'

These examples then show that an ATB dependency can sneak in a violation of the traditional CSC: the fact that (70) is better than (69), which violates the CSC, indicates that (70) does not violate the CSC (the reason why [70] is still degraded is discussed below regarding [89]).

The same contrast is found in English, although it is weaker since wh-phrases must move to different +wh-SpecCPs in English, which results in a wh-island violation. The relevant examples are given below.

(71) ???*Which manuscript$_j$ do you wonder who$_i$ [John talked to e$_i$ about reviewing e$_j$] and [Peter talked to e$_i$ about publishing it]?*

(72) *Which manuscript$_j$ do you wonder whether [John talked to Mary about reviewing e$_j$] and [Peter talked to Bill about publishing it]?*

The examples are rather long with a number of movement/sideward-movement dependencies and involve extraction from an island, so they are all expected to be degraded. (We will see below [cf. [89]] that (71) involves an additional violation.) Still, (71) is judged as better than (72), on a par with the contrast in (69)–(70) (the contrast being weaker in [71]–[72] due to the factor noted above).

We thus have here another case where the CSC can be violated, namely, by piggybacking on ATB, which can be accounted for under the proposed approach to the CSC/ATB.

### 6.7.3 Non-ATB ATB

Under the current analysis it is actually in principle not necessary that the same element moves from each conjunct to void the CSC effect. In principle, a different element can move from each conjunct: this would suffice to delabel the conjuncts, voiding the CSC effect. However, the problem with such extraction is the intervention effect: the first conjunct intervenes for extraction from the second conjunct. The effect is voided with ATB under Nunes's account of ATB. The account, however, does not extend to non-ATB constructions. It thus appears that the intervention effect forces ATB: the reason why it must be the same element that moves from each conjunct is the intervention effect.

Nevertheless, let us try to take advantage of the fact that possessor/left-branch extraction (LBE) is possible from conjuncts in SC and see what happens with multiple LBE that extracts different left-branches from different conjuncts. An issue that would arise if multiple LBE were to be performed in the SC counterpart of *Mary likes whose house and which car* (as the input to LBE) is that the remnants of the extraction would participate in a coordination but there would be no coordinator there, since, as discussed above, the coordinator would be carried along under the movement of the wh-phrase in the second conjunct, which may raise a problem. Interestingly, this kind of multiple extraction is possible if the coordinator is repeated (as noted by S. Stjepanović, p. c.), as shown below with multiple AP LBE (see [84] for evidence that we are indeed dealing with movement here).[28]

---

[28] SC quite generally allows AP LBE; for relevant discussion see e.g. Bošković (2012, 2013a), Corver (1992), Stjepanović (2010), Talić (2019).

(73) ?Crvena$_i$ i   bijeli$_j$ su se meni   t$_i$ suknja i   t$_j$ kaput dopali.
red    and white are self me.DAT   dress and   coat pleased
'The red dress and the white coat pleased me.'

(74) ?Crvena$_i$, bijeli$_j$ i   šareni$_k$ su se meni   t$_i$ suknja, t$_j$ kaput i   t$_k$ šešir
red   white and colorful are self me.DAT   dress   coat and   hat
dopali.
pleased

It seems plausible that we are dealing here with pronunciation of a lower copy of the coordinator, which is needed to indicate coordination. In Bošković (2019) I argue that more is actually going on here: (73) involves formation of coordination after movement (i.e coordination-formation in the moved position of the APs).[29] Cases where structures that are typically formed by external merge are formed via internal merge have been noted before. One such case involves van Riemsdijk's (1989) regeneration in Germanic, where in a D-NP structure, NP undergoes movement, with another D merged with it in the moved position. At any rate, it is beyond the scope of this paper to tackle the issue of the possibility of coordination-formation after movement (see also Zhang 2010). The reader should just bear in mind the possibility that the coordination we see in the moved position in (73)–(74) is created after movement (see Bošković 2019), though nothing in the discussion below crucially depends on that.

Consider then (74), repeated below.

(75) ?Crvena$_i$, bijeli$_j$ i   šareni$_k$ su se meni   [t$_i$ suknja], [t$_j$ kaput] i   [t$_k$
red   white and colorful are self me.DAT   dress   coat and
šešir] dopali.
hat    pleased

---

It should be noted that there is an interfering factor with examples like (73)–(74) for some speakers. Under the most natural pronunciation, the fronted adjectives are focalized and followed by a pause. This creates an issue for clitic placement since *su* and *se* are enclitics. This kind of examples are, however, possible without clitics too, as shown by (i), from Bošković (2019) (see Bošković 2019 for counterparts of SC non-ATB ATB examples discussed in this section without clitics, where this interfering factor does not arise; all the relevant contrasts remain the same).

(i)   Crvene$_i$ i   bijele$_j$ ona suknje$_i$ i   kapute$_j$ prodaje.
red    and white she skirts   and coats   is.selling
'She is selling red skirts and white coats.'

**29** Recall that in SC, the second conjunct can move to SpecConjP, tucking in under the first conjunct, with the conjunction adjoining to it (see fn 25). Given this, I suggest in Bošković (2019) that the conjunction in (73) takes the rest of the clause as its complement, with the APs moving to the Specs of ConjP, the second AP tucking in under the first one, with the conjunction adjoining to the lower Spec, all of which are independently attested in SC (see Bošković 2019 for another possibility).

Note first that we are not dealing here with typical trace-voiding of intervention effects. We have seen that turning an intervener into a trace voids intervention effects: in (75), the interveners are not traces, only their edge is. Focusing on the first two conjuncts, in contrast to (63), where the whole first conjunct moves, in (75) only the edge of this conjunct moves. In other words, in (63) the intervener is a trace, in (75) only the edge of the intervener is a trace (see Bošković 2012 for arguments that AP is located at the TNP-edge in SC, which is actually what enables its extraction). (76) gives the relevant structure. This means we are not dealing here with run-of-the-mill trace-voiding of intervention effects.

(76)    white$_j$ [$_{TNP}$ t$_i$ dress] t$_j$

What is even more interesting is that ATB is forced here: (77), where extraction does not take place from the last conjunct, is unacceptable.

(77)    *Crvena$_i$ i     bijeli$_j$ su se meni     [t$_i$ suknja], [t$_j$ kaput] i     [šareni šešir]
        red         and white are self me.DAT       dress         coat     and colorful hat
        dopali.
        pleased

These examples raise a number of puzzling questions. First, how come the intervention effect is voided in (75), given that the intervener is not a trace, only its edge is. This is actually similar to the ATB case in (67), which shows that intervention is also voided under ATB. In (67), the potential intervener has a trace at its edge, just as in (75). However, the above analysis of (67) crucially appealed to the fact that (67) involves traditional ATB, applying to it Nunes's account of ATB. Under that analysis, movement from the second conjunct does not cross the first conjunct. Since under that analysis it is crucial that the construction involves traditional ATB, i. e. that it is the same element that is extracted from each conjunct, the analysis cannot be extended to (75). The lack of intervention effects is not the only puzzling aspect of (75). The contrast between (75) and (77) indicates that the ATB requirement is at work here. Extraction must take place from each conjunct. However, what is striking is that it is not the same element that is extracted from each conjunct, but different elements. An ATB requirement is then apparently imposed on a non-ATB construction (I will refer to this as non-ATB ATB). Moreover, this holds for (75), involving three conjuncts, but not for the CSC-exceptional case in (15), involving two conjuncts, i. e., the ATB requirement seems to be imposed in (78) but not (79).

(78)    NP&NP&NP

(79)    NP&NP

This is actually not quite correct. The ATB requirement is not imposed on (78) if extraction takes place from the first conjunct only.

(80) ?*Crvena$_i$ se meni [t$_i$ suknja], bijeli kaput i šareni šešir dopadaju.*
 red self me.DAT dress white coat and colorful hat pleasing
 'I like a red dress, white coat, and colorful hat.'

The number of conjuncts then does not matter but from which conjunct extraction takes place: if it takes place only from the initial conjunct, the ATB requirement is not imposed, if it takes place from a non-initial conjunct, it is imposed: extraction must then take place from each conjunct.

How can all these puzzling aspects of (75) and related constructions be accounted for? This section will propose an account of the paradigm in question that crucially relies on the labeling framework, hence it can be interpreted as providing evidence for it. What we are trying to capture is what I refer to as non-ATB ATB, where extraction must take place from each conjunct but it is different elements that are extracted from the conjuncts. Note first that the existence of non-ATB ATB is not surprising under the current approach, where to void the CSC it is simply necessary to extract from each conjunct (everything else being equal, which often it is not, due to the intervention effect that the first conjunct induces for extraction from the second conjunct). The timing of labeling and the satisfaction of CL will be important in the discussion below. In this respect, I will continue to assume that CL must be satisfied when ConjP is formed and that labeling occurs as soon as it is possible.

Crucial to the discussion below will be trace-voiding of intervention effects. The case we are considering here is different from those discussed in the literature in this respect. While in the standard cases the trace itself is the intervener, in the cases we are considering the trace is the edge of the intervener. We will see below that this can be naturally captured in the labeling framework. Due to the factors discussed below, the trace at the edge of the intervener here has the effect of turning the intervener into an unlabeled element. In other words, in the relevant cases where the intervention effect is voided, the intervening element is unlabeled (due to the presence of a trace at its edge, see below). This then leads me to propose (81), which, as discussed in section 6.1, is rather natural given the current understanding of intervention effects.

(81) Unlabeled elements do not function as interveners.

The intuition is the following: given that extraction from one conjunct that crosses another conjunct induces an intervention effect, the effect can be voided if the intervener is turned into an unlabeled element, given (81), which is precisely what extraction from the first conjunct does. So, not to induce an intervention effect, when extraction takes place from the second conjunct it also must take place from the first conjunct. Since all this affects labeling, CL will then force extraction from all conjuncts, even those that are not on the path of the extraction from a conjunct we are trying to "save".

The idea here is then to block labeling of the first conjunct in (75) at the point when extraction from the second conjunct takes place. There are several ways of implementing this. I will use here a particular implementation that relies on a proposal from work in progress that the presence of an uninterpretable feature blocks labeling via feature-sharing in XP-YP configurations (see also Bošković to appear a). I will also assume, following Bošković (2007), that movement in general is driven by the presence of an uninterpretable feature, uK, on the moving element. This proposal fits the labeling framework quite naturally. The natural expectation in this framework is that all, or at least most, movement is labeling-driven, i. e. it takes place to resolve labeling problems. This is in fact what occurs when XP and YP merge without feature-sharing: movement then takes place to resolve the labeling problem. What happens here is that the problem, and the reason for movement, is present in the pre-movement structure (I will refer to it as the base-position of movement). In other words, the base-position of movement drives the movement: something would go wrong in the base-position of movement if it doesn't take place—there is nothing in the higher structure that motivates it. This is in fact exactly the characteristic of Bošković's (2007) approach to movement, which is implemented through the presence of a uK feature on the moving element, which then forces movement (in other words, both the labeling approach of Chomsky 2013 and Bošković 2007 involve base- rather than target-driven movement). It therefore seems natural to adopt Bošković's uK assumption here. This means that in (82), *Jovanove* has the uK feature which drives the relevant movement operation: the uK feature blocks feature-sharing, with movement taking place to resolve the labeling problem. The labeling problem does not arise in (83), where the relevant uK feature is not present (it if were, *Jovanove* would have to move).[30]

(82)    *Jovanove$_i$ on voli   [t$_i$ knjige]*.
       John's    he loves   books

(83)    *On voli Jovanove knjige.*    (SC)

---

**30** I leave open whether a uK feature would block labeling more generally, including the head-phrase case (if the phrase has it; I also leave open whether head-movement is uK-driven in this manner).

To account for the non-ATB ATB paradigm we need to slightly complicate this overall picture. Moving elements always have a uK feature, which blocks labeling via feature-sharing. However, this uK feature can be added to the relevant element either before or after the relevant merger. If uK is added to XP prior to XP merging with YP, the presence of the uK feature will block feature-sharing, and labeling via feature-sharing, forcing XP to move. This is not the case if it is added after XP and YP undergo merger. Since labeling takes place as soon as it is possible, in this case XP and YP will be able to undergo feature-sharing and labeling.

Now, in (75), repeated below, for movement from the second conjunct to be able to cross the first conjunct the latter cannot be labeled so that it does not function as an intervener (cf. [81]).

(75) ?Crvena$_i$, bijeli$_j$ i  šareni$_k$ su se meni  [t$_i$ suknja], [t$_j$ kaput] i  [t$_k$ 
red   white and colorful are self me.DAT  dress   coat  and
šešir] dopali.
hat  pleased

This means that the edge of the first conjunct must also undergo movement, so that it can have the uK feature that blocks labeling. This uK feature is added to the AP prior to the AP-NP merger; it blocks feature-sharing so that the first conjunct is not labeled. But given CL, none of the conjuncts in (75) can then be labeled. This forces extraction out of each conjunct: each conjunct must "host" movement so that the labeling is blocked. This is indeed the case in (75). However, this is not the case in (77), repeated below, where no movement takes place out of the last conjunct.

(77) *Crvena$_i$ i  bijeli$_j$ su se meni  [t$_i$ suknja], [t$_j$ kaput] i  [šareni šešir]
red   and white are self me.DAT  dress   coat  and colorful hat
dopali.
pleased

The last conjunct is then labeled in (77) (recall that labeling occurs as soon as it is possible), while the other conjuncts are not—this yields a CL violation.

In (15), on the other hand, the uK feature is not added to the possessor immediately: the possessor first undergoes merger, which results in feature-sharing and labeling that in turn satisfies CL (the second conjunct is labeled). The uK feature is then added, with the possessor undergoing movement. This was not an option in (75)/(77) since movement from the second conjunct would then cross a labeled element, resulting in an intervention effect. uK must be added here to the relevant element in the first conjunct immediately so that this conjunct is not labeled. CL then forces all conjuncts not to be labeled, which in turn forces each conjunct to "host" extraction.

There is an issue of the ordering of AP-movements that needs to be clarified. Focusing on the first two conjuncts in (75), to void the intervention effect the first conjunct needs to be unlabeled at the point when movement from the second conjunct crosses it. The next phase head in (75) is v.[31] There are several possibilities here, bearing in mind Chomsky's assumption that in an XP-YP configuration that does not involve feature-sharing, turning XP or YP into a trace enables labeling (by the other element). Bošković (2012) and Despić (2011) argue that AP is base-generated at the edge of its TNP in SC, c-commanding out of it (see in fact [13]–these works show that SC possessors are actually APs morphologically and structurally). We can then assume that all movements to the same phase head take place simultaneously, with the order of the moved elements reflecting their c-command relations before the movement. Alternatively, the first AP, which c-commands the second AP, can move before the second AP if we assume either that the next round of labeling occurs at the next phasal level, when the phase is completed (see Chomsky 2013, this means only after all movements to the edge of the vP phase take place) or that movements to the edge of the same phase that create multiple Specs are a single operation that cannot be split by anything else: only after all these movements take place other operations, including labeling that is made possible by traces, can take place. On all these options the first conjunct is unlabeled when movement from the second conjunct crosses it. AP-movement from the second conjunct to the vP phase could even in principle be allowed to take place before AP-movement from the first conjunct given that, as noted above, in the cases under consideration the co-ordination structure is in a sense "re-created" in a higher position, with another ConjP. As noted in Bošković (2019), it seems natural to assume that there should be some parallelism between the two coordinations where the order of the conjuncts in the higher ConjP should correspond to their order in the lower ConjP. This would filter out derivations where this is not the case (the order of the conjuncts in the higher ConjP indeed corresponds to the lower ConjP, see Bošković 2019).[32]

---

[31] LBE with longer remnants in general sounds best if the remnant precedes the verb (I assume it is VP-adjoined in [75]).

[32] If the multiple vPSpecs could in principle move higher up in any order, the orders not conforming with the parallelism would then be filtered out.

It should be noted that given (81), ATB cases like (67) could be accounted for even without sideward movement (only if the existence of a c-command relation between the moving elements or the presence of the higher ConjP is not crucially needed in implementing the order of the movements). The conjunct intervention effect would be voided in (67) under (81) given that the con-

Note that we are dealing with actual extraction in the relevant cases, as confirmed by their island-sensitivity. Thus, the presence of an adjunct island (the *because* clause) between the extracted APs and the remnant NPs causes ungrammaticality in (84).

(84) *\*Crvena, bijeli i   šareni je otišao zato što su se meni   suknja,*
   red   white and colorful is left   because are self me.DAT dress
   *kaput i   šešir dopali.*
   coat and hat   pleased
   'He left because I liked a red dress, white coat, and colorful hat.'

Interestingly, the non-ATB ATB whose existence was revealed by the discussion above can be mixed with true ATB. There are only two fronted APs in (85), with three nouns in the lower coordination. Yet, in contrast to (77), (85) is acceptable.

(85) ?*Crvena i   bijeli su se meni   suknja, kaput i   šešir dopali.*
   red   and white are self me.DAT dress   coat and hat pleased

However, (85) is acceptable only on a particular meaning: 'red dress, white coat, and white hat', where a traditional ATB dependency is formed between 'white coat' and 'white hat' with respect to 'white'. What makes this possible is that both 'coat' and 'hat' are masculine: the adjective that modifies them is also masculine (*crvena* and *suknja* are feminine).

(86) ?*Crvena$_i$ i   bijeli$_j$ su se meni   [t$_i$ suknja], [t$_j$ kaput] i   [t$_j$ šešir]*
   red   and white are self me.DAT   dress   coat and   hat
   *dopali.*
   pleased

Notice now that, in contrast to (85), (87) is unacceptable.

(87) *\*Bijeli i   crvena su se meni   kaput, suknja i   šešir dopali.*
   white and red   are self me.DAT coat   dress and hat pleased

Apparently, a traditional ATB dependency can only be formed between contigious NPs here. There can be no ATB between 'red dress' and 'red hat' since the adjective needs to agree with the nouns, which have different gender (*suknja* is

---

junct is unlabeled (being a target of successive-cyclic movement). However, it is not clear how certain more complicated cases discussed below that involve interaction between standard ATB and non-ATB ATB and parallelisms with PG constructions could be accounted for without Nunes's analysis, hence I continue to assume it below.

feminine, *šešir* masculine). Also, there can be no ATB between 'white coat' and 'white dress' since these nouns also have different gender (*kaput* is masculine, *suknja* feminine). Interestingly, there can apparently be no ATB between 'white coat' and 'white hat'. There is no gender disagreement here since the nouns have the same gender. We seem to be dealing here with a locality effect on traditional ATB-formation: it is not possible to skip an intervening NP.

(88) *Bijeli$_i$ i    crvena$_j$ su se meni    [t$_i$ kaput], [t$_j$ suknja] i    [t$_i$ šešir]
     white and red    are self me.DAT         coat        dress          and     hat
     *dopali.*
     pleased

This is rather interesting under the sideward-movement approach. Sideward movement was originally proposed by Nunes (2004) for PG constructions, to create a dependency that voids traditional islands. That we see a locality effect here is quite interesting from this perspective. It is a different kind of a locality effect though: it does not involve traditional islandhood, it is more akin to intervention effects (traditional islands and intervention effects are treated rather differently in the current theory; this was also the case with the GB accounts in Chomsky 1986 and Rizzi 1990, where they actually involved different configurations: domination vs c-command).

The effect in question, which I will refer to as the ban on non-contiguous ATB, is also at work in examples (70) and (71), discussed above. It contributes to the unacceptability of (71) and it is the reason for the degraded status of (70) (recall that, under the current analysis, in contrast to (69), (70) does not violate the CSC, hence the contrast between these examples). Thus, the ATB dependency between t$_j$-s in (70), repeated below, skips a potential ATB site (t$_i$).

(70) ??*Koga$_j$ je koja    kola$_i$ [ubijedio    t$_j$ da    kupi t$_i$] i    [umalo nagovorio t$_j$*
     who is which car       persuaded      that buys          and almost convinced
     *da    proda kuću]?*
     that sells house
     'Who did he persuade to buy which car and almost convinced to sell the house?'

It is apparently not possible to form an ATB dependency between e$_j$ and e$_k$ across e$_i$ in (89), while it is possible to form it between all three, or between e$_j$ and e$_k$ (see [86]), or e$_i$ and e$_j$, as in (90), with an ATB dependency between 'red dress' and 'red shirt' [*košulja* is feminine]).

(89)    e$_i$...e$_j$....e$_k$

(90) ?Crvena$_i$ i  bijeli$_j$ su se meni  [t$_i$ suknja], [t$_i$ košulja] i  [t$_j$ kaput]
red  and white are self me.DAT  dress  shirt  and  coat
dopali.
pleased

A similar effect is actually found with PGs, which Nunes also treats with sideward movement—we then may be dealing here with a more general effect on sideward movement. Thus, it is not possible to skip a potential PG site in (91).

(91)  a.  Who did you praise e to the sky [after criticizing e] [in order to surprise e]?
b.  Who did you praise e to the sky [after criticizing e] [in order to surprise **him**]?
c.  *Who did you praise e to the sky [after criticizing **him**] [in order to surprise e]?

(Nissenbaum 2000:547)

(92) gives PG examples that are closer to the ATB examples from above (c/d are more detailed representations of a/b). While both examples involve extraction from an island, (92b/d) is better than (92a/c): the former represents a sideward-movement dependency between e$_j$ and e$_k$ from (89) and the latter between e$_i$ and e$_k$, which violates the ban on non-contiguous sideward-movement.

(92)  a.  *Which article do you wonder who John talked to about reviewing after talking to?
b.  ??Which article do you wonder who John talked to about reviewing after printing?
c.  *Which article$_1$ do you wonder who$_2$ John talked [to t$_2$] [about reviewing t$_1$] after talking to PG$_2$?
d.  ??Which article$_1$ do you wonder who$_2$ John talked [to t$_2$] [about reviewing t$_1$] after printing PG$_1$?

Summing up, this section has revealed a new type of ATB, where movement must take place from each conjunct but different elements are moving from the conjuncts. That such cases exist is not surprising under the current account, which does not in principle require that the same element is extracted from the conjuncts. However, non-ATB ATB is rather limited due to other factors. One such factor concerns intervention effects, where higher conjuncts block extraction from lower conjuncts. We have, however, seen that in a particular context the intervention effect can be voided. It is well-known that traces void intervention effects. The discussion in this section has uncovered cases where intervention effects are voided if the edge of the intervener, rather than the intervener itself, is a trace. This trace-voiding intervention effect can be naturally captured in the labeling framework through the generalization that unlabeled elements do not function as interveners, a rather natural generalization given the nature of intervention effects, as noted in section 6.1.

Focusing on the non-ATB ATB case under consideration, extraction must occur from each conjunct although it is different elements that are extracted from the conjuncts. Under the proposed account, in this case the ATB requirement is also imposed by CL. For extraction from a lower conjunct to take place across a higher conjunct without an intervention effect, the edge of the conjunct that is crossed needs to be turned into a trace, the effect of which is that the higher conjunct is unlabeled at the relevant point of the derivation. CL then forces the edge of each conjunct to be a trace (even the lower conjuncts that are not crossed by the relevant movement), so that each conjunct is unlabeled. Each conjunct then must be extracted from even when different elements undergo extraction.

Before concluding this section I briefly note two additional candidates for non-ATB ATB.[33] As observed by Hiroaki Tada and Satoshi Oku (p. c.), Japanese numeral constructions may provide another such case. As noted above, extraction is possible from the first but not the second conjunct of coordinated ClassPs in Japanese (see [32], fn 23). Importantly, extraction from the second conjunct is possible if it also takes place from the first (non-clitic conjunction *sosite* can optionally occur between the fronted NPs in [94]).

(93) John-ga  [$_{VP}$ [$_{PP}$ yaoya-kara]     [mikan-o  3-ko] to  [banana-o
    John-NOM      vegetable.store-from orange-ACC 3-CL  and banana-ACC
    5-hon] katta.
    5-CL    bought
    'John bought [3 oranges and 5 bananas] from a vegetable store.'

(94) John-ga   mikan-o$_i$   (sosite) banana-o$_j$   yaoya-kara
    John-NOM orange-ACC and         banana-ACC vegetable.store-from
    (sorezore)    [t$_i$ 3-ko] to  [t$_j$ 5-hon] katta.
    respectively   3-CL  and    5-CL    bought
    (Hiroaki Tada, p. c.)

---

**33** The relevant constructions merit a much closer scrutiny than they can be given here. (I discuss non-ATB ATB, including limits and constraints on it, in more detail in Bošković [2019]. The reader is also refered to Bošković [to appear a] regarding an interfering factor that arises in this respect with *tough* constructions.)

These examples appear to represent another case of non-ATB ATB, where movement takes place out of each conjunct, but it is different elements that are moving (see Bošković 2019).

Furthermore, the ATB requirement is imposed here. Thus, (97), where extraction takes place from each conjunct, is better than (96), where extraction takes place from the first and the second, but not the third conjunct.

(95)  John-ga    yaoya-kara         [mikan-o   3-ko] to  [banana-o 5-hon]
      John-NOM vegetable.store-from orange-ACC 3-CL  and banana-ACC 5-CL
      to   [budou-o  2-fusa] katta.
      and grape-ACC 2-CL    bought
      'John bought 3 oranges, 5 bananas and 2 bunches of grapes from a vegetable store.'

(96)  ?*John-ga   mikan-o$_i$   (sosite) banana-o$_j$   yaoya-kara
       John-NOM orange-ACC and        banana-ACC vegetable.store-from
       (sorezore)   [t$_i$ 3-ko] to  [t$_j$ 5-hon] to  [budou-o 2-fusa] katta.
       respectively  3-CL and       5-CL     and grape-ACC 2-CL    bought

(97)  John-ga    mikan-o$_i$   (sosite) banana-o$_j$  (sosite) budou-o$_k$
      John-NOM orange-ACC and         banana-ACC and         grape-ACC
      yaoya-kara           (sorezore)   [t$_i$ 3-ko] to  [t$_j$ 5-hon] to  [t$_k$ 2-fusa]
      vegetable.store-from respectively  3-CL and        5-CL     and      2-CL
      katta.
      bought
      (Hiroaki Tada, p. c)

Another relevant case is discussed in Postal (1998) and Zhang (2010), who argue that each wh-phrase is separately extracted from the conjuncts in (98).[34]

(98) *Which book$_i$ and which magazine$_j$ did [John buy t$_i$] and [Bill read t$_j$] respectively?*

As noted in Bošković (2019), the ATB requirement is also imposed here, as the unacceptability of (99)–(100) shows.

---

**34** Postal gives strong evidence to this effect (note e. g. the possibility of binding into the individual conjuncts in *[Which man]$_i$ and [which woman]$_j$ did respectively the doctor talk to t$_i$ about himself$_i$ and the lawyer talk to t$_j$ about herself$_j$*; such licensing is also possible with parasitic gaps), and Zhang argues that (98) involves coordination-formation after movement (she also notes that *respectively* is not required, as shown by *The dogs and the roosters barked and crowed all night*).

(99) *Which book$_i$ and which magazine$_j$ did [John buy t$_i$], [Bill read t$_j$] and [Mary write a novel] respectively?

(100) *Which book$_i$ and which magazine$_j$ did [Mary write a novel], [John buy t$_i$] and [Bill read t$_j$] respectively?

I leave a detailed discussion of such cases for another occasion (see Bošković 2019), merely reiterating that the current approach does in principle allow non-ATB ATB.

## 6.8 Postal's exception

Postal (1998) discusses a semantically-defined context which allows extraction from conjuncts, where the conjuncts are temporally ordered, as in (101): the event characterized by the first conjunct precedes that of the second conjunct.

(101) a. *the stuff which$_i$ Arthur [sneaked in] and [stole t$_i$]*
(Postal 1998:53)
b. *Here's the whiskey which$_i$ I went to the store and [bought t$_i$].*
(Ross 1967:103)

There are strong constraints on such CSC violations. Thus, they are only possible with VP conjuncts.

(102) a. **the cheese which$_i$ Frank went to the store and his wife bought t$_i$*
b. *the book which$_i$ Gail will drive there and (*will) buy t$_i$*
(Postal 1998:58)

Furthermore, extraction is not possible from the first conjunct.[35]

(103) *What$_i$ did he [buy t$_i$], went home, and [ate t$_i$]?

When there are more than two conjuncts, extraction can occur from some, or all non-initial conjuncts—there is no ATB requirement.

(104) *the stuff which$_i$ Harry went to the store, bought t$_i$, went home, and ate t$_i$*
(Postal 1998:66)

The current analysis enables us to account for (101) as well as the restrictions from (102)–(103) and the lack of the ATB requirement displayed by (104). The construc-

---

[35] The last conjunct must be extracted from (see below), hence the trace in the last conjunct.

tion in question is clearly exceptional, hence it merits an analysis that is at least to some extent exceptional. I suggest that what is exceptional here is that the coordination is not fully parallel, the first conjunct is a vP while the other conjuncts are (or can be, see below) bare VPs. More precisely, given that the subject in traditional SpecvP does not undergo feature-sharing with its sister, which is a vP (see Chomsky 2013; the discussion in this section follows the first set of assumptions from fn 18), the first conjunct is actually unlabeled at the point when the coordination is formed. The suggestion is that this kind of coordination, which doesn't fully conform with CL, is only possible under the temporal sequence condition, which I assume also exceptionally licenses the "discharge" of the external θ-role of the verb in conjuncts where vP is not present. This immediately captures the bare-VP restriction, i. e. (102).

Regarding (103), the details of labeling are important. As noted above, what is exceptionally licensed regarding CL here is the situation where the first conjunct is unlabeled (recall that the subject in traditional SpecvP does not undergo feature-sharing) and other conjuncts are VPs. However, the extraction in (103) changes this situation. As discussed above, an object undergoing wh-movement undergoes object shift, the landing site of object shift being higher than the subject base-position. Object shift results in phi-feature-sharing, which labels the relevant phrase. This then departs from the exceptional labeling configuration noted above, which results in a CL violation.

Why is extraction from other conjuncts possible, in fact in a non-ATB manner (see [104])? This is surprising, since independently of CL, extraction that occurs in a non-ATB manner should yield an intervention effect. In fact, the first conjunct should be an intervener for any extraction from lower conjuncts, even if there is only a single extraction, as in (101). Recall, however, that the first conjunct is actually unlabeled in (101) and that unlabeled elements do not function as interveners. The first-conjunct intervention effect is then voided in (101).[36]

Why is it that lower conjuncts do not cause intervention effects either, as indicated by the fact that extraction from non-initial conjuncts need not proceed in an ATB manner (it need not affect each conjunct, cf. [104])? This is actually not surprising.[37] An ATB dependency can be formed via sideward movement between

---

[36] Recall that I assume that if labeling cannot occur immediately (which is the case with phrase-phrase merger configurations that do not involve feature-sharing), it occurs at the next phasal level. Subject movement to SpecTP will enable v to label. However, the labeling occurs only after the CP phase is completed, hence after wh-movement from the second conjunct to SpecCP (this wh-movement then crosses an unlabeled element).

[37] A clarification is in order regarding the PIC. In Uriagereka's (1999) original multiple spell-out proposal, not only the Spec of phase XP, but also its complement is accessible from the outside,

the two traces in (104), so that actual movement takes place only from the second conjunct, movement from this conjunct crossing only an unlabeled element, as discussed above.

This does not force movement to start from the second conjunct. Consider (105).

(105)     the cheese which$_i$ Harry [went to the store], [took out his wallet], [grabbed a five dolar bill], [bought t$_i$], [went home], [took a shower], and [then ate t$_i$] (Postal 1998:57)

The conjuncts above the *[bought t$_i$]* conjunct in (105) can all be (traditional) vPs (i. e. unlabeled; as discussed below, only the last conjunct must be a VP). Movement from the *[bought t$_i$]* conjunct then only crosses unlabeled elements (no problem arises with movement of the subject, which can proceed in ATB fashion from the vP conjuncts in question).

Interestingly, Postal (1998:75) notes that temporal CSC extractions are disalowed in French.

(106)     *le pain que$_1$ Jacques a couru au marché, acheté t$_1$, foncé chez luiz et mangé t$_1$
'the bread which$_1$ Jacques ran to the market, bought t$_1$, rushed home, and ate t$_1$'

What could be the relevant difference between French and English? I suggest it is the well-known difference regarding V-movement: French is a V-movement language and English isn't.[38] Lasnik (1995) analyzes this difference by positing a feature in the verb in French which requires French verbs to move, while no such feature is present in English verbs: they are lexically bare in the relevant sense, hence need not raise, undergoing PF merger with the inflectional affix under PF-adjacency. (As for the v-V relation, if there is V-to-v movement, not just PF merger between these heads in English, under Lasnik's approach it would be driven by a property of v, not V.) Given this, bare VP coordination is simply not possible in

---

only what is dominated by the complement is not. Bošković (2015) argues for a return to this conception of the PIC, a consequence of which is that a phasal complement need not move via the phasal edge. I also adopt it here. This means that movement from the VP conjunct in e. g. (101) need not proceed via the conjunct edge (not much would actually change if edge movement were to take place, we would only need to modify the condition under which temporal sequence conjuncts allow for a relaxation of CL).

**38** Even participles and infinitives raise in French (Pollock 1989, Belletti 1990).

French (since the verb must raise), it is only possible in bare non-featural V languages (in Lasnik's terms), where verbs do not raise.

The analysis predicts that examples like (101) will only be allowed in non-V-raising languages. While I leave a confirmation of the prediction for future research, I note here that they are disallowed in SC, also a V-movement language (Bošković 2001, Stjepanović 1999).

(107) *hljeb koji$_i$ se ušunja u prodavnicu i kupi t$_i$
bread which self sneaked-in to store and bought
'the bread which he sneaked into the store and bought.'

Postal (1998:59) also notes that temporal CSC extractions disallow *respectively* dependencies.

(108) *the wine and beer which$_1$ Jack and Bob will go to the store and buy t$_1$ respectively*

If such dependencies require the presence of the subject trace in the second conjunct, which seems plausible, (108) can also be captured under the current, bare VP analysis of temporal CSC extractions.

Finally, Postal (1998) and Lakoff (1986) note that extraction must occur from the last conjunct.

(109) *the stuff which$_i$ Harry went to the store, bought t$_i$, went home, and ate it* (cf. [104])

We have seen above (cf. [105]) that VP coordination need not start with the second conjunct. I suggest that only the last conjunct must be a VP and take the forced movement from the last conjunct to indicate that a bare VP cannot tolerate the presence of a lexical object. In fact, having in mind Chomsky's (2001) requirement that something must move out of vP, if the requirement holds for VP when there is no vP above it, object movement will be forced here (since the verb cannot move, and the subject is not even present). The suggestion can be tested with constructions not discussed by Postal and Lakoff, where the last conjunct has an intransitive verb. Such cases are also unacceptable, as shown by (110), as expected under the suggested account.

(110) *the stuff which$_i$ Harry went to the store, bought t$_i$, went home, and fell asleep*

## 6.9 Conclusion

The paper has proposed a deduction of one part of the CSC, namely the ban on extraction from conjuncts, which also captures the ATB exception. The paper has actually reformulated the traditional CSC based on a number of cases where extraction from conjuncts was shown to be possible. In particular, the CSC was shown to hold only for successive-cyclic movement from conjuncts, as in *$Who_i$ did you see $[t_i$ friends of $t_i]$ and Sue. The restriction of the CSC effect to successive-cyclic movement can be captured in Chomsky's (2013) labeling approach, where successive-cyclic movement changes the category of the element it targets. The gist of the account is the following: Conjuncts are phases. Movement from a conjunct then has to proceed successive-cyclically via the conjunct edge. Such successive-cyclic movement delabels the conjunct, changing its category. As a result, if movement takes place only from one conjunct, a violation of the Coordination-of-Likes requirement ensues, the violation being remedied if movement takes place from each conjunct, as with ATB.

The analysis restricts the CSC effect to successive-cyclic movement, which was shown to have strong empirical motivation based on a number of cases where elements which are base-generated at the conjunct edge, or move there independently of successive-cyclic movement, were shown to be extractable. These cases include left-branch extraction in SC, $r$-pronouns in Dutch, V-2 movement in German, clitic doubling in Dutch and Romance, quantifier-float in Japanese, article-incorporation in Galician, and object shift in English. The temporal sequence exception to the CSC was also accounted for. It was also shown that ATB-movement can license an additional extraction from a conjunct from which ATB-movement takes place. Furthermore, the discussion in the paper has revealed the existence of a new type of ATB where movement must take place out of each conjunct though it is not the same element that is extracted from the conjuncts, as in traditional ATB, but different elements.

The proposed analysis was shown to have a number of additional theoretical consequences. Thus, the paper has established the generalization that unlabeled elements do not count as interveners, a rather natural generalization given the nature of intervention effects, where features of the intervener matter (projecting features requires projecting a label, i. e. labeling). The discussion also shed light on the ban on wh-movement from SpecIP to SpecCP, which is widely observed crosslinguistically. I have argued for a return to split IP, in the spirit of Pollock (1989), and shown that subjects undergoing wh-movement cannot move to the highest projection in the split IP even when this movement is not immediately followed by movement to SpecCP. If the projection in question is involved in agreement-licensing, as in the original AgrsP/TP split, we can also account for the fact that in many languages subject wh-movement affects agreement.

Additionally, the paper has argued that conjuncts are phases and provided evidence for Nunes's sideward-movement account of ATB. Overall, to the extent that the proposed analysis is successful it provides evidence for the phase theory (including a particular contextual approach to phases) and Chomsky's (2013) system, which allows unlabeled elements during the derivation.

## Bibliography

Abels, Klaus. 2007. Towards a restrictive theory of (remnant) movement. *Linguistic Variation Yearbook* 7:57–120. https://doi.org/10.1075/livy.7.04abe (accessed 15 September 2019).

Beavers, John, & Ivan Sag. 2004. Coordinate ellipsis and apparent non-constituent coordination. *Proceedings of the International Conference on Head-Driven Phrase Structure Grammar* 11:48–69.

Belletti, Adriana. 1990. *Generalized verb movement*. Turin: Rosenberg and Sellier.

Belletti, Adriana. 2005. Extended doubling and the VP periphery. *Probus* 17 (1):1–35. https://doi.org/10.1515/prbs.2005.17.1.1 (accessed 15 September 2019).

den Besten, Hans, & Gert Webelhuth. 1990. Stranding. In Günther Grewendorf & Wolfgang Sternefeld (eds.), *Scrambling and Barriers*, 77–92. Amsterdam: John Benjamins.

Bobaljik, Jonathan, & Dianne Jonas. 1996. Subject positions and the roles of TP. *Linguistic Inquiry* 27 (2):195–236. https://www.jstor.org/stable/4178934 (accessed 15 September 2019).

Boeckx, Cedric. 2003. *Islands and chains*. Amsterdam: John Benjamins.

Boeckx, Cedric. 2007. *Understanding minimalist syntax*. Oxford: Blackwell.

Bošković, Željko. 1997a. *The syntax of nonfinite complementation: An economy approach*. Cambridge, MA: MIT Press.

Bošković, Željko. 1997b. On certain violations of the Superiority Condition, AgrO, and economy of derivation. *Journal of Linguistics* 33 (2):227–254. https://doi.org/10.1017/S0022226797006476 (accessed 15 September 2019).

Bošković, Željko. 2000. Sometimes in SpecCP, sometimes in-situ. In Roger Martin, David Michaels, & Juan Uriagereka (eds.), *Step by step: Essays on minimalist syntax in honor of Howard Lasnik*, 53–87. Cambridge, MA: MIT Press.

Bošković, Željko. 2001. *On the nature of the syntax-phonology interface: Cliticization and related phenomena*. Amsterdam: Elsevier.

Bošković, Željko. 2002. A-movement and the EPP. *Syntax* 5 (3):167–218. https://doi.org/10.1111/1467-9612.00051 (accessed 15 September 2019).

Bošković, Željko. 2004. Be careful where you float your quantifiers. *Natural Language and Linguistic Theory* 22 (4):681–742. https://doi.org/10.1007/s11049-004-2541-z (accessed 15 September 2019).

Bošković, Željko. 2005. On the locality of left branch extraction and the structure of NP. *Studia Linguistica* 59 (1):1–45. https://doi.org/10.1111/j.1467-9582.2005.00118.x (accessed 15 September 2019).

Bošković, Željko. 2007. On the locality and motivation of Move and Agree: An even more minimal theory. *Linguistic Inquiry* 38 (4):589–644. https://doi.org/10.1162/ling.2007.38.4.589 (accessed September 2019).

Bošković, Željko. 2008. On successive-cyclic movement and the freezing effect of feature checking. In Jutta Hartmann, Veronika Hegedűs, & Henk van Riemsdijk (eds.), *Sounds of silence: Empty elements in syntax and phonology*, 195–233. Amsterdam: Elsevier.

Bošković, Željko. 2011. Rescue by PF deletion, traces as (non)interveners, and the *that*-trace effect. *Linguistic Inquiry* 42 (1):1–44. https://doi.org/10.1162/LING_a_00027 (accessed September 2019).

Bošković, Željko. 2012. On NPs and clauses. In Günther Grewendorf & Thomas Zimmermann (eds.), *Discourse and grammar: From sentence types to lexical categories*, 179–242. Berlin: de Gruyter.

Bošković, Željko. 2013a. Phases beyond clauses. In Lilia Schürcks, Anastasia Giannakidou & Urtzi Etxeberria (eds.), *The nominal structure in Slavic and beyond*, 75–128. Berlin: De Gruyter.

Bošković, Željko. 2013b. Traces do not head islands: What can PF deletion rescue? In Yoichi Miyamoto, Daiko Takahashi, Hideki Maki, Masao Ochi, Koji Sugisaki, & Asako Uchibori (eds.), *Deep insights, broad perspectives: Essays in honor of Mamoru Saito*, 56–93. Tokyo: Kaitakusha.

Bošković, Željko. 2014. Now I'm a phase, now I'm not a phase: On the variability of phases with extraction and ellipsis. *Linguistic Inquiry* 45 (1):27–89. https://doi.org/10.1162/LING_a_00148 (accessed 15 September 2019).

Bošković, Željko. 2015. From the Complex NP Constraint to everything: On deep extractions across categories. *The Linguistic Review* 32 (4):603–669. https://doi.org/10.1515/tlr-2015-0006 (accessed 15 September 2019).

Bošković, Željko. 2016a. On the timing of labeling: Deducing Comp-trace effects, the Subject Condition, the Adjunct Condition, and tucking in from labeling. *The Linguistic Review* 33 (1):17–66. https://doi.org/10.1515/tlr-2015-0013 (accessed 15 September 2019).

Bošković, Željko. 2016b. Getting really edgy: On the edge of the edge. *Linguistic Inquiry* 47 (2):1–33. https://doi.org/10.1162/LING_a_00273 (accessed 15 September 2019).

Bošković, Željko. 2016c. What is sent to spell-out is phases, not phasal complements. *Linguistica* 56:25–56.

Bošković, Željko. 2018. On movement out of moved elements, labels, and phases. *Linguistic Inquiry* 49 (2):247–282. https://doi.org/10.1162/LING_a_00273 (accessed 15 September 2019).

Bošković, Željko. 2019. On the limits of across-the-board movement. Ms, University of Connecticut.

Bošković, Željko. to appear a. On smuggling, the freezing ban, labels, and *tough*-constructions. In Adriana Belletti & Christopher Collins (eds.), *Smuggling in syntax*. Oxford University Press.

Bošković, Željko. to appear b. On the Coordinate Structure Constraint, islandhood, phases, and rescue by PF-deletion. In George Fowler, James Lavine, and Ronald F. Feldstein (eds.), *A festschrift for Steven Franks*. Bloomington, IN: Slavica.

Bowers, John. 1993. The syntax of predication. *Linguistic Inquiry* 24 (4):591–656. https://www.jstor.org/stable/4178835 (accessed 15 September 2019).

Cecchetto, Carlo. 2000. Doubling structures and reconstruction. *Probus* 12 (1):93–126. https://doi.org/10.1515/prbs.2000.12.1.93 (accessed 15 September 2019).

Chaves, Rui. 2006. Coordination of unlikes without unlike categories. *Proceedings of the International Conference on Head-Driven Phrase Structure Grammar* 13, 102–122.
Chomsky, Noam. 1957. *Syntactic structures*. The Hague: Mouton.
Chomsky, Noam. 1986. *Barriers*. Cambridge, MA: MIT Press.
Chomsky, Noam. 1995. *The minimalist program*. Cambridge, MA: MIT Press.
Chomsky, Noam. 2000. Minimalist inquiries. In Roger Martin, David Michaels, & Juan Uriagereka (eds.), *Step by step: Essays on minimalist syntax in honor of Howard Lasnik*, 89–155. Cambridge, MA: MIT Press.
Chomsky, Noam. 2001. Derivation by phase. In Michael Kenstowicz (ed.), *Ken Hale: A life in language*, 1–52. Cambridge, MA: MIT Press.
Chomsky, Noam. 2008. On phases. In Robert Freidin, Carlos Otero, & Maria Zubizarreta (eds.), *Foundational issues in linguistic theory: Essays in honor of Jean-Roger Vergnaud*, 133–166. Cambridge: MIT Press.
Chomsky, Noam. 2013. Problems of projection. *Lingua* 130:33–49. https://doi.org/10.1016/j.lingua.2012.12.003 (accessed 15 September 2019).
Chomsky, Noam. 2015. Problems of projection: Extensions. In Elisa Di Domenico, Cornelia Hamann, & Simona Matteini (eds.), *Structures, strategies and beyond: Studies in honour of Adriana Belletti*, 3–16. Amsterdam: John Benjamins.
Cinque, Guglielmo. 1999. *Adverbs and functional heads*. Oxford: Oxford University Press.
Corver, Norbert. 1992. On deriving left branch extraction asymmetries: A case study in parametric syntax. *Proceedings of the North East Linguistics Society (NELS)* 22, 67–84.
van Craenenbroeck, Jeroen, & Marjo van Koppen. 2008. Pronominal doubling in Dutch dialects: Big DPs and coordinations. In Sjef Barbiers, Olaf Koeneman, Marika Lekakou, & Margreet van der Ham (eds.), *Microvariation in syntactic doubling*, 207–249. Bingley: Emerald.
Despić, Miloje. 2011. *Syntax in the absence of Determiner Phrase*. Storrs, CT: University of Connecticut dissertation.
Despić, Miloje. 2013. Binding and the structure of NP in Serbo-Croatian. *Linguistic Inquiry* 44 (2):239–270. https://doi.org/10.1162/LING_a_00126 (accessed 15 Spetember 2019).
Epstein, Samuel, & Daniel Seely. 2002. Rule applications as cycles in a level-free syntax. In Samuel Epstein & Daniel Seely (eds.), *Derivation and explanation in the Minimalist Program*, 65–89. Oxford: Blackwell.
Erlewine, Michael. 2016. Anti-locality and optimality in Kaqchikel Agent Focus. *Natural Language and Linguistic Theory* 34 (2):429–479. https://doi.org/10.1007/s11049-015-9310-z (accessed 15 September 2019).
Grosu, Alexander. 1973. On the nonunitary nature of the coordinate structure constraint. *Linguistic Inquiry* 4 (1):88–92. https://www.jstor.org/stable/4177753 (accessed 15 September 2019).
Johnson, Kyle. 2002. Restoring exotic coordinations to normalcy. *Linguistic Inquiry* 33:97–156.
Johnson, Kyle. 2009. Gapping is not (VP-) ellipsis. *Linguistic Inquiry* 40 (1):289–328. https://doi.org/10.1162/002438902317382198 (accessed 15 September 2019).
Kayne, Richard. 1989. Facets of Romance past participle agreement. In Paola Benincà (ed.), *Dialect variation and the theory of grammar*, 85–103. Dordrecht: Foris.
Kayne, Richard. 1994. *The antisymmetry of syntax*. Cambridge, MA: MIT Press.
Kayne, Richard. 2002. Pronouns and their antecedents. In Samuel Epstein & Daniel Seely (eds.), *Derivation and explanation in the Minimalist Program*, 133–166. Oxford: Blackwell.
Lakoff, George. 1986. Frame semantic control and the Coordinate Structure Constraint. *Proceedings of the Chicago Linguistic Society (CLS)* 22: 154–167.

Lasnik, Howard. 1995. Verbal morphology: *Syntactic structures* meets the Minimalist Program. In Héctor Campos and Paula Kempchinsky (eds.), *Evolution and revolution in linguistic theory: Essays in honor of Carlos Otero*, 251–275. Washington, D.C.: Georgetown University Press.

Lasnik, Howard. 1999. *Minimalist analysis*. Oxford: Blackwell.

Machado-Rocha, Ricardo. 2016. *O redobro de clítico no português brasileiro dialetal*. Belo Horizonte: Universidade Federal de Minas Gerais dissertation.

McCloskey, James. 2000. Quantifier float and *wh*-movement in an Irish English. *Linguistic Inquiry* 31 (1):57–84. https://doi.org/10.1162/002438900554299 (accessed 15 September 2019).

Messick, Troy. 2020. The derivation of highest subject questions and the nature of the EPP. *Glossa: A Journal of General Linguistics* 5 (1):13. 1–12. http://doi.org/10.5334/gjgl.1029 (accessed 30 May 2020). Rutgers University.

Mizuguchi, Manabu. 2014. Phases, labeling, and *wh*-movement of the subject. Paper presented at English Linguistic Society of Japan 32, Gakushuin University, 8–9 November.

Müller, Gereon. 2010. On deriving CED effects from the PIC. *Linguistic Inquiry* 41 (1):35–82. https://doi.org/10.1162/ling.2010.41.1.35 (accessed 15 September 2019).

Nissenbaum, Jon. 2000. *Investigations of covert phrase movement*. Cambridge, MA: MIT dissertation.

Nunes, Jairo, 2004. *Linearization of chains and sideward movement*. Cambridge: MIT Press.

Oda, Hiromune. 2017. Two types of the Coordinate Structure Constraint and rescue by PF deletion. *Proceedings of the North East Linguistics Society (NELS)* 47:343–356.

Oda, Hiromune. 2019. Decomposing and deducing the Coordinate Structure Constraint. Ms., University of Connecticut.

Pollock, Jean-Yves. 1989. Verb movement, Universal Grammar, and the structure of IP. *Linguistic Inquiry* 20 (3):365–424. https://www.jstor.org/stable/4178634 (accessed 15 September 2019).

Postal, Paul. 1998. *Three investigations of extraction*. Cambridge, MA: MIT Press.

Rackowski, Andrea, & Norvin Richards. 2005. Phase edge and extraction: A Tagalog case study. *Linguistic Inquiry* 36 (4):565–599. https://doi.org/10.1162/002438905774464368 (accessed 15 September 2019).

Richards, Norvin. 2001. *Movement in language*. Oxford: Oxford University Press.

van Riemsdijk, Henk. 1989. Movement and regeneration. In Paola Benincà (ed.), *Dialect variation and the theory of grammar*, 105–136. Dordrecht: Foris.

Rizzi, Luigi. 1990. *Relativized Minimality*. Cambridge, MA: MIT Press.

Rizzi, Luigi. 2016. Labeling, maximality and the head-phrase distinction. *The Linguistic Review* 33 (1):103–127. https://doi.org/10.1515/tlr-2015-0016 (accessed 15 September 2019).

Ross, John Robert. 1967. *Constraints on variables in syntax*. Cambridge, MA: MIT dissertation.

Runić, Jelena. 2014. *A new look at clitics, clitic doubling, and argument ellipsis: Evidence from Slavic*. Storrs, CT: University of Connecticut dissertation.

Sag, Ivan, Gerald Gazdar, Thomas Wasow, and Steven Weisler. 1985. Coordination and how to distinguish categories. *Natural Language and Linguistic Theory* 3 (2):117–171. https://doi.org/10.1007/BF00133839 (accessed 15 September 2019).

Saito, Mamoru. 2016. (A) case for labeling: Labeling in languages without phi-feature agreement. *The Linguistic Review* 33 (1):129–175. https://doi.org/10.1515/tlr-2015-0017 (accessed 15 September 2019).

Schachter, Paul. 1977. Constraints on coordination. *Language* 53 (1):86–103. https://www.

jstor.org/stable/413057 (accessed 15 September 2019).
Shlonsky, Ur. 2015. A note on labeling, Berber states and VSO order. In Sabrina Bendjaballah, Noam Faust, Mohamed Lahrouchi, & Nicola Lampitelli (eds.), *The form of structure, the structure of form: Essays in honor of Jean Lowenstamm*, 349–360. Amsterdam: John Benjamins.
Stjepanović, Sandra. 1999. *What do second position cliticization, scrambling, and multiple wh-fronting have in common*. Storrs, CT: University of Connecticut dissertation.
Stjepanović, Sandra. 2010. Left branch extraction in multiple wh-questions: A surprise for question interpretation. In Wayles Browne, Adam Cooper, Alison Fisher, Esra Kesici, Nikola Predolac, & Draga Zec (eds.), *Proceedings of Formal Approaches to Slavic Linguistics (FASL) 18*, 502–517. Ann Arbor: Michigan Slavic Publications.
Stjepanović, Sandra. 2014. Left branch extraction and the Coordinate Structure Constraint. *Proceedings of the North East Linguistics Society (NELS)* 44:157–170.
Stjepanović, Sandra. to appear. Extraction out of Coordinate Structure Conjuncts. In Tania Ionin and Jonathan MacDonalds (eds.), *Proceedings of Formal Approaches to Slavic Linguistics (FASL) 26*. Ann Arbor, MI: Michigan Slavic Publications.
Takahashi, Daiko. 1994. Minimality of movement. Storrs, CT: University of Connecticut dissertation.
Talić, Aida. 2019. Upward P-cliticization, accent shift, and extraction out of PP. *Natural Language and Linguistic Theory* 39 (3):1103–1143. https://doi.org/10.1007/s11049-018-9424-1 (accessed 15 September 2019).
Ticio, Emma. 2003. *On the structure of DPs*. Storrs, CT: University of Connecticut dissertation.
Torrego, Esther. 1987. On empty categories in nominals. Ms., University of Massachusetts, Boston.
Uriagereka, Juan. 1988. *On government*. Storrs, CT: University of Connecticut dissertation.
Uriagereka, Juan. 1995. Aspects of the syntax of clitic placement in Western Romance. *Linguistic Inquiry* 26 (1):79–123. https://www.jstor.org/stable/4178889 (accessed 15 September 2019).
Uriagereka, Juan. 1999. Multiple Spell-Out. In Samuel Epstein & Norbert Hornstein (eds.), *Working minimalism*, 251–282. Cambridge, MA: MIT Press.
Watanabe, Akira. 1993. *AGR-based Case theory and its interaction with the A'-system*. Cambridge, MA: MIT dissertation.
Watanabe, Akira. 2006. Functional projections of nominals in Japanese: Syntax of classifiers. *Natural Language and Linguistic Theory* 24 (1):241–306. https://doi.org/10.1007/s11049-005-3042-4 (accessed 15 September 2019).
Williams, Edwin. 1978. Across-the-board rule application. *Linguistic Inquiry* 9 (1):31–43. https://www.jstor.org/stable/417803 (accessed 15 September 2019).
Wurmbrand, Susi. 2013. QR and selection: Covert evidence for phasehood. *Proceedings of the North East Linguistics Society (NELS)* 42:619–632.
Zhang, Niina. 2010. *Coordination in syntax*. Cambridge: Cambridge University Press.
Zwart, Jan-Wouter. 1993. *Dutch syntax: A minimalist approach*. Groningen: University of Groningen dissertation.

Ivona Kučerová
# 7 Labeling as two-stage process: Evidence from semantic agreement

**Abstract:** This chapter provides novel empirical evidence that the distinction between grammatical and semantic agreement can be tied to two stages of labeling of a phase, namely, labeling by features projected from narrow syntax and labeling by the syntax-semantics interface (CI) (Chomsky, 2013, 2015). I use the term grammatical agreement as a shortcut for a morphological realization of features projected to the label from narrow syntax, be they valued or unvalued (then the morphology realizes them as a morphological default), and semantic agreement for a morphological realization of the feature representation provided during labeling by CI. The latter morphological realization is faithful to the intended semantic denotation but does not necessarily isomorphically realize $\phi$-feature bundles present in narrow syntax (e. g., feminine gender on anaphors referring to grammatically neuter nouns, as in German *Mädchen* 'girl'; Wurmbrand 2017). The distinction between the two types of feature bundles in the label can be empirically distinguished when we compare the locality domains of syntactic relations based on agree, and locality domains mediated by phase heads (anaphoric agreement). I argue that agree must be based on features projected from narrow syntax, and only as last resort the valuation may reflect features from the CI labeling. In contrast, anaphoric relations are primarily based on CI labeled features.

The proposal furthers our understanding of locality restrictions on grammatical versus semantic agreement and provides a principled account of otherwise puzzling locality differences. Furthermore, it contributes to our understanding of the representation of labels and the division of labor among modules of the grammar. Under the proposed model, syntax is a fully autonomous module, with no recourse to semantic information. Instead, interpretability of features arises only at the syntax-semantics interface. No notion of (un)interpretable features as, e. g., in Smith (2015), is needed. Empirical support for the proposal comes from nominal, anaphoric and conjunct agreement in Italian, Czech and English.

## 7.1 Introduction

Under the Y-model, narrow syntax builds structure and the interfaces interpret it. The notion of interpretability is, however, multiply ambiguous: while at the syntax-morphology branch interpretability means that the output of the narrow-syntax computation is readable and realizable by the morphology module (as in the Distributed Morphology framework, e.g., Halle and Marantz 1993), the syntax-semantics interface ultimately yields an interpretation in a compositional semantics sense (see, for instance, the explicit model presented in Heim and Kratzer 1998) but the primary purpose of the syntax-semantics interface is presumably parallel to that of the syntax-morphology interface, i.e., to make the narrow-syntax representation legible and realizable by the semantic module. Neither of these notions of interpretability matches the original notion of interpretable versus uninterpretable syntactic features of Chomsky (2000) and following work where the notion of interpretability concerns feature checking prior the narrow-syntax representation is externalized via the interfaces.

The lack of terminological clarity becomes particularly problematic in the domain of semantic interpretability of $\phi$-features. Some authors argue that features like gender and number come to the narrow syntax derivation in two flavors: some instances of gender and number features are purely formal, while others are semantically interpretable. The proposals tend to associate the interpretable $\phi$-features with a higher functional projection, such as D, and the formal version with a lower projection, such as n (sometimes directly, sometimes via another semantically interpretable feature, such as humanness, e.g., Veselovská 1998, Kramer 2009, Pesetsky 2013, Smith 2015, Landau 2016), or they leave the distinction purely to the interpretability of the feature (Kramer 2015). Some authors, most prominently Wiltschko (2009), explore the idea that the difference is not only that of a structural height but of syntactic complementation versus adjunction as well.

This chapter puts forward a rather different view that fully utilizes the Y-model architecture, i.e., it is centered around syntax as a combinatorial module which does not utilize any semantic information. In particular, I argue that there is no notion of semantic interpretability within the narrow syntax module. Instead, $\phi$-features become interpretable only in the course of the derivation, namely, at the syntax-semantics interface, as part of a two-stage labeling of phases: first by features projected from narrow syntax, then by features labeled by the syntax-semantics interface (CI; Chomsky 2013, 2015). The role of phase heads is then to map narrow syntax features (first labeling stage) onto features within the phase label making them legible to the semantics module (second labeling stage). Since these features become associated with semantically interpreted objects, they become indirectly interpretable via these objects. Furthermore, I argue that the association can yield a new set of $\phi$-features that can value features left unvalued from narrow syntax and can participate in processes mediated by phase heads, such as anaphoric agreement (e.g., Kratzer 2009). Thus, there is only one type of $\phi$-features in narrow syntax. The appearance of a structurally higher features being interpretable is a direct consequence of the role of phase heads (D for gender and number) in mapping narrow-syntax representations onto the syntax-semantics interface. This chapter explores two interrelated sets of data that support this theoretical position: the so called semantic versus grammatical agreement, and anaphoric agreement. The empirical novelty of the chapter lies in its focus on locality restrictions on interpretability of $\phi$-features, instead of on the question of interpretability of $\phi$-features per se, thus highlighting the role of the individual grammar modules and uncovering new empirical patterns.

## 7.2 Grammatical versus semantic agreement within and with nominals

Most of the current theoretical work that recognizes that only some $\phi$-features are semantically interpreted, while others are not, centers on two empirical phenomena: (i) nominals with a set of grammatical $\phi$-features that do not match the intended interpretation, and (ii) nominals with a set of grammatical $\phi$-features that matches more than one semantic interpretation. The former case can be exemplified by nouns like *děvče* 'girl' in Czech or *Mädchen* 'girl' in German (e. g., Wurmbrand 2017). The gender of these nouns is grammatically neuter but the noun itself denotes a female. As the Czech examples in (1) demonstrate, such a noun obligatorily triggers neuter agreement in a local agree domain (subject-predicate agreement, agreement within the extended nominal projection); however, cross-sentential agreement can either be neuter or feminine. I. e., the agreement can match the morpho-syntactically realized gender (here, neuter), or it can match the semantically intended gender (here, feminine).

(1) To/ *ta pracovité/ *pracovitá děvče šlo/ *šla
that.N.SG/ *F.SG industrious.N.SG/ *F.SG girl.N.SG went.N.SG/ *F.SG
na jahody. Hned jich mělo/ měla plný košík.
on strawberries immediately of_them had.N.SG/ F.SG full basket
'The industrious girl went strawberry-picking. She quickly filled a basket.'

As (2) demonstrates, anaphoric agreement can switch between grammatical and semantic agreement even within the same clause. Since Czech is a pro-drop language, a cross-sentential agreement is mediated by an anaphoric agreement[1] be-

---

[1] I use the term anaphoric agreement somewhat loosely to have a cover term for a valuation of $\phi$-features on pronouns.

tween a pro element and the linguistic antecedent present in the previous sentence. Thus, a local agreement must be based on agree with the morpho-syntactic features of the nominal but the anaphoric relation can be based either on the morpho-syntactic features realized on the nominal, or on the $\phi$-features matching the intended interpretation (feminine for a female).[2]

(2) Petr podal děvčeti jeho/ její kabát.
 Petr passed to-girl.N.SG its/ her coat
 'Petr gave the girl$_i$ her$_i$ coat.'

Note that Czech is a *pro*-drop language. This means that a cross-sentential agreement in (1) is mediated by an anaphoric agreement between a *pro* and the linguistic antecedent present in the previous sentence.[3] I argue that the cross-sentential agreement and the anaphoric agreement have the same structural underpinning, albeit in distinct locality domains. Thus the cut between grammatical and semantic agreement is not between a local and long-distance agree but between agree and whatever operation underlies the anaphoric relation. The descriptive generalization of the pattern we have seen so far is given in (3).

(3) *Descriptive generalization for type 'girl.N' nouns:*
 a. A local agreement must be based on agree with the morpho-syntactic features of the nominal. [in our examples, neuter]
 b. An anaphoric agreement (relation) can be based either on the morpho-syntactic features realized on the nominal, or on the $\phi$-features match-

---

[2] Nothing in the basic characterization hinges on Czech being a *pro*-drop language. We could replace the covert pronominal subjects of (1) with their overt counterpart, as in (i). The profile of the data doesn't change but the examples are downgraded because overt pronominal subjects are natural only in contrastive contexts or as expletives.

(i) To/ *ta pracovité/ *pracovitá děvče šlo/ *šla na jahody.
 that.N.SG/ *F.SG industrious.N.SG/ *F.SG girl.N.SG went.N.SG/ *F.SG on strawberries
 'The industrious girl went strawberry-picking.'
 a. ?Ono jich hned mělo plný košík.
  3.SG.N of_them immediately had.N.SG full basket
 b. ?Ona jich hned měla plný košík.
  3.SG.F of_them immediately had.F.SG full basket
 'She quickly filled a basket.'

[3] The anaphoric agreement must refer to the linguistic antecedent, otherwise the grammatical – neuter – agreement would be unexpected.

ing the intended interpretation. [in our examples, neuter or feminine for a female][4]

The pattern is reminiscent of the behavior of so called imposters, i. e., nominals which grammatical features do not match their intended interpretation, as in English *yours truly* (e. g., Collins and Postal 2012). While subject-predicate agreement with imposters is strictly based on their morpho-syntactic φ-features, (4), their locally bound pronouns can either share the morpho-syntactically expressed φ-features of its antecedent, or can be based on the intended interpretation, as in (5).

(4)   Yours truly is/*am unhappy.

(Collins and Postal, 2012, 3, (5c))

(5)   Your Majesty should praise yourself / herself.

(Collins and Postal, 2012, vii, (1b))

The variability in the morphological expression of the anaphor is licensed only if the immediate antecedent is an imposter. If the immediate antecedent is a pronoun referring back to the imposter, then the morphological form of the anaphor is strictly based on the morphological features of the pronoun, not that of the preceding imposter, as in (6).

(6)   a.   The present authors$_1$' children feel that they$_1$ need to defend their$_1$ interests.
      b.   The present authors$_1$' children feel that we$_1$ need to defend our$_1$ interests.
      c.   *The present authors$_1$' children feel that they$_1$ need to defend our$_1$ interests.
      d.   *The present authors$_1$' children feel that we$_1$ need to defend their$_1$ interests.

(Collins and Postal, 2012, 141, (2))

Thus, non-pronominal DPs can give rise to two distinct anaphoric agreement patterns but pronouns cannot.

(7)   *Descriptive generalization of variability in anaphoric agreement:*
      Only non-pronominal DPs can give rise to two distinct anaphoric agreement patterns.

---

[4] In a language with different markedness properties, for example, Arabic where feminine is default, the concrete features would play out differently but the general characterization in terms of morpho-syntactic features versus the intended interpretation is expected to remain unchanged.

Two interrelated questions arise: (i) Under what conditions can $\phi$-features on a nominal yield a new set of features, namely, features that match the intended semantic interpretation?, and (ii) What is the structural underpinning of anaphoric agreement and why does its locality domain differ from syntactic agree?

Before we can answer these questions we need to consider another set of nominals, i.e., those in which the morpho-syntactically realized $\phi$-features yield more than one interpretation. This group of nominals can be exemplified by Russian nominals such as *vrač* 'doctor', i.e., nominals that morphologically appear to be masculine but if the intended referent is female, these nominals trigger feminine agreement in their local domain (e.g., extended nominal projection; see, e.g., Corbett 1983 and Pesetsky 2013). Italian nouns of profession, such as *chirurgo* 'surgeon' exhibit the same pattern (e.g., Kučerová 2018). If the noun denotes a male (or is unspecified for natural gender), all agreeing elements must be masculine, as in (8). In contrast, if such a noun denotes a female, the predicate agreement is feminine but the agreement within the extended nominal domain can either be feminine or masculine, as in (9).[5]

(8)  il       chirurg-o  è    andat-o  
     the.M  surgeon.M  has  gone.M  
     'the (male) surgeon is gone'

(9)  a.  la       chirurgo  è    andat-a  
         the.F  surgeon    has  gone.F  
     b.  il       chirurgo  è    andat-a  
         the.M  surgeon    has  gone-F  
         'the female surgeon is gone'

Crucially, the switch in the local agreement pattern, as in (9), is subject to markedness. I.e., a morphologically masculine noun can trigger feminine predicate agreement but a morphologically feminine noun cannot trigger a masculine predicate agreement, as in (10). See also Bobaljik and Zocca (2011) for a discussion of cross-linguistic prevalence of markedness in these patterns.

---

**5** If the noun is morphologically marked as feminine, all agreeing elements must be feminine, as in (i). I take these cases aside as they are orthogonal to the main focus of this chapter.

(i)  la       chirurg-a  è    andat-a  
     the.F  surgeon-F  has  gone.F  
     'the female surgeon is gone'

(10) La/ *il brava/ *bravo guarda si e'persa nel
the.F.SG/ M.SG good.F.SG/ M.SG guard.F.SG her/him lost.F.SG in the
bosco.
woods
'The guard lost his/her way in the forest.'
(modeled after Ferrari-Bridgers 2007)

The markedness restriction, however, only holds for a local agreement. The anaphoric agreement can freely be based on the intended gender even if the antecedent is in a morphologically marked form and triggers obligatory marked (feminine) agreement, as in (11) from Czech.

(11) Viděls tu/ *toho vysokou/ *vysokého osobu$_i$, co
saw-you that.ACC.F.SG/ M.SG tall.ACC.F.SG/ M.SG person.F.SG what
stála/ *stál u baru?
stood.ACC.F.SG/ M.SG by bar
'Did you see that tall person$_i$ that stood by the bar?'
  a. Marie mi ho$_i$ představila.
     Marie to-me him introduced
     'Marie introduced him$_i$ to me.'
  b. Marie mi ji$_i$ představila.
     Marie to-me her introduced
     'Marie introduced her$_i$ to me.'

The markedness restriction is not limited to the masculine-feminine opposition. As the Czech example in (12) demonstrates, neuter nouns in a three-gender system match the behavior of feminine nouns, i. e., local agree is obligatorily determined by the grammatical features of the noun but anaphoric agreement can be based either on grammatical (here, neuter), or semantic features (masculine, feminine).

(12) Přišlo tam takové vyžle. Marii se
came.N.SG there such.N.SG skinny_person.N.SG Marie.DAT REFL
nelíbil/ nelíbila/ ?nelíbilo.
not-liked.M.SG/ F.SG/ N.SG
'There was a skinny person$_i$ there. Marie didn't like him$_i$/ her$_i$/ them.SG$_i$.'

Thus with respect to locality of agreement, nouns like *osoba* and *guarda* behave like *děvče* in that agree with them is based on the grammatical gender but anaphoric agreement with them is variable.

The only difference is that while the morpho-syntactic gender on *děvče* never matches the intended semantic interpretation (feminine), the morpho-syntactic gender on *osoba* and *guarda* (feminine) can. Note also that the grammatical gender of 'girl' type nouns never matches the intended semantic interpretation (natural gender). The grammatical gender of 'person' type nouns can (*osoba* 'person.F' can denote a female) but not always (*vyžle* 'skinny person.N') which is a direct consequence of the lexical underspecification of the natural gender of the referent for this type of nouns. The interaction of grammatical features and the intended interpretation is summarized in (13).[6]

(13) *Does agreement match gender-features morphologically expressed on the nominal, or the intended interpretation? (descriptive summary for a 3-way gender system)*

|  | type 1 (*děvče* 'girl.N') | unmarked type 2 (*chirurgo* 'surgeon.M') | marked type 2 (*osoba* 'person.F') |
|---|---|---|---|
| agr within DP | features | either | features |
| subj-pred agr | features | interpretation | features |
| anaphoric agreement | either | either | either if n, otherwise interpretation |

---

[6] For reasons of space, this chapter entirely leaves out interactions of grammatical versus semantically-interpretable number. Number is also subject to this type of variation, as witnessed by nouns of the committee type in English, and there is a distinction between number based on the intended interpretation (the more frequent case, as in *a pen* vs *pens*; see, e. g., Kratzer 2009 for an argument that number is primarily semantic) and grammatical number of pluralia tantum (e. g., Corbett 2000). As an anonymous reviewer correctly pointed out, number seems to differ from gender in that it allows a switch to the intended interpretation in a local agree relation, as in (i). However, there is a non-trivial confound: Cases of local semantic agreement I am familiar with involve movement which affects locality. As pointed out by Sauerland and Elbourne (2002), the plural agreement with collective nouns in English requires a wide-scope reading of the nominal. Similarly, Babyonyshev (1997) ties the emergence of semantic agreement with numerals in Russian to derived positions as well. To fully explore the similarities and possible differences between gender and number goes beyond the scope of this chapter.

(i) A northern team is/are certain to be in the final.
  a. is: ∃ > certain, certain > ∃
  b. are: ∃ > certain, *certain > ∃

(Sauerland and Elbourne, 2002, 288, (14))

The other difference is that number value is in and of itself semantically interpreted but gender only triggers a presupposition. It is not obvious whether the interpretive difference has a syntactic counterpart in the type of features number and gender are in narrow syntax. Note, for example, that for Kratzer (2009) number is not associated with a DP but it arises only at the level of vP. Thus, if there is a number feature in the narrow syntax of a DP it must be a different object that the semantic number Kratzer is interested in.

Thus marked type 2 nouns ('person') can be unified with type 1 nouns ('girl') but unmarked type 2 nouns ('surgeon') seem to differ. Yet, I argue we can unify them as well but we will have to take into account a morphological realization of unvalued syntactic features.

Before we proceed with the discussion, a note on existing literature is in order. The fact that values of $\phi$-features do not always match their denotation, and that under such conditions, some grammatical processes may be based on the 'semantically informed' value of the feature has previously been accounted for by proposing that there is more than one gender feature in the structure: one interpretable, one uninterpretable, with the interpretable feature often being merged higher (e. g., Kramer 2009, 2015, Pesetsky 2013, Smith 2015, Landau 2016, Wurmbrand 2017). Putting aside the non-trivial theoretical consequences of semantic information being part of the narrow-syntax computation,[7] it is not clear how this line of reasoning could account for the full range of the data discussed in this chapter, especially the locality properties. If a probe unselectively probes for a gender feature, the interpretable feature should always be closer. In turn, we wouldn't expect to see the distinction between local agree and anaphoric agreement, of the type discussed for *děvče*, (1)–(2). If the probe was selective, then we should never find optionality within anaphoric agreement and we shouldn't see a split between agree within an extended nominal projection in contrast to subject-predicate agreement, as in (9). If such a split was explainable, let say, by the height of the interpretable feature, we would expect the split to appear everywhere, not only with morphologically unmarked gender, i. e., for instance, (10) should have the same agreement profile as (9), contrary to the facts.

## 7.3 Proposal: What is in the label?

The empirical pattern discussed in the previous section raises two questions: (i) Under what conditions can $\phi$-features on a nominal yield a new set of features, namely, features that match the intended semantic interpretation?, and (ii) What is the structural underpinning of anaphoric agreement and why does its locality domain differ from syntactic agree? We will start by answering the former question. The proposed answer will then naturally extend to the latter question as well (to be discussed in section 7.3.3).

---

[7] Assuming 'interpretable' features in narrow syntax seems to be a remnant of Generative Semantics. Such an assumption is incompatible with the Y-model.

The core observation is that the relevant $\phi$-feature variation manifests itself only in agreement. I assume that agreement is a morphological realization of a syntactic relation, namely, agree. Since agree targets labels as a representation of a more complex syntactic structure, in order to understand agreement patterns, we must first understand what $\phi$-features are in the label.[8] I will argue that in order to account for the empirical distinction between grammatical and semantic agreement, we have to explore not only what features form a label but also at what point of the derivation, the label gets established. Concretely, I will propose that grammatical agreement is based on an early stage of labeling, namely, that associated with feature projection in the narrow-syntax module, and that semantic agreement is based on a later stage of labeling, namely, that associated with the label being accessed (minimally searched, using the technical term of Chomsky 2013, 2015) by the syntax-semantics interface (CI).

Let us discuss the proposal in a technical detail. I assume that $\phi$-features in narrow syntax are never semantically interpreted. Interpretability of $\phi$-features arises only indirectly at the syntax-semantics interface via an association with a semantic index.[9] As for the feature values, I assume that features can be valued or unvalued, and that agree consists of matching and valuation (Chomsky 2000, Adger 2003, Pesetsky and Torrego 2007). If a $\phi$-feature is valued in narrow syntax, it either comes to the derivation valued from the lexicon, or it is valued by agree with an instantiation of a valued feature of the same type. Crucially, I argue that if a $\phi$-feature cannot be valued in narrow syntax, it can be valued at the syntax-semantics interface. Such a valuation is highly restricted: I argue that it is restricted by the Maximize Presupposition principle of Heim (1991) as part of phase spell-out & labeling.

The labeling process proposed in Chomsky (2013, 2015) implicitly assumes that labeling is a two-stage process. I explicate the individual stages here. The first stage of labeling is based on syntactic features that are present in the narrow-syntax derivation, i. e., features that get automatically projected to within narrow syntax. That the first stage of labeling is based on the narrow-syntax representa-

---

**8** By label I mean a feature set that represents a syntactic structure that for purposes of syntactic operations such as merge or agree behaves as a unit. For example, a label of an extended nominal projection (DP) is a set of features that represent the DP for purposes of external/internal merge etc.

**9** The $\phi$-feature-like interpretive effects can arise also via the lexical denotation of a root. For example, a root for a noun like 'woman' denotes a female via its lexical semantics. Note that this semantic denotation of natural gender is by definition assertive. I will argue that the interpretive effect associated with $\phi$-features is presuppositional.

tion guarantees the primacy of syntax in the overall derivation.[10] Once all syntactic features are checked and projected, the phase is spelled-out and the structure undergoes labeling by the syntax-semantics interface (CI).[11] I argue that the primary objective of this stage of labeling is to ensure that the label is legible to the semantics module. I argue that as part of the second stage of labeling, syntactic features in the label can be rebundled and otherwise adjusted for purposes of externalization, in a manner parallel to feature adjustments identified for the realization of syntactic structures at the syntax-morphology interface (e. g., as in the Distributed Morphology framework of Halle and Marantz 1993). Note that when the phase is syntactically complete, only the complement of the phase head is externalized (spelled-out). The label and the edge of the phase remains accessible to the syntactic computation of the next phase.

The consequence of the two-stage labeling process is that if there are $\phi$-features in the label, they can be projected to the label within narrow syntax, or they could be result of labeling by the syntax-semantics interface. Namely, if there is a valued gender feature in the narrow-syntax derivation of a DP, this valued feature must project to the label. If a probe probes for a gender feature, it must get valued by this syntactically projected feature. However, if there is no valued gender feature in the narrow-syntax derivation of a DP, I argue that under certain circumstances the syntax-semantics interface can fill in a semantically appropriate value. The next two subsections discuss the proposed derivations in a detail.

### 7.3.1 Labeling in syntax

Let us start with examining the agreement pattern attested in Italian and exemplified in (8)–(9), repeated below.

---

[10] The core assumption here is that syntax builds structures, interfaces interpret these structures.

[11] Chomsky (2013, 2015) does not explicitly acknowledge the necessity of the two stages but if the labeling process is to reflect narrow-syntax features and if CI plays a role in the labeling process, there must be two processes taking place in two stages of the derivation. As pointed out by an anonymous reviewer, two stages of labeling are explicitly proposed in Bošković (2016). In this work, labeling interacts with movement, i. e., there is a labeling stage prior movement and a labeling stage after movement of certain syntactic objects. Bošković's approach is rather different from the approach of labeling proposed in this chapter as his two stages of labeling reflect narrow-syntax processes, not an interaction of narrow syntax and the CI interface. This being said, it is quite possible that there is a deeper connection between the two approaches as movement out of a phase interacts with spell-out. To fully explore this connection goes beyond the scope of this chapter.

(14) il    chirurg-o è andat-o
     the.M surgeon.M has gone.M
     'the (male) surgeon is gone'

(15) a. la    chirurgo è andat-a
        the.F surgeon  has gone.F
     b. il    chirurgo è andat-a
        the.M surgeon  has gone-F
        'the female surgeon is gone'

I assume that historically all nouns in a language like Italian or Czech, i. e., languages with a grammatical gender system, were associated with a gender from the lexicon.[12] However, there is a limited lexical domain in which nouns lost their gender specification, i. e., nouns of professions that were traditionally performed by males but are currently increasingly performed by females. In turn, some nouns that used to be grammatically specified for masculine gender have changed their grammatical representation in order to reflect this sociological shift and have become structurally genderless.[13] Thus, we can directly investigate two types of nominals: nouns *with* a valued gender feature from the lexicon, and nouns *without* a valued gender feature from the lexicon.

For concreteness, let us assume that D is merged as a bundle of unvalued $\phi$-features.[14] The unvalued feature on D gets valued by matching feature on n. The features on n are valued from the lexicon (to match idiosyncratic indices of the root representation; Acquaviva 2014). In turn the valued gender feature projects to the label of the DP. A derivation of a noun with gender valued from the lexicon – here 'girl' with the gender feature valued as neuter – is given in (16).

---

[12] See Acquaviva (2014) for a formal model of such a system and arguments why in a language like Italian gender is an intrinsic part of the root lexical representation. Cf. Borer (2014) for an argument that roots do not have to combine with categorial heads as long as they project a nominal feature like gender.

[13] See Kučerová (2018) for structural tests demonstrating that Italian names of professions we investigate here are based on category-neutral roots, unlike their gendered counterparts.

[14] This is rather simplistic as e. g., Ritter (1995) and Béjar and Rezac (2003) argue that person is merged as a valued person on D. Similarly, there's a number of sophisticated arguments for a Number P etc. The current simplification is inconsequential as the focus is on features that project to the label in narrow syntax, i. e., the only relevant factor is that their value is introduced within the narrow-syntax computation.

(16) *Derivation of a noun with gender from the lexicon (děvče 'girl.N'):*
   a. *Base generation & agree:*

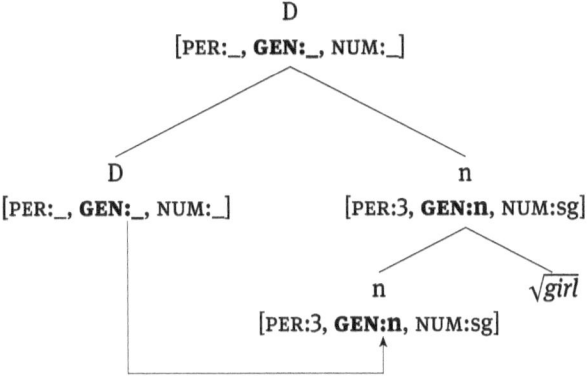

   b. *Valuation & syntactic labeling:*

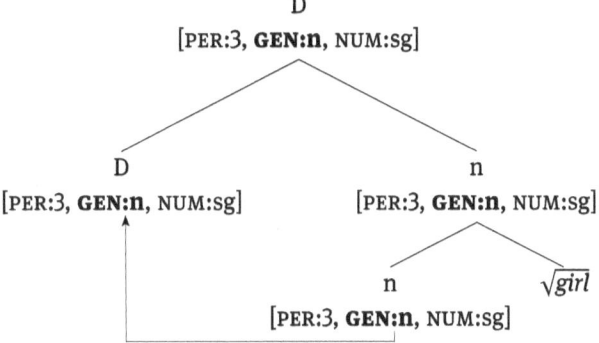

A consequence of this derivation is that agreement with such a DP is strictly based on the grammatical gender feature from the lexicon. In the case of the noun 'girl.GIRL' this means that all instances of agreement based on agree (e. g., subject-predicate agreement) will be in neuter. Observe that the derivation would proceed in the same way for any common noun with a gender specified from the lexicon.

The narrow-syntax derivation of a noun without a valued gender from the lexicon is minimally different. As we can see in (17), if a noun like *chirurgo* 'surgeon' enters the derivation, D still probes for the gender feature on n. But since there is no valued gender on n, the feature on D remains unvalued and this unvalued feature projects to the label in narrow syntax.

(17) *Derivation of a noun without gender from the lexicon (chirurgo 'surgeon'):*
 a. *Base generation & agree:*

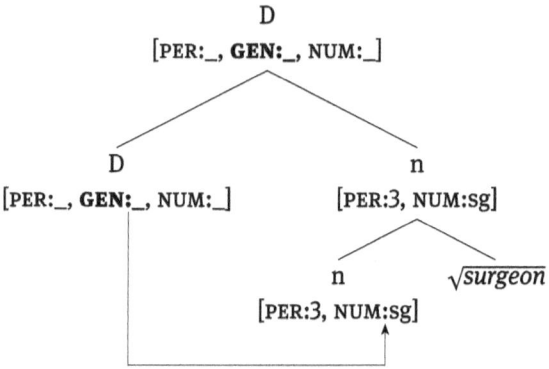

 b. *Valuation & syntactic labeling:*

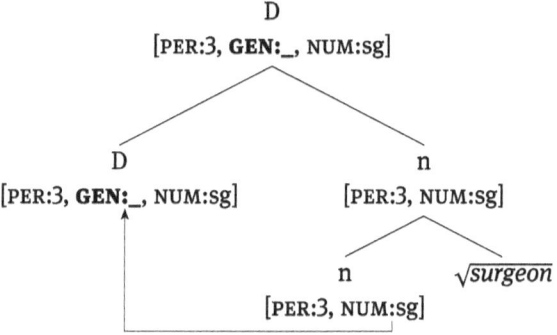

Once we adopt a dissociation of matching and valuation, the derivation converges even if the gender feature projected in syntax is unvalued. In turn, if such a DP is spelled-out, morphology realizes the unvalued gender feature as a morphological default. For Italian, the default realization is masculine. We thus obtain a masculine DP realization, such as that in (15b). The question is how we can model the fact that the same DP can be realized with a "semantically informed" value, as in (15a).

## 7.3.2 Labeling in the syntax-semantics interface

I follow Cooper (1983), Heim (2008) and others in that a gender feature is presuppositional. This means that its semantic denotation can be captured as an admissibility condition on the 'referent'. Technically, the semantic denotation of the masculine and feminine gender is defined as an identity function, i. e., the function takes the value of a semantic index under a certain assignment and returns the value of this index under the same assignment only if the gender presupposition is satisfied. If the returned value is not of the appropriate gender, the function will remain undefined and the structure will not be interpretable. For concreteness, the formulas in (18) are defined for individuals but the gender presupposition mechanism is more general, as the same facts obtain of indefinites and quantifiers.[15]

(18)  a.  $[[\text{GEN}:f_i]]^{w,g} = \lambda x_e. g(i)$ is female in $w$: x
      b.  $[[\text{GEN}:m_i]]^{w,g} = \lambda x_e. g(i)$ is a person in $w$: x

Note that the subscript *i* in the denotation of a gender feature is to indicate that the admissibility restriction arises only in the context of a semantic index. Thus, the interpretation function interprets an assignment index (*i*) associated with the gender, not the actual gender feature. This insight is crucial for the current proposal. I argue that labeling by the syntax-semantics interface associates narrow-syntax features from the label (the result of the narrow-syntax labeling) with a semantic index. The semantic module (LF) interprets this index, and morphology, and in turn, agreement, reflects $\phi$-features associated with the semantic index.

In order to unpack this claim we first need to consider the structure of a semantic index and have a concrete model of how such an index becomes part of the derivation. Following Heim and Kratzer (1998) I assume that an index in and of itself does not carry a meaning. Its meaning is associated with a denotation only via an assignment function at LF. Thus, a semantic index is an object that can be part of the derivation prior semantics proper. Technically, a semantic index is a complex structure which includes a numerical pointer and a reference to person, possibly to other $\phi$-features (Heim 2008, Minor 2011, Sudo 2012). For instance, <5, ③> is an ordered pair that maps a numerical identifier 5 to third person (i. e., [–participant]) at LF. An assignment function then maps this index, for example, to individual named Peter. Note that the output of the assignment function does not have to be an individual, for example, when the index is a variable bound by a quantifier.

I argue that a semantic index becomes part of the DP label during labeling by the syntax-semantics interface. Concretely, an index is built as part of the minimal search by CI for the purposes of labeling. For concreteness, I assume that

---

[15] Thanks to an anonymous reviewer who pointed out the importance of a more general formulation.

the numerical identifier is base-generated as an external argument of D (Williams 1981, Higginbotham 1985, Grimshaw 1990, Winter 2000, Borer 2005).[16] First, the features of the phase label, in our case $\phi$-features, project into the label in the narrow-syntax part of the labeling process. These features immediately become available to the CI-labeling process. I follow Kučerová (2018) in that the syntactic feature central to the process is person. The reasoning is that person feature is a designated feature that associates a DP with a semantic index as a representation of a DP for the purposes of a semantic interpretation. During the minimal search by CI, the system searches the edge of the phase, i. e., the phase head and its specifier(s) and identifies all features relevant to person, here the numerical identifier in the specifier of the DP. As part of labeling by CI, a person feature projected from syntax gets bundled with a numerical identifier. This new feature bundle effectively becomes a semantic index. The derivation in (19) exemplifies how such a new bundle is formed for a noun like Peter.[17]

(19) *Baseline case (Peter):*
    a. *Numerical identifier and syntactic labeling:*

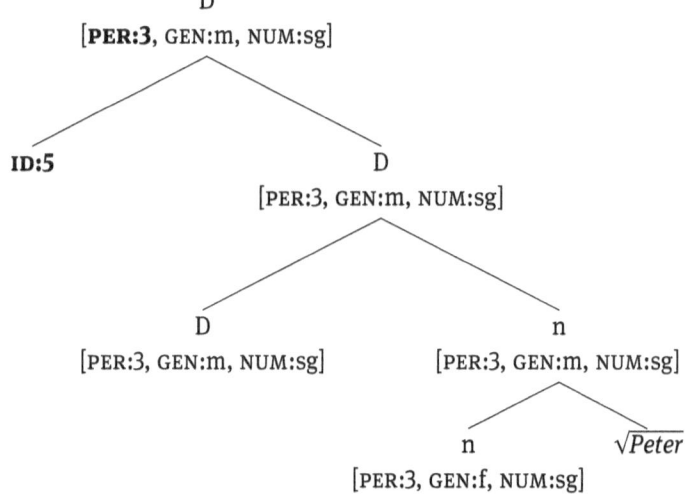

---

[16] There is a long linguistics tradition of associating D with an individual-denoting function (Williams 1981, Higginbotham 1985, Grimshaw 1990, Wiltschko 1998, Winter 2000, Borer 2005, Longobardi 2008, Landau 2010). Note we need a more general process because of non-individual denoting nominals but we can still build on this structural insight.

[17] For concreteness, I treat the proper name as structurally identical to a common noun. Note also that the name is selected for its stereo-typical gender association.

b. *Semantic index added to the label:*

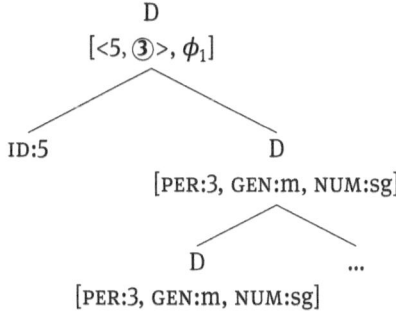

With this baseline derivation in place, we can turn to nominals that come to the derivation without a valued gender. Following Sudo (2012) who proposes that a semantic index contains indices of presupposed ϕ-features I argue that an unvalued gender feature in the label of a DP can get enriched by gender indices associated with their semantic index. This enrichment arises modulo Maximize Presupposition (Heim, 1991), i. e., a requirement that if a presupposition is satisfied in the given context and if there is a structure that satisfies this presupposition then such a structure must be chosen over a structure that does not satisfy this presupposition. I. e., the enrichment of the unvalued gender feature can yield a morphological realization of the presuppositional gender feature within the semantic index. I. e., if there is no valued gender feature in the label, then the morphology module realizes the gender value of the presuppositional indices. In turn, the morphological output satisfies the Maximize Presupposition requirement. An example of a derivation with enrichment of the semantic index modulo Maximize Presupposition is given in (20). Here the root noun is the Italian noun *chirurgo* 'surgeon'; the derivation is for a context in which the noun denotes a female.

(20)  *Nominal without a valued gender feature (*surgeon *'chirurg')*
   a.  *Numerical index & syntactic labeling (simplified):*

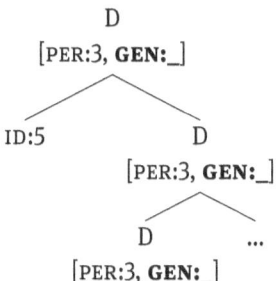

b. *Semantic index added to the label:*

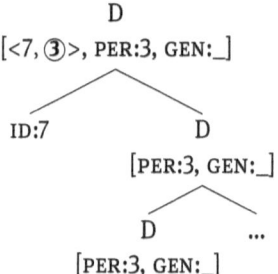

c. *Index enriched by gender (where 7 → Mary):*

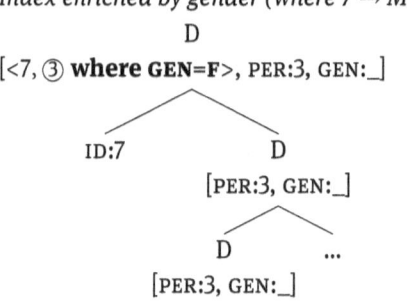

Once the DP is labeled both by features projected from narrow syntax and by the syntax-semantics interface, the morphological spell-out of the DP can be based on two different sources of information. Either the morphological realization is based on the syntactic feature in the label, that is, the unvalued feature, or it can be based on the presuppositional gender associated with the semantic index. If the morphological realization is based on the unvalued feature, the output will be based on morphological default and the extended nominal projection of the DP will be masculine, as in (14).

The other option is that the morphology module will realize the presuppositional gender associated with the semantic index in the label (modulo Maximize Presupposition). In this case, the gender of the extended nominal projection will get realized as feminine, as in (15). Note that since the gender feature in the label forms a chain with other instances of unvalued gender feature within the DP, the morphological realization of the chain uniformly uses either the unvalued gender feature, or it spreads the presuppositional gender across the whole chain.

The question that immediately arises is how morphology could access a CI-label without violating the Y-model. Note that only the complement of a phase head is sent to spell-out. That is, the edge of phase $\alpha$ remains accessible to a further derivation after the complement of this phase head has been sent to the morphology interface. The edge of phase $\alpha$ gets sent to morphology only after the complement of the next phase head gets spelled-out. At this point, the label of α has been fully labeled by CI and the morphology module can use the enriched semantic information.

Crucially, the previous discussion refers to enrichment and morphological realization instead of valuation of the syntactic gender value in the label. The reason is that the optionality of the gender realization within the DP contrasts with the subject-agreement facts. While the gender within the extended nominal projection can either be masculine or feminine, the gender on the agreeing predicate is feminine, irrespective of the gender on D. I argue that there is a fundamental asymmetry between the valuation within the DP and external agree. The label per se does not probe for the unvalued features. The chain formation is triggered by D and it is complete before the label is semantically enriched. Probing the label by an unvalued gender feature on a probe, e. g., a predicate, is rather different in that at the point agree is established, the semantically enriched feature bundle (the semantic index with its presuppositional indices) has already been formed. In turn, the unvalued gender feature of the probe gets valued via the enriched information. That is to say, if a feature participating in agree can get valued, it must get valued. If there is a valued syntactic feature in the label, agree must get valued by this feature because of the primacy of syntax. Only if there is no syntactically valued feature in the label, the predicate can get valued by the gender associated with the semantic index (modulo Maximize Presupposition). More precisely, if there is a such enriched feature bundle, agree must be based on this enriched value. In turn, the predicate agrees in feminine irrespective of the morphological spell-out of the DP, (21).[18]

(21) a. la chirurgo è andat-a
 the.⟨F⟩ surgeon has gone.⟨F⟩
 *last resort valuation for spell-out of DP & agree*
 b. il chirurgo è andat-a
 the.⟨M⟩ surgeon has gone-⟨F⟩
 *last resort valuation only for agree*

 'the female surgeon is gone'

One consequence of the obligatory agree-based realization of the presupposed feature is that the Maximize Presupposition principle is satisfied even if the gen-

---

[18] If there was no presuppositional gender associated with the semantic index, the feature on the goal would remain unvalued and would get realized as morphological default. Patterns of this sort are attested, for example, in Czech in agreement with numerals that lack φ-features in their label.

der feature is not morphologically realized on the DP itself. Hence we obtain optionality in the marking of the DP.[19]

With the system set up as is, we must make sure that the system does not overgenerate.[20] To see that the system indeed does not overgenerate we need to consider again nouns with a gender valued from the lexicon, such as Czech *děvče* 'girl.N' or *osoba* 'person.F'. As we have seen, the label of these nouns contains valued gender feature projected from narrow syntax (neuter for 'girl', feminine for 'person') and a semantic index enriched by a presuppositional gender (feminine if the intended referent is a female, masculine if it is a male). The fully labeled structures are given in (22) for 'girl', assuming a feminine referent, and for 'person' in (23), assuming a masculine referent.

(22) *Syntactic and CI labeling for 'girl', where 7 → Mary:*

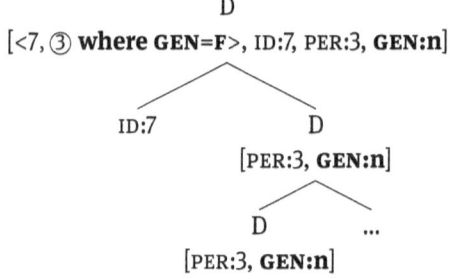

(23) *Syntactic and CI labeling for 'person', where 7 → Peter:*

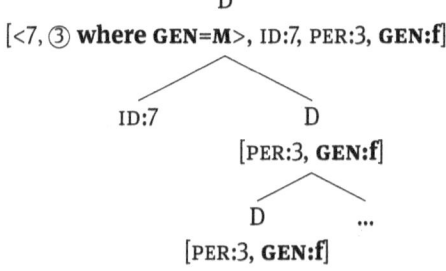

---

**19** I assume some competition between 'faithfulness' of morphological structures to the value of syntactic features versus 'faithfulness' of morphological realizations to the intended semantic interpretation, here governed by Maximize Presupposition, is at play.

**20** Overgeneration is not necessarily a problem within the narrow-syntax module as it can get amended by some form of an interface 'filter'. However, since the enrichment happens already at the interface level, there is no later point in the derivation when the undesired derivations could be filtered out.

As the structures indicate, the presuppositional gender of the index cannot have any effect on the morphological realization of the DP itself and on agree if such a DP becomes a probe. The reason is that there is a valued syntactic gender feature in the label and this feature cannot be overwritten by the interface enrichment. We see here that the valuation modulo Maximize Presupposition is a last resort. It can take place if and only if the value is not determined from syntax.[21]

This section provided an answer to our first research question, namely, to the question under what conditions can $\phi$-features on a nominal yield a new set of features, namely, features that match the intended semantic interpretation. I have argued that new $\phi$-feature values are derived only if the label contains no valued gender feature from syntax and if there is presuppositional gender associated with the semantic index in the label. The question is whether the presuppositional gender indices are part of the label even if they cannot be morphologically realized because of there being a syntactically valued gender. The next section argues that the presuppositional indices are indeed always present. The empirical evidence comes from anaphoric agreement and the discussion will provide an answer to our second question, namely, that of what the structural underpinning of anaphoric agreement is and why its locality domain differs from syntactic agree.

### 7.3.3 Anaphoric agreement

Kratzer (2009) provides empirical evidence that there is no direct structural relationship between a pronoun and its antecedent. Instead, anaphoric agreement is always mediated by a phase head.[22] Under Kratzer's proposal a pronoun is merged as a minimal pronoun and 'inherits' its features from the local phase head. I follow Kratzer with a minor modification: I argue that binding is licensed at LF but

---

[21] The pattern also seems to suggest that for Maximize Presupposition it is sufficient if there is only one morphological realization of the presupposed value. The data do not provide a clear answer but in my opinion, this is not a correct interpretation of the fact. What we see here is that morphology and semantics can never communicate directly. The obligatory morphological realization of the presuppositional gender on the agreeing predicate is a consequence of syntactic probe probing for a CI-labeled label.

[22] The idea that phase heads (v, C, D) gather features of arguments in their local domain, such as semantic indices, person features, $\phi$-features etc., and that this phase head representation mediates syntactic relations has been independently argued for by a number of scholars, e. g., Adger and Ramchand (2005), Ritter and Wiltschko (2014), Zubizarreta and Pancheva (2017), Pancheva and Zubizarreta (2018). The central idea of this family of work is that a phase head collects these features for semantic anchoring purposes.

its syntactic underpinning is established in narrow syntax.[23] For concreteness, I model a minimal pronoun as an unvalued semantic index and a bundle of unvalued $\phi$-features. The value of the semantic index is assigned via a local phase head. I argue that the valuation of unvalued $\phi$-features is parallel to the realization of unvalued gender feature proposed in the previous section. Namely, the unvalued features can get morphologically realized in two different ways. The first option is that the morphology module realizes the presuppositional features associated with the semantic index (module Maximize Presupposition). The other option is that morphology copies morpho-syntactic features of the antecedent, i. e., of the label that shares its semantic index. This process of sharing morphological realization over a syntactically established chain corresponds to the notion of Feature Transmission proposed in Heim (2008) and Kratzer (2009). Let us see how the proposed derivation plays out for nouns of our interest, i. e., nouns with a syntactically valued gender feature and with a distinct presuppositional gender feature, such as the Czech noun *děvče* 'girl.N'. The relevant example is in (2), repeated below as (24).

(24)    Petr podal děvčeti       jeho/      její       kabát.
        Petr passed to-girl.**N.SG** its. N.SG / her. F.SG coat
        'Petr gave the girl$_i$ her$_i$ coat.'

As this example demonstrates, a noun like *děvče* obligatorily triggers neuter agreement, the reason being that there is a valued gender feature in the label of the DP (neuter). The very same noun can, however, locally bind a pronoun that shares its syntactically valued gender feature (neuter; *jeho* 'its') or a pronoun which is based on its presuppositional gender feature (feminine; *její* 'her'). The derivation in (25) exemplifies how the duality of morphological realization of the bound pronoun arises. As we can see in (25a), the local phase head that mediates the binding relationship between the antecedent ('girl') and the bound pronoun within the direct object first gathers the semantic index from the label of the DP in its specifier. This semantic index is enriched by a presuppositional gender feature (feminine). In the next step, the semantic index is shared with the possessive pronoun, (25b). Once the morphology realizes the pronoun, there are two possible routes the morphology output can take. If the morphology module realizes the morpho-syntactic features of the label of the antecedent across the complete chain that shares the semantic index, the pronoun gets realized as neuter, (25b). The morphological realization can be local as well. Then the pronoun gets morphologically realized

---

**23** According to Kratzer (2009) binding takes place at LF. See also Charnavel and Sportiche (2016) that binding is established within a phase.

based on the presuppositional indices associated with its semantic index, i. e., feminine, (25b).

(25)  a.  *Semantic indices on the phase head (Appl):*

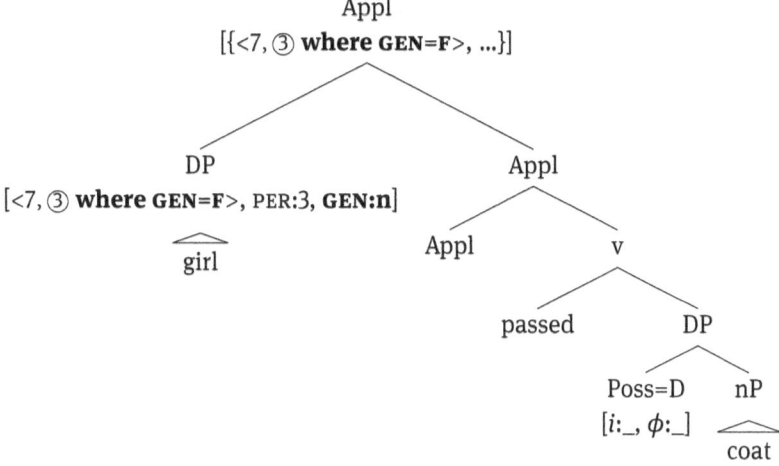

b.  *Unvalued index of the minimal pronoun valued via the phase head:*

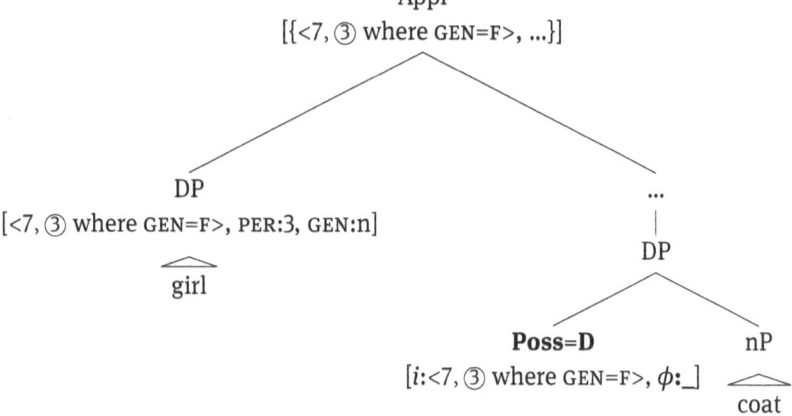

c.  *ϕ-features of the possessive pronoun valued by Feature Transmission:*

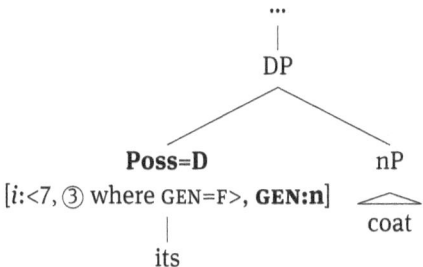

c'. *ϕ-features of the possessive pronoun valued directly from the index (modulo Maximize Presupposition):*

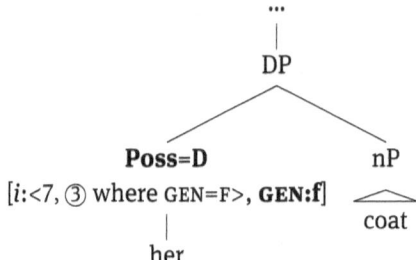

To summarize, the argument put forward here is that anaphoric agreement is always mediated by a phase head. Since the feature representation of the phase head refers to the semantic index of the antecedent, the bound pronoun can inherit either the syntactic ϕ-features of its antecedent, or its features can get valued by presuppositional features associated with the semantic index. Thus even if we cannot see the presupposed features on the index in the overt realization of the DP or its syntactically agreeing elements, the features become morphologically realized in anaphoric relations.

The separation between agree based directly on the features present in the label of the probe, with syntactically projected features having precedence, and anaphoric agreement being mediated by a semantic index on a local phase head has consequences for locality of these two structural relations. While agree must use a valued syntactic feature for valuation, anaphoric agreement can be based on presuppositional features of the shared semantic index even if the antecedent has a valued gender feature in the label. Consequently, local agree is restricted to syntactically projected features in the label, locality properties of anaphoric agreement are restricted by their relevant phase heads and locality properties of the head's feature valuation. Next section explores locality interactions mediated by phase heads.

### 7.3.4 Pronouns as antecedents

We have seen that the morphological form of a locally bound pronoun can either be based on morphological copying of features present in the chain mediated by a phase head, or it can be locally derived from the agreeing semantic index itself. Now we turn to morphological realizations of pronouns that are established across a sentential boundary, i. e., via a C head. There are two cases to consider:

the cross-sentential agreement type, exemplified in (1), and the binding by imposters type, exemplified by (6), repeated below as (26) and (27), respectively.

(26)  To/       *ta   pracovité/      *pracovitá děvče  šlo/      *šla
      that.N.SG/ *F.SG industrious.N.SG/ *F.SG    girl.N.SG went.N.SG/ *F.SG
      na jahody.    Hned      jich    mělo/    měla plný košík.
      on strawberries immediately of_them had.N.SG/ F.SG full basket
      'The industrious girl went strawberry-picking. She quickly filled a basket.'

(27)  a.  The present authors$_1$' children feel that **they$_1$** need to defend **their$_1$** interests.
      b.  The present authors$_1$' children feel that **we$_1$** need to defend **our$_1$** interests.
      c.  *The present authors$_1$' children feel that **they$_1$** need to defend **our$_1$** interests.
      d.  *The present authors$_1$' children feel that **we$_1$** need to defend **their$_1$** interests.

(Collins and Postal, 2012, 141, (2))

I argue that the agreement pattern in (26) is mediated by a covert pronominal element (*pro*), as in (28). In turn, the data in both cases are parallel in that both the bound pronoun in the imposter case and the predicate in the 'girl' case must be based on the morphological realization of the antecedent (the overt pronominal subject in the English case or *pro* in the Czech case).[24]

(28)  To        děvče   ...
      that.N.SG girl.N.SG
      'The girl...'
      a.  pro    Hned        jich      mělo     plný košík.
          pro.**N.SG** immediately of_them had.**N.SG** full basket
      b.  pro    Hned        jich      měla     plný košík.
          pro.**F.SG** immediately of_them had.**F.SG** full basket
      'She quickly filled a basket.'

The question is why a full DP can give rise to two pronominal binding patterns but if the antecedent is a pronoun, the local relationship is obligatorily based on the morphological features of the pronoun. I argue that the pattern follows from the proposal put forward for anaphoric agreement within a clause. In the first step of the derivation for the imposter case, the bound pronoun and the pronominal

---

[24] We could use overt pronouns instead of *pro* but the utterances would be downgraded because of information-structure requirements on overt pronouns. See footnote 2.

subject get coindexed via their local phase head (v). At this point of the derivation, the coindexation is not valued by a semantic index yet, as the index must come from the previous linguistics discourse. Similarly for the *pro* case: *pro* gets merged as a minimal pronoun in the specifier of vP and it shares its index with v. The predicate probes for *pro* and in turn agree establishes a matching link with the unvalued $\phi$-features of the covert pronoun. The actual valuation of the shared semantic index awaits until v inherits a semantic index from the C head, with the semantic index being associated with the linguistically present antecedent (either in the matrix clause or in the previous clause). Once the semantic index is established, the value is shared via the established chain. The morphology module then realizes the complete chain, either using morphological features present on the antecedent (by Feature Transmission; neuter singular for the Czech case, (28a); third plural for the imposter case, (27a)), or presuppositional gender features associated with the shared semantic index (feminine singular for the Czech case, (28b); first plural for the imposter case, (27b)). The result is that the morphological realization must be uniform within the clause, irrespective of whether the relevant relationship is based on agree (the Czech case) or on anaphoric agreement (the imposter case). The mixed patterns are ungrammatical.

### 7.3.5 More on heads with an unvalued semantic index

The logic of the argument is that whenever there is a phase head that collects semantic indices, a syntactic agree with such a phase head can ignore grammatical gender and can be based on semantic gender derived from the indices. We can test this prediction by investigating other configurations in which a local agree is mediated by a phase head that collects semantic indices of its local DPs. I argue that conjoined DPs provide a testing ground for this prediction.

Following Munn (1993), Bošković (2009), Bhatt and Walkow (2013), I assume that DP conjunction forms semantic plurality. Since a formation of semantic plurality is a process that requires access to the semantic component, more precisely to semantic indices, the label of a ConjP must contain a reference to semantic indices of the individual conjuncts. The English examples in (29) demonstrate the basic insight. Whether or not the predicate agreement with the conjoined DP will be plural depends on whether the two nominals are associated with two distinct indices. Thus when the predicate probes for the label of the conjunction, the label must contain a set of two distinct indices in order for the unvalued number feature on the probe to be valued as plural.

(29) a. his best friend$_i$ and editor$_j$ **is** by his bedside $\qquad i = j$
 b. his best friend$_i$ and editor$_j$ **are** by his bedside $\qquad i \neq j$

We can use this insight and extend it to our discussion of nominals with a syntactically valued gender feature but with a distinct presuppositional gender feature associated with their semantic index. Recall that if noun comes to the derivation with a valued gender from the lexicon and if the grammatical gender does not match its natural gender, a predicate must agree with the grammatical gender, as in (10), repeated below as (30). The reason is that syntactic agree must respect the valued syntactic feature projected to the label (here, feminine).

(30) La/ *il brava/ *bravo guarda si e'persa nel
 the.F.SG/ M.SG good.F.SG M.SG guard.F.SG her/him lost.F.SG in the
 bosco.
 woods
 'The guard lost his/her way in the forest.'
 (modeled after Ferrari-Bridgers 2007)

Interestingly, when such a noun is embedded in a conjoined DP, the label of the conjoined DP does not contain syntactic gender features projected from narrow syntax. Instead, the label contains the semantic index. Since the semantic index is enriched by a presuppositional gender feature, the presuppositional gender feature becomes available for local agree. As we can see in (31), if the noun *guardia*.F.SG 'guard' refers to a female, the predicate agreement treats the noun as feminine (the combined agreement of the female-denoting 'guard' and the feminine noun 'sister'), (31a). If, however, the noun denotes a male, the combined agreement is masculine, as in (31b).[25]

(31) a. La guardia e sua sorella sono andate al cinema sta
 the guard.F and self sister have gone.F.PL to-the movies this
 sera
 evening
 'The guard and her sister went to the movies tonight.'
 b. La guardia e sua sorella son andati al cinema sta
 the guard.F and self sister have gone.M.PL to-the movies this
 stera
 evening
 'The guard and his sister went to the movies tonight.'
 [adapted from Ferrari-Bridgers (2007, 151, (4))]

---

**25** Bošković (2009) argues that last-conjunct agreement in Serbo-Croatian is possible with grammatical gender but not semantic gender. I leave these facts aside because the syntactic analysis of first and last conjunct agreement is rather complex.

## 7.4 Conclusions

This chapter has argued for a model of grammatical and semantic agreement that removes all semantic information from narrow syntax. Instead, $\phi$-features become interpretable only indirectly via association of syntactic person feature with a semantic index. I proposed a system in which labeling proceeds in two stages. First, features are projected from the narrow-syntax derivation. Then the features become subject to labeling by the syntax-semantics interface. The second stage of labeling can rebundle the features present in the syntactically projected label. I have argued that the association of the person feature with a semantic index takes place during the labeling of the syntax-semantics component. The chapter explores the interaction of the syntactically projected features and the CI-labeled features in two interrelated domains: in the domain of local syntactic agree and in anaphoric agreement where the feature sharing process is mediated by phase heads. In turn, the proposal furthers our understanding of locality restrictions on grammatical versus semantic agreement and provides a principled account of otherwise puzzling locality differences. The proposal further contributes to our understanding of the representation of labels and the division of labor among modules of the grammar. Under the proposed model syntax is a fully autonomous module, with no recourse to semantic information. Instead, interpretability of features arises only at the syntax-semantics interface.

## Bibliography

Acquaviva, Paolo. 2014. Distributing roots: Listemes across components in Distributed Morphology. *Theoretical Linguistics* 40:277–286.

Adger, David. 2003. *Core syntax: A minimalist approach*. Oxford: Oxford University Press.

Adger, David, and Gillian Ramchand. 2005. Merge and move: Wh-dependencies revisited. *Linguistic Inquiry* 36:161–193.

Babyonyshev, Maria A. 1997. Structural connection in syntax and processing: Studies in Russian and Japanese. Doctoral Dissertation, Massachusetts Institute of Technology.

Béjar, Susana, and Milan Rezac. 2003. Person licensing and the derivation of PCC effects. *Amsterdam Studies in the Theory and History of Linguistic Science Series* 4:49–62.

Bhatt, Rajesh, and Martin Walkow. 2013. Locating agreement in grammar: An argument from agreement in conjunctions. *Natural Language & Linguistic Theory* 31:951–1013.

Bobaljik, Jonathan David, and Cynthia Levart Zocca. 2011. Gender markedness: the anatomy of a counter-example. *Morphology* 21:141–166.

Borer, Hagit. 2005. *Structuring sense: An exo-skeletal trilogy*. New York: Oxford University Press.

Borer, Hagit. 2014. Wherefore roots? *Theoretical Linguistics* 40:343–359.

Bošković, Željko. 2009. Unifying first and last conjunct agreement. *Natural Language & Linguistic Theory* 27:455–496.

Bošković, Željko. 2016. On the timing of labeling: Deducing Comp-trace effects, the Subject Condition, the Adjunct Condition, and tucking in from labeling. *The Linguistic Review* 33:17–66.

Charnavel, Isabelle, and Dominique Sportiche. 2016. Anaphor binding: What French inanimate anaphors show. *Linguistic Inquiry* 47:35–87.

Chomsky, Noam. 2000. Minimalist inquiries: The framework. In *Step by Step*, ed. R. Martin, D. Michaels, and J. Uriagereka, 89–155. Cambridge, MA: MIT Press.

Chomsky, Noam. 2013. Problems of projection. *Lingua* 130:33–49.

Chomsky, Noam. 2015. Problems of projection: Extensions. In *Structures, strategies and beyond. Studies in honour of Adriana Belletti*, ed. Elisa Di Domenico, Cornelia Hamann, and Simona Matteini, 3–16. Amsterdam: John Benjamins.

Collins, Chris, and Paul Martin Postal. 2012. *Imposters: A study of pronominal agreement*. Cambridge, Mass.: MIT Press.

Cooper, Robin. 1983. *Quantification and syntactic theory*. Dordrecht: Reidel.

Corbett, Greville. 2000. *Number*. Cambridge: Cambridge University Press.

Corbett, Greville G. 1983. *Hierarchies, targets and controllers: Agreement patterns in Slavic*. London: Croom Helm.

Ferrari-Bridgers, Franca. 2007. The predictability of gender in Italian. *Lingua et Linguistica* 1:146–167.

Grimshaw, Jane. 1990. *Argument structure*. Cambridge, Massachusetts: MIT Press.

Halle, Morris, and Alec Marantz. 1993. Distributive morphology and the pieces of inflection. In *The view from Building 20: Essays in linguistics in honor of Sylvain Bromberger*, 111–176. Cambridge, MA: MIT Press.

Heim, Irene. 1991. Artikel und Definitheit. In *Semantik: Ein internationales Handbuch der zeitgenössischen Forschung*, ed. Arnim von Stechow and Dieter Wunderlich, 487–535. Berlin: Mouton de Gruyter.

Heim, Irene. 2008. Features on bound pronouns. In *Phi-theory: Phi features across interfaces and modules*, ed. Daniel Harbour, David Adger, and Susana Béjar, 35–56. Oxford: Oxford University Press.

Heim, Irene, and Angelika Kratzer. 1998. *Semantics in generative grammar*. Oxford: Blackwell.

Higginbotham, James. 1985. On semantics. *Linguistic inquiry* 16:547–593.

Kramer, Ruth. 2009. Definite markers, phi-features, and agreement: a morphosyntactic investigation of the Amharic DP. Doctoral Dissertation, University of California Santa Cruz.

Kramer, Ruth. 2015. *The morphosyntax of gender*. Oxford – New York: Oxford University Press.

Kratzer, Angelika. 2009. Making a pronoun: Fake indexicals as windows into the properties of pronouns. *Linguistic Inquiry* 40:187–237.

Kučerová, Ivona. 2018. $\phi$-features at the syntax-semantics interface: Evidence from nominal inflection. *Linguistic Inquiry* 49:813–845.

Landau, Idan. 2010. The explicit syntax of implicit arguments. *Linguistic Inquiry* 41:357–388.

Landau, Idan. 2016. DP-internal semantic agreement: A configurational analysis. *Natural Language & Linguistic Theory* 34:975–1020.

Longobardi, Giuseppe. 2008. Reference to individuals, person, and the variety of mapping parameters. In *Essays on nominal determination: From morphology to discourse management*, ed. Henrik Høeg Müller and Alex Klinge, 189–211. Amsterdam–Philadelphia: John Benjamins Publishing Company.

Minor, Sergey. 2011. Complex indices and a blocking account of the sequence of tenses. Ms., CASTL, Tromsø.

Munn, Alan Boag. 1993. Topics in the syntax and semantics of coordinate structures. Doctoral Dissertation, University of Maryland, College Park, MD.

Pancheva, Roumyana, and Maria Luisa Zubizarreta. 2018. The person case constraint. *Natural Language & Linguistic Theory* 36:1291–1337.

Pesetsky, David. 2013. *Russian case morphology and the syntactic categories*. Cambridge, MA: MIT Press.

Pesetsky, David, and Esther Torrego. 2007. The syntax of valuation and the interpretability of features. In *Phrasal and clausal architecture. Syntactic derivation and interpretation. In honor of Joseph E. Emonds*, ed. Simin Karimi, Vida Samiian, and Wendy K. Wilkins, 262–294. Amsterdam: John Benjamins.

Ritter, Elizabeth. 1995. On the syntactic category of pronouns and agreement. *Natural Language and Linguistic Theory* 13:405–443.

Ritter, Elizabeth, and Martina Wiltschko. 2014. Featuring animacy and humanness. A talk presented at the Dog days workshop at University of Toronto, August 2014.

Sauerland, Uli, and Paul Elbourne. 2002. Total reconstruction, PF movement, and derivational order. *Linguistic Inquiry* 33:283–319.

Smith, Peter Williams. 2015. Feature mismatches: Consequences for syntax, morphology and semantics. Doctoral Dissertation, University of Connecticut, Storrs, CT.

Sudo, Yasutada. 2012. On the semantics of phi features on pronouns. Doctoral Dissertation, Massachusetts Institute of Technology, Cambridge, MA.

Veselovská, Ludmila. 1998. Possessive movement in the Czech nominal phrase. *Journal of Slavic linguistics* 6:255–300.

Williams, Edwin. 1981. Argument structure and morphology. *The linguistic review* 1:81–114.

Wiltschko, Martina. 1998. On the syntax and semantics of (relative) pronouns and determiners. *Journal of Comparative Germanic Linguistics* 2:143–181.

Wiltschko, Martina. 2009. What's in a determiner and how did it get there? In *Determiners: universals and variation*, ed. Jila Ghomeshi, Ileana Paul, and Martina Wiltschko, 25–66. Amsterdam: John Benjamins.

Winter, Yoad. 2000. Distributivity and dependency. *Natural language semantics* 8:27–69.

Wurmbrand, Susi. 2017. Formal and semantic agreement in syntax: A dual feature approach. In *Language Use and Linguistic Structure: Proceedings of the Olomouc Linguistics Colloquium 2016*, ed. Joseph Emonds and Markéta Janebová, 19–36. Olomouc: Palacký University.

Zubizarreta, Maria Luisa, and Roumyana Pancheva. 2017. A formal characterization of person-based alignment. The case of Paraguayan Guaraní. *Natural Language & Linguistic Theory* 35:1161–1204.

# Index

φ-features 183–188, 191, 192, 194, 197–199, 201, 203–206, 208, 210
φ-agreement 90, 94–96, 119, 125

across-the-board-movement 4, 133, 134
adjectives 62, 63, 71, 72, 82, 122
agree 46, 66, 94, 96, 168, 186, 188, 189, 191, 192, 195, 196, 201, 203, 206, 208–210
agreement 3, 5, 90, 95, 96, 100, 124, 137, 139, 153, 183, 185–193, 195, 197, 204, 207–210
AgrsP 153, 154, 178
all-stranding 107–109, 124
anaphoric agreement 184–189, 191, 203, 206–208, 210
argument ellipsis 20, 74, 75
autonomous syntax 183, 210

Bangla 3, 62, 63, 65, 67–80, 83, 84
binding 70, 114–116, 124, 203, 204, 207
blocking effect 61, 63, 66
Brazilian Portuguese 144

clitic doubling 135, 144, 145, 177
contextual approach to phasehood 20
Coordinate Structure Constraint (CSC) 134
coordination 6, 144, 147, 149–153, 161, 162, 168, 174–176
Coordination of Likes 5
CP 3, 5, 6, 19, 20, 36–39, 44, 45, 47, 65, 66, 78, 79, 84, 89, 90, 95–97, 100–103, 107–111, 113, 114, 118, 122, 125, 137, 148, 149

DP 3–5, 22, 62, 66, 68–70, 72–80, 83, 84, 90, 95, 110, 118–124, 126, 138, 193–196, 198–204, 206, 208, 209
DP vs. NP language 80
Dutch 109, 110, 121, 135, 142–144, 177

EPP 124, 151, 153
exceptional case-marking 163
extraction marking 90–92, 96, 97, 100, 119, 120

finiteness 12–15
French 75, 175, 176

Galician 120, 135, 141, 145, 156, 177
German 68, 73, 103, 106, 111, 112, 122, 135, 142, 143, 177, 185

head-movement 140, 141

imperfective 13, 14, 19
– secondary 18, 19, 23, 25, 28, 29
imposters 187, 207
intervention (effects) 66, 67, 133, 135, 136, 155–158, 161, 163–167, 169–171, 174, 177
inversion 98–100
islands 100, 102, 133, 134, 139, 147, 149, 156, 169
Italian 74, 150, 156, 188, 194, 196, 199

Japanese 20, 74, 135, 145, 157, 158, 171, 177

Kaqchikel 150
Kinande 150

labeling 1, 4, 5, 133, 135–142, 146, 147, 150, 154, 164–167, 171, 174, 177, 183, 192, 193, 195–199, 202, 210
labels 136, 152, 174, 210
left-branch extraction 110, 121, 135, 161, 177
lexical aspect 16, 23

multiple spell-out 90, 100, 119, 123, 124

object shift 135, 146, 174, 177

parasitic gaps 114, 117, 118, 124, 158
partial wh-movement 101–103
perfective 12, 14–16, 19, 22, 23, 25, 26
– lexical 23, 25
– superlexical 15, 17, 19, 27, 29, 30
phase 1–7, 15, 19–26, 29–31, 35–39, 45–47, 49, 51, 52, 54, 61, 62, 66, 67, 74–81, 83–86, 89, 125, 133, 135, 136, 138, 140, 147–149, 151, 153, 159, 167, 177, 178, 184, 193, 198, 200, 205
Phase-Impenetrability condition 136
pied-piping 101–105, 119, 123

PP  4, 90, 111, 112, 118, 119, 121, 123, 124, 126, 143
pronoun copying  106, 107

*r*-pronouns  133, 135, 142, 155, 177

scope  114–117, 124, 150, 162
Serbo-Croatian  71, 73, 76–80, 122, 139
sideward movement  135, 154, 158, 159, 169, 170, 174
Spanish  41, 46, 74, 144
spell-out  39, 80, 102, 105–107, 192, 200, 201
split IP  155, 177
stranding  75, 79, 90, 100, 107–111, 119, 123, 124
strict aspectual antecedent  21, 23–26, 29–31
successive cyclicity  4, 89, 90, 100, 114, 118, 119, 125
successive-cyclic movement  3, 4, 94, 96, 107, 108, 111, 117, 118, 125, 136–138, 140, 142, 144, 146, 147, 153, 154, 159, 177

syntax-morphology interface  184, 193
syntax-semantics interface  5, 184, 185, 192, 193, 196, 197, 200, 210

TP  19–21, 36–39, 44, 45, 47, 51, 54, 152, 153, 178
transfer  1

verb phrase  89, 90, 92, 98, 99, 103–105, 107, 108, 113, 117
verb-second (V2)  94
viewpoint aspect  16, 18, 19, 23, 24

wh-copying  105, 106
wh-movement  36, 40, 45, 47, 54, 100, 101, 103, 105, 106, 136, 147, 150, 152, 154, 155, 174, 177, 178

www.ingramcontent.com/pod-product-compliance
Lightning Source LLC
Chambersburg PA
CBHW030651230426
43665CB00011B/1040